Managing Human Resources in Cross-Border Alliances

Across the globe companies are seeking alliances with companies in other countries and forming cross-border alliances (CBAs). These collaborations are some of the most complex and exciting in the business world. But while CBAs offer multinational companies a way into the global marketplace, there is no guarantee of success.

Managing Human Resources in Cross-Border Alliances looks at the business and human resources issues that arise through these collaborations, positing that it is the handling of these issues that can determine the CBA's success. The book takes readers through the two main kinds of CBA, international joint ventures (IJVs) and international mergers and acquisitions (IM&As), explaining how each type works and which human resource (HR) issues arise. As well as analyzing these issues and explaining the relevant management, economics, and sociological theories, it uses short end-of-chapter case examples and in-depth end-of-text case studies to provide numerous practical examples.

The first major textbook that seriously studies HR issues in a cross-border alliances context, this book offers both students of HR/international business and practicing HR professionals frameworks for truly understanding the complexities of the area.

Randall S. Schuler is Professor of Human Resource Strategy and Director of the MHRM Program at Rutgers University, and is Research Associate at the Graduate School of Business Administration Zurich. **Susan E. Jackson** is Professor of Human Resource Strategy and Director of the Doctoral Program in Industrial Relations and HR at Rutgers University, and is Research Associate at the Graduate School of Busines Administration Zurich. **Yadong Luo** is Professor of Management in the Department of Management at the University of Miami.

Routledge Global Human Resource Management Series

Routledge Global Human Resource Management is an important new series that examines human resources in its global context. The series is organized into three strands: Content and issues in global Human Resource Management (HRM); Specific HR functions in a global context; and comparative HRM. Authored by some of the world's leading authorities on HRM, each book in the series aims to give readers comprehensive, indepth and accessible texts that combine essential theory and best practice. Topics covered include cross-border alliances, global leadership, global legal systems, HRM in Asia, Africa and the Americas, industrial relations and global staffing.

Managing Human Resources in Cross-Border Alliances
Randall S. Schuler, Susan E. Jackson and Yadong Luo

Globalizing HRM
Paul Sparrow, Chris Brewster and Hilary Harris

Managing Human Resources in Cross-Border Alliances

Randall S. Schuler, Susan E. Jackson, and Yadong Luo

Routledge
Taylor & Francis Group

LONDON AND NEW YORK

First published 2004 by Routledge
11 New Fetter Lane, London EC4P 4EE

Simultaneously published in the USA and Canada
by Routledge
29 West 35th Street, New York, NY 10001

Routledge is an imprint of the Taylor & Francis Group

Typeset in Times New Roman by
Keystroke, Jacaranda Lodge, Wolverhampton
Printed and bound in Great Britain by
TJ International Ltd, Padstow, Cornwall

British Library Cataloguing in Publication Data
A catalogue record for this book is available from the British Library

Library of Congress Cataloging in Publication Data
Schuler, Randall S.
    Managing human resources in cross-border alliances / Randall S. Schuler,
Susan E. Jackson, Yadong Luo.
        p. cm. – (Routledge global human resource management series; 1)
    Simultaneously published in the USA and Canada.
    Includes bibliographical references and index.
    1. International business enterprises—Employees. 2. Human capital.
    I. Jackson, Susan E. II. Luo, Yadong. III. Title. IV. Series.
    HD6336 .S38 2003
    658.3—dc21   2002153072

ISBN 0–415–36946–0 (hbk)
ISBN 0–415–36947–9 (pbk)

Contents

Illustrations

Figures

Tables

Boxes

Foreword

This book is the first volume in the series Routledge Global Human Resource Management. The series examines human resource management (HRM) policies and practices in domestic and multinational companies throughout the world.

Several books in this series, including this first volume, are devoted to HRM practices in multinational companies. Some books focus on specific areas of HRM policies and practices, such as renumeration, staffing, training and development, and labor relations. Other books address special topics that arise in multinational companies. This first book, for example, addresses the special topic of managing cross-border alliances.

In addition to books on HRM in multinational companies, several other books in the series adopt a comparative approach to understanding human resource management. The books on comparative human resource management describe the HRM policies and practices found in domestic firms located in various countries and regions of the world. The comparative books utilize a common framework that makes it easier for the reader systematically to understand the rationale for the human resource management practices in different countries.

The series Routledge Global Human Resource Management is intended to serve the growing market of scholars and practitioners who are seeking a deeper and broader understanding of the role and importance of human resource management in companies as they operate throughout the world. With this in mind, all books in the series provide a thorough review of existing research and numerous examples of companies around the world. Mini-company stories and examples are found throughout the chapters. In addition, each book in the series includes at least one detailed case description that serves as a convenient practical illustration of topics discussed in the book.

Because a significant number of scholars and practitioners throughout the world are involved in researching and practicing the topics examined in this series of books, the authorship of the books and the experiences of companies cited in the books reflect a vast global representation. The authors in the series bring with them exceptional knowledge of the HRM topics they address, and in many cases have been the pioneers for their topics. So we feel fortunate to have the involvement of such a distinguished group of academics in this series.

The publisher and editor also have played a major role in making this series possible. Routledge has provided its global production, marketing, and reputation to make this series feasible and affordable to academics and practitioners throughout the world. In addition, Routledge has provided its own highly qualified professionals to make this series a reality. In particular we want to indicate our deep appreciation for the work of our editor, Catriona King. She has been behind the series from the very beginning and has been invaluable in providing the needed support and encouragement to us and to the many authors in the series. She, along with her staff, has helped make the process of completing this series an enjoyable one. For everything they have done, we thank them all.

Randall S. Schuler, Rutgers University/GSBA Zurich
Paul Sparrow, Manchester University
Susan E. Jackson, Rutgers University/GSBA Zurich
Michael Poole, Cardiff University

Preface

Across the world, companies are seeking alliances with other companies. Although the pace at which this occurs tends to vary with such forces as economic conditions worldwide, the reality seems to be that alliances will continue to be a critical part of global businesses for some time to come. And while alliances are varied in type, size, duration, and complexity, those that are most complex and interesting for us are cross-border alliances (CBAs).

We describe two major types of cross-border alliances: international joint ventures (IJVs) and international mergers and acquisitions (IM&As). Each of these offers a multinational company a unique way to involve itself in the global market. However, neither offers a guarantee of success. In fact, the evidence suggests that both IJVs and IM&As are filled with challenges, many of which go unmet, with the result that the alliance fails. A close look at this evidence suggests that many failures are linked to a neglect of human resource issues. Furthermore, many of the successes seem to be associated with systematic attention and time devoted to managing the many human resource issues.

Based upon the experiences of many companies, some of which have had success in CBAs and some of which have had failure in CBAs, a pattern of understanding has begun to emerge regarding the management of human resource issues in cross-border alliances. This understanding, which is grounded in both the experiences of multinational companies (MNCs) and academic research, enables us to offer a more thorough schema by which CBAs can be created and managed with a greater chance of success.

Our hope is that this book will enable practitioners to think systematically about the human resource issues to be managed in cross-border alliances, while at the same time encouraging scholars to continue systematic research on these issues. Because IJVs and IM&As are two unique forms of cross-border alliances, we offer separate frameworks for understanding each of them. Each framework suggests several guidelines for managing human resource issues effectively in cross-border alliances. In offering these guidelines, we do not intend to suggest hard-and-fast rules; instead, the guidelines should serve as tips for MNCs seeking to enter into cross-border alliances in the near term. For researchers, the guidelines offered might be viewed as propositions that are worthy of further investigation.

This book contains eight chapters. Chapter 1 introduces the concepts of "cross-border alliance" and "human resource management" (HRM) as they are used throughout the book. Chapters 2 and 3 are devoted to describing the nature of IJVs and their related human resource (HR) issues. Chapters 4 and 5 provide similar treatment for international mergers and acquisitions. Chapters 6 and 7 address several topics that are relevant to both IJVs and IM&As, including trust, cooperation, conflict management, collaboration, structure, exit, and managing cultural diversity. Chapter 8 describes how members of an HRM department can facilitate the effective management of IJVs and IM&As. Virtually everyone in a company can participate in the management of cross-border alliances. However, HR professionals – including both the HR leader and the HR staff – should be uniquely capable of leading a systematic discussion of human resource management issues in CBAs.

Finally, in addition to the primary chapters, two detailed case studies of company experiences are provided in the Appendixes. These cases are used throughout the book to illustrate key points, but the full Appendixes may prove useful to those who are interested in additional details.

The ideas and suggestions offered throughout this book are grounded in the experiences of numerous managers at the companies cited in these chapters. We thank them for the information and insights they have shared related to managing CBAs. We also thank Paul Stonham, editor of the *European Management Journal* at the European School of Management in Oxford, for his permission to use the cases on the Davidson-Marley BV international joint venture; James Scoville at the University of Minnesota for granting us permission to use his case, Precision Measurement of Japan; and Hugh Scullion, Strathclyde University, for contributing the case example of Rolls-Royce PLC. Finally, we wish to express our thanks to Joanna Eriksen at Rutgers University for all of her efforts in preparing the manuscript of this book. Without her professional dedication, this project would not have been completed in a timely and efficient manner.

Randall S. Schuler
Susan E. Jackson
Yadong Luo

Abbreviations

ABGC	(an unnamed) Asian-based global (air) carrier
CBA	cross-border alliance
CEO	chief executive officer
COO	chief operating officer
DB	Deutsche Bank
GATT	General Agreement on Tariffs and Trade
HR	human resource
HRM	human resource management
IJV	international joint venture
IM&As	international mergers and acquisitions
IPO	initial public offering
IT	information technology
J&J	Johnson & Johnson
JV	joint venture
MHI	Mitsubishi Heavy Industries
MITI	(Japanese) Ministry of International Trade and Industry
MNC	multinational company
MNE	multinational enterprise
OD	organizational development
OEM	original equipment manufacturer
PMI	Precision Measurement, Inc.
PM-J	Precision Management of Japan
R&D	research and development
RR	Rolls-Royce
SCT	status characteristics theory
TEC	Takezawa Electric Company
VCR	video cassette recorder
WTO	World Trade Organization

Managing human resources in cross-border alliances

1

I personally see more consolidations, more partnerships, more strategic alliances, and more acquisitions.

Jac Nasser
Former CEO, Ford Motor

Merging a U.S. and a European company, as we have done, is a particularly complicated process. The management styles are totally different. People have different views on how to manage a global organization. The British and American philosophies are so apart on those subjects they're almost impossible to reconcile.

Jan Leschly
Former CEO, GlaxoSmithKline

The media often portray business organizations as warring enemies that define their own success by the demise of their competitors. Executives sometimes use similar imagery to motivate their "troops." What such images ignore are the strong interdependencies among business organizations and the degree to which cooperation results in mutual gains. Just as nations have discovered the benefits of economic cooperation, businesses have learned that success often depends on forming strategic alliances. As a result of the formation of strategic alliances among companies often viewed as fierce competitors, industries are sometimes completely transformed (Freidheim, 1998).

Successfully managing strategic alliances is surprisingly difficult, however. The recent DaimlerChrysler cross-border merger illustrates some of the management challenges inherent in managing cross-border alliances. Competitive forces in the global auto industry initially led the two companies to merge. The combination looked good on paper, but cultural differences interfered with management's ability to quickly reap the economic benefits they had anticipated. Clashes due to differences in country cultures and company cultures nearly doomed the new company's success. It seemed to take years for management to focus on a common vision and agree to the need for a single unifying culture. Although the alliance seems now to be succeeding, the initial years of difficulty might have been avoided if the managers had understood and appreciated the many human resource (HR) issues that would require their attention (Apfelthaler *et al.*, 2002).

Strategic alliances among firms

In general, *strategic alliances* involve two or more firms agreeing to cooperate as partners in an arrangement that is expected to benefit both firms. Sometimes strategic alliances involve one firm taking an equity position in another firm. In the most extreme case, one firm acquires the other firm. But less extreme equity positions are also common. Ford, for example, has equity in both U.S. and non-U.S. auto parts producers, but it has not acquired these companies. Many strategic alliances do not affect legal ownership, however. In the airline industry, a common type of alliance is between an airline and an airframe manufacturer. In high-tech industries, strategic alliances allow older, established firms to gain access to the hot new discoveries being made by scientists in universities and in small, creative organizations. For example, the U.S. biotechnology industry is characterized by networks of nonequity relationships between new biotechnology firms dedicated to research and new product development, and established firms in industries that can use these new products, such as pharmaceuticals. In return for sharing technical information with the larger firms, the smaller firms gain access to their partners' resources for product testing, marketing, and distribution (Liebeskind *et al.*, 1996).

In this book, we focus on strategic alliances between firms that have their headquarters in different countries. We refer to these as *cross-border alliances* (CBAs). Presumably, such alliances are formed because they promise to help the firms involved achieve some of their strategic objectives. Thus, CBAs can be defined as partnerships that are formed between two or more firms from different countries for the purpose of pursuing mutual interests through sharing their resources and capabilities (Doz and Hamel, 1998; Yan and Luo, 2000).

As is true for strategic alliances in general, there are many types of CBAs. Two broad categories of CBAs are those that involve equity investments and those that involve no shared equity or joint capital investment.

Nonequity cross-border alliances

A nonequity CBA is an investment vehicle in which profits and other responsibilities are assigned to each party according to a contract. Each party cooperates as a separate legal entity and bears its own liabilities. In recent years, many cooperative programs between firms involve joint activities without the creation of a new corporate entity. Instead, carefully defined rules govern the allocation of tasks, costs, and revenues.

Nonequity alliances have great freedom to structure their assets, organize their production processes, and manage their operations. This flexibility can be highly attractive for a foreign investor interested in property development, resource exploration, and other production projects in which the foreign party incurs substantial up-front development costs. A partner can build into the contract an accelerated return on its share of investment to allow it to recoup its equity share by the end of the term. Further, this type of alliance can be developed quickly to take advantage of short-term business opportunities, then dissolved when its tasks are completed. Because of their ability to provide foreign investors with returns in excess of their proportional contributions to the alliances' total registered capital, nonequity alliances have been the vehicles of choice for build–operate–transfer infrastructure projects. Among the many types of nonequity alliances are joint exploration projects, research and development consortia, co-production agreements, co-marketing arrangements, and long-term supply agreements.

Atlantic Richfield's offshore oil *exploration consortia* in Brazil, Ecuador, and Indonesia are examples of joint exploration projects. The arrangement allows for the exploration costs to be borne by the foreign partner, and later the development costs are shared by the home partner. Microsoft's *R&D consortium* with Qinhua University in China is another example of an international non-equity alliance. This agreement specifies a method for allocating costs to the partners, but the revenue of each partner depends on what each company independently does with the technology created.

An example of a *co-production agreement* is the alliances between Boeing and Japan Aircraft Development Corporation (itself a consortium of Mitsubishi, Kawasaki, and Fuji). Each partner is responsible for manufacturing a particular part of the product, and therefore each partner's costs are a function of its own efficiency in producing that part. However, revenue is a function of sales of the 767 by the dominant partner, Boeing. An example of a *co-service arrangement* is provided by the alliance between Delta Air Lines and Air France. These partners seek to align their commercial policies and procedures, coordinate transatlantic operations, and combine frequent flier programs. Although Delta and Air France each retain independent fleet plans, they look for ways jointly to improve operating efficiencies.

Co-marketing arrangements provide a platform in which each party can reach a larger pool of international consumers. For example, Praxair (United States) and Merck KGA (Germany) established their global alliance in 1999, through which each uses the other's distribution channels to bring an offering combining Praxair's gases and Merck's wet chemicals to semiconductor customers. This co-marketing alliance gives both parties an entrance into the other's main markets. Praxair has a strong distribution infrastructure in North America but is a small player in Europe and Asia. Merck, in contrast, is strong in Europe and Asia but absent from the U.S. wet chemical market.

In a typical *long-term supply agreement*, the manufacturing buyer often provides the supplier with updated free information on products, markets, and technologies, which in turn helps ensure the input quality. IKEA, for example, not only offers such information to its dozens of foreign suppliers but also provides them with free periodic training. Correspondingly, many of IKEA's foreign suppliers are committed to becoming its long-term exclusive suppliers.

Finally, a *co-management arrangement* is a loosely structured alliance in which cross-border partners collaborate in training (technical or managerial), production management, information systems development, and value-chain integration (e.g., integrating inbound logistics with production or integrating outbound logistics with marketing). Partnership provides an organizational vehicle for firms quickly and efficiently to acquire these managerial skills, which cannot be bought from a public market. Co-management arrangements occur because international companies often realize that their managerial skills are insufficient for running businesses abroad and, meanwhile, local companies often find that they can benefit from foreign counterparts' international experience and organizational skills. Therefore, foreign and local companies can benefit from complementary managerial expertise they contributed through an alliance (Child and Faulkner, 1998; Cyr, 1995; Hennart and Reddy, 1997; Muson, 2002; Pucik, 1988).

Equity-based cross-border alliances

International joint ventures and international mergers and acquisitions are two major types of equity-based CBAs. Such arrangements typically represent a long-term collaborative strategy. Furthermore, as we explain throughout this book, equity-based alliances require active day-to-day management of a wide variety of HR issues. Some of the HR issues that are critical to the success of equity-based CBAs may also arise in nonequity CBAs, but they may be less central to the success of the alliance. In equity-based CBAs, however, long-term success is impossible unless HR issues are managed effectively. While there are many lessons that can be transferred from our discussion of equity-based CBAs to managing HR issues in nonequity alliances, most of our discussion focuses on describing the challenges of managing human resources in equity-based CBAs. More specifically, we focus on international joint ventures and international mergers and acquisitions.

International joint ventures

An *international joint venture* (IJV) is one type of equity-based CBA. Alliance partners form a joint venture when they create a separate legal organizational entity representing the partial holdings of two or more parent firms. In IJVs, the headquarters of at least one partner is located outside the country of the joint venture. Joint ventures are subject to the joint control of their parent firms. The parent firms, in turn, become economically and legally interdependent with each other.

Firms form IJVs for many reasons. In some countries, the host government provides strong incentives to foreign firms to use joint ventures as a mode of entry into the country's markets. Another reason to form joint ventures is to gain rapid access to new markets. Learning is yet another objective behind many IJVs. By partnering with local companies instead of entering a market on their own, foreign firms can more quickly develop their ability to operate effectively in the host country. IJVs also provide a means for competitors within an industry to leverage new technology and reduce costs. In the auto industry, for example, Ford, General Motors, DaimlerChrysler, Nissan, and Renault formed an international joint venture, Covisint, in order to manage their supply chains using business-to-business e-commerce (Greenhalgh, 2000). Ford's former CEO Jac Nasser explained the reasoning behind the formation of this IJV:

> We see this technology [e-business] as so powerful that, for it to be optimized, we need it to become an industry standard. So, rather than have 15 different standards out there . . . we figured out that it would be more efficient if the basic architecture was common.

Assuming Covisint succeeds, it will fundamentally alter supply chain relationships within the automobile industry.

For various reasons, managing IJVs successfully is difficult, and many ultimately fail. IJV failures often stem from poor management of human resource issues. Prior to formation of an IJV, human resource management (HRM) professionals can help the potential partners assess their cultural compatibility. As the new entity is formed, recruiting and selecting of key executives to staff the IJV becomes critical. With the staff in place, HRM practices that align employees' skills and motivations with the business objectives of the IJV can determine whether it ultimately achieves the desired outcomes.

International mergers and acquisitions

Companies today need to be fast, efficient, profitable, flexible, adaptable and future-ready, and to have a dominant market position. Without these qualities, it is virtually impossible to be competitive in today's global economy. In addition to participating in strategic alliances to develop the capabilities they need to compete, many firms evolve and grow through mergers or acquisitions. Among the most significant transnational merger and acquisition deals in recent years are those involving Daimler–Chrysler, Chase–J.P. Morgan, McKinsey–Envision, UBS–Paine Webber, Credit Suisse–DLJ, Celltech–Medeva, SKB–Glaxo, NationsBank–Bank of America, Vivendi–Universal, Pfizer–Warner Lambert, Nestlé–Purina, and Deutsche Telekom–Voice Stream. Although global economic and market conditions move up and down, the future appears ripe for a continuation of international merger and acquisition activity.

In a merger, two companies agree to join their operations together to form a new company in which they participate as equal partners. In an acquisition, one firm buys a controlling or full interest in another firm with the understanding that the buyer will determine how the combined operations will be managed. The majority of acquisitions are friendly – that is, the acquired firm solicits bids and enters into an acquisition voluntarily. Sometimes, however, a firm becomes a takeover target. Although mergers and acquisitions are technically different, it is common to refer to all these means for combining the operations of two firms as mergers and acquisitions (M&As) (Charman, 1999; Deogun and Scannell, 2001).

Some observers argue that the increased pace of international mergers and acquisitions (IM&As) is a major driving force behind the development of multigovernment agreements and rules for business conduct (Tyson, 2001). IM&A deals can have enormous economic and social consequences. They can quickly put the major competitors within a country out of business, and they can determine whether, how, and where people work. Gaining government approval for international M&As is sometimes difficult, but the initial step of gaining approval usually proves to be far easier than successfully managing the new entity.

As is true for IJVs, IM&As unfold through many stages. At each stage, success requires effectively managing many HR issues. This involves identifying the HR issues and their implications for human resource management activities.

Human resource management

Human resource management refers to all of the dedicated activity that an organization uses to affect the behaviors of all the people who work for it. Because the behaviors of employees influence profitability, customer satisfaction, and a variety of other important measures of organizational effectiveness, managing human resources is a key strategic challenge for all companies, and particularly so for those engaged in CBAs.

Human resource management activities

Every organization, from the smallest to the largest, engages in a variety of *human resource management activities*. HRM activities include formal policies and everyday practices for managing people. Policies are statements that offer a general statement of how people will be managed. For example, there may be a policy to reward employees for their performance in the organization. HRM practices then take the next step and provide a more specific statement of how people will be managed. For example, the practice of paying commissions based on individual sales performance is a practice that would be consistent with an HRM policy of rewarding employees for performance. Another practice that would also be consistent with this policy would be offering team-based incentives that are tied to the performance of a team against stated team goals.

Companies have many choices in the variety and nature of the formal HRM policies and practices that can be created. Their creation in any specific company often reflects a wide variety of factors, including the past traditions of the firm, the leadership of the HRM department, the preferences of top management, the strategic activities (such as CBAs) and products of the company, presence of union representation, and government regulations. Research and evidence from company experiences demonstrate rather convincingly that some HRM policies and practices are better suited for some companies than others. The more systematically HRM policies and practices are matched to the company, the more effective the company is likely to be (Becker *et al.*, 1997).

The many specific HRM policies and practices referred to in this book include HR planning, job analysis, recruitment, selection, retention, training and development, performance management, remuneration (compensation), and so on. When an organization systematically coordinates and integrates all of these activities, it creates a *human resource management system*.

The design and implementation of effective HRM activities and systems requires substantial staff expertise. Although line managers from all areas of an organization must be involved in the process, professional HRM knowledge is essential also. Chapter 8 considers the HRM profession itself with respect to CBAs. The chapter specifically addresses what competencies are needed to succeed in managing CBAs and how the HRM department needs to be structured when firms enter into various forms of CBAs. Throughout Chapters 1–7, however, we discuss the roles of all relevant staff in CBAs. These staff are identified as members of the HRM Triad.

The HRM Triad

Used wisely, HRM activities can transform a lackluster company into a star performer or facilitate a successful CBA. Used unwisely, they create havoc or spell doom to an alliance. In some companies, existing approaches to managing human resources reflect chance and happenstance. Instead of analyzing how their HRM systems affect all aspects of the business, some organizations continue to do things the same way year after year. Ask why salespeople in the shoe section are paid on commission and people in toys are not, and you are likely to be told, "That's just the way we've always done it." When companies do change the way they manage people, they may do so for the wrong reason. Why did that small retail food chain just send all its middle managers to off-site wilderness training? "Everybody in the industry's doing it – we can't be the only ones who don't." Why did your insurance company start randomly listening in on calls from customers? "The new telecommunications system we installed last year included it as a no-cost feature, so we decided we should use it."

Similarly, some companies fail to consider, or choose to ignore, HRM activities in cross-border alliances. Yet, whether a CBA chooses its human resource policies and practices carefully or somewhat haphazardly, those policies and practices can have powerful effects. To be sure that those effects are *positive* rather than destructive requires actively involving three key groups of players, whom we refer to as the HRM Triad (Jackson and Schuler, 2003):

- HR professionals;
- line managers; and
- the employees (and their representatives) who are affected by the human resource policies and practices.

There is a saying at Merck that "human resources are too important to be left to the HRM department." No department can, by itself, effectively manage a company's human resources (Huselid *et al.*, 1997). The special expertise of HRM professionals is used by, and in cooperation with, line managers, other administrative staff, and all first-line employees in every department. This cooperation is very important in CBAs because there are so many HR issues that need to be systematically managed to enhance the chances of alliance's success.

Line managers have always been responsible

Regardless of whether a line manager ever holds a formal position in HRM, she or he is held accountable for the task of managing people. In small businesses, owners must have HR expertise as they build the company from the ground up. Eventually, as a company grows, the owner may contract out some of the administrative aspects related to managing people (e.g., payroll), or delegate some of the responsibilities to a specialist, or both. As the company grows larger, more specialists may be hired – either as permanent staff or on a contract basis to work on special projects, such as designing a new pay system. As with other business activities, these specialists will not bear all the responsibility for the project. For example, many companies have a marketing department; nevertheless, they employ people outside that department to conduct marketing activities. Similarly, most companies have a few people with special expertise in accounting; nevertheless, employees throughout the company perform accounting activities. The same is true for the managing of human resources.

This book treats managing human resources as a responsibility shared by everyone in all the companies involved in the CBA: line employees *and* professionals in the human resources department *and* top-level executives *and* even entry-level new hires. Consistent with the stakeholder model described below, involvement in the process of managing human resources can even extend to people outside the alliance members, such as managers in supplier firms, customers, union representatives, and members of community organizations.

HRM professionals provide special expertise

"HRM professionals" refers to people with substantial specialized and technical knowledge of HRM issues, laws, policies, and practices. The leaders of HRM units and the specialist and generalist staff who work within the function usually are HRM professionals, although this is not always the case. Sometimes organizations fill the top-level HRM position with a person who has a history of line experience but no special expertise in the area of HRM. According to one survey of 1,200 organizations, this is a growing trend, reflecting increasing recognition of the importance of people to business success (Jackson and Schuler, 2003). Line managers who are doing a "tour of duty" in the HRM department would be appropriately referred to as HRM managers, but they would not be considered HRM professionals – at least not until they have gained substantial experience and have perhaps taken a few executive development courses devoted to HRM. External experts who serve as HRM consultants or vendors for the organization may be HRM professionals, also. But do not assume that a consultant or vendor is an HRM professional just because he or she offers HRM products or services.

Employees share responsibility

The responsibilities of line managers and HRM professionals are especially great; nevertheless, they share responsibility with the third key partner in the HRM Triad, namely all of the other employees (and their representatives) who are affected by HRM policies and practices. Regardless of their particular jobs, all of the employees in an organization share some of the responsibility for effective HRM. Some employees write their own job descriptions and even design their own jobs. Many employees provide input for the appraisal of their own performance or the performance of their colleagues and supervisors, or both. Many organizations ask employees to participate in annual surveys whereby they can express their likes and dislikes about the organization's approach to managing people. Perhaps most significantly, employees assess their own needs and values and must manage their own careers in accordance with these. Of course, where employees are represented by unions, union representatives play a significant role in a company's attempt to merge with or acquire another company. The company's approach to HRM can also play an important part in its decision to create a joint venture.

As we move forward, we all need to position ourselves for the future. Learning about how effective organizations are managing human resources is an essential step for getting into position and for evaluating the success of our CBA.

The multiple stakeholder model

Ultimately, the success of an organization is determined by the evaluations of its major stakeholders. Stakeholders are individuals or groups that have interests, rights, or ownership in an organization and its activities. Stakeholders who have similar interests and rights are said to belong to the same stakeholder group. Customers, suppliers, employees, society, and other organizations (e.g., alliance partners) are examples of stakeholders, as illustrated in Figure 1.1.

We argue throughout this book that an organization's approach to managing human resources – including how it manages the people involved in CBAs – is central to its success in satisfying key stakeholders (Jackson and Schuler, 2003; Yan and Luo, 2001). Stakeholders benefit from the organization's successes and can be harmed by its failures and mistakes. Similarly, the organization has an interest in maintaining the general well-being and effectiveness of key stakeholders. If one or more of the stakeholder groups break off their relationships with the organization, the organization suffers.

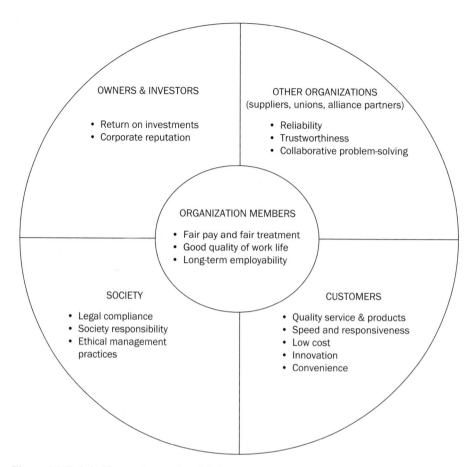

Figure 1.1 Stakeholders and examples of their concerns

© Susan E. Jackson and Randall S. Schuler

For any particular organization, some stakeholder groups may be relatively more important than others. The most important groups – the primary stakeholders – are those whose concerns the organization must address in order to ensure its own survival (Jones, 1995; Robson, 2001). When success is defined as effectively serving the interests of these groups, their needs define a firm's fundamental objectives. These objectives, in turn, drive the organization's approaches to managing employees.

Each organization weighs the concerns of stakeholders somewhat differently, but it ignores any particular stakeholder at its own peril. Executives who once enjoyed enormous autonomy and wielded considerable personal power in running their companies now focus increasingly on maximizing shareholder value. Companies that once attended little to customers now find that in almost every industry it is a buyers' market, and sellers have become captives of the customer. Employers who once acted as if they were in charge of the employment relationship are now so desperate for good people that they are beginning to let employees decide where company offices should be located, what hours they will work, and under what conditions (Davenport, 2000).

The principle that effective management requires attending to all relevant stakeholders is as true for managing human resources as for other management tasks. Human resource management practices cannot be designed solely to meet the concerns of employees. Nor can they be designed by considering only their consequences for the bottom line (i.e., profits). Organizations that are the most effective in managing people develop HRM systems that meet the needs of all key stakeholders. In order to develop a stakeholder-friendly approach to managing human resources, it is necessary to understand the concerns of each stakeholder group. This goal can perhaps be more successfully attained through the HRM Triad. We describe the main stakeholder groups next and briefly note how the concerns of each group can influence an organization's HRM practices. In a CBA, these concerns are multiplied by the number of companies involved. Thus the complexity of making a CBA successful increases dramatically.

Owners and investors

Most owners and investors invest their money in companies for financial reasons. At a minimum, owners and shareholders want to preserve their capital for later use, and ideally they want to experience a growth in it. To achieve these goals, their capital should be invested primarily in profitable companies. Because an organization's approach to managing human resources can enhance or diminish its profitability, many investors prefer companies with good reputations in the area of HRM management.

The job of institutional investors, which is to make money by choosing which companies to invest in, has become increasingly complex as difficult-to-measure assets have become more important. Tangible assets, such as inventory, equipment, real estate, and financial assets, are relatively easy to measure. In the old economy, investors focused on measuring tangible assets in order to determine a firm's value. In the new economy, however, investors recognize that many intangible assets can be just as valuable as tangible assets. Intangible human assets include such things as reputation as an employer-of-choice, depth of employee talent and loyalty, and the firm's ability to innovate and change. In organizations such as investment banks, consulting firms, and advertising agencies, there is almost nothing there except intangible human assets. Investing in these companies often means hoping that the best employees will continue working at and for the company (Handy, 1998; Wong, 2000). As one study of initial public offering (IPO) companies showed, companies that attend to HRM issues are rewarded with more favorable initial investor reactions as well as longer-term survival (Welbourne and Andrews, 1996). Accountants may have difficulty attaching monetary values to a firm's human resources, but this does not stop investors from paying attention.

Owners and investors are particularly interested in CBAs because they can affect the value of the companies involved. For example, the value of an acquiring company may go down if it fails to make sense to investors. Alternatively, successful mergers or acquisitions can lead to the financial success of firms such as General Electric, Nestlé, and Johnson & Johnson.

Customers

Improving customer satisfaction is a primary means through which HRM practices affect success. Reducing costs, improving product quality, and improving service quality all are ways to improve customer satisfaction (Wilkinson *et al.*, 1997). Service companies win or lose during the time of contact between employees and customers. This time of contact is now referred to by many people as the moment of truth – a phrase coined by Jan Carlzon as he was writing about his experiences as CEO and Chairman of Scandinavia Airlines System (quoted in Grunroos, 1990: xv). The moment of truth, it turns out, is often the moment when customers get a glimpse of how a firm manages its human resources and its business. When the internal climate of the organization is positive, with employees generally getting along well and not leaving the company at too rapid a pace, customers report that they are more satisfied and intend to return (Johnson, 1996).

Customer satisfaction can be adversely affected if a CBA results in an altered product or service or an increase in its price. This consequence may occur in an acquisition if the acquirer pays too much and is required to assume substantial debt. Here costs may increase and staff levels may be reduced and morale levels may be decreased.

Society

For organizations such as public schools (in the U.S. sense), nonprofit foundations, and government agencies, the concerns of owners – that is, taxpayers and contributors – often are essentially those of society at large. But for privately owned companies and those whose shares are publicly traded, the concerns of owners – that is, investors – may be quite different from those of society in general. Under free market capitalism, the primary managerial obligation is to maximize shareholders' profits and their long-term interests (Friedman, 1970). Friedman argued that using resources in ways that do not clearly maximize investor interests amounts to spending the owners' money without their consent – and is equivalent to stealing. According to Friedman, a manager can judge whether a decision is right or wrong by considering its consequences for the company's economic needs and financial well-being. If it improves the financial bottom line it is right, but if it detracts from the financial bottom line, it's wrong. A CBA that results in failure clearly detracts from the bottom line and consequently runs counter to long-term investor interest.

Formal laws and regulations establish relatively clear guidelines for how society expects a company to behave, but effective companies respond to more than simply these formal statements. They understand that the enactment of formal laws and regulations often lags behind public opinion by several years. Long before legislation is agreed to, communities communicate their expectations and attempt to hold organizations accountable for violations of those expectations. In turn, proactive organizations stay attuned to public opinion and use it as one source of information that may shape their own management practices. With heightened public interest in corporate social responsibility, many companies are discovering that they cannot avoid having people evaluate how well they perform in this respect (Ruf *et al.*, 1998). Consequently, they need to be aware of the impact they can have or may have on communities in which they operate. This can become very critical in IM&As, where the social costs that may come from the resulting staff reductions can become significant for the communities affected. In these communities, which face possible loss of jobs and tax revenues, people may protest against the merger or acquisition. This is what happened when the board of the Hershey Trust (located in the United States) announced that it was seeking to diversify its portfolio and was thus willing to sell its stake in the Hershey Food Company to an acquirer, such as Nestlé (a Swiss company).

Other organizations

Companies of all types are becoming increasingly interdependent with other organizations. Other organizations that can be considered major stakeholders include suppliers, unions, and alliance partners, among others.

- *Suppliers*. Suppliers provide the resources a company needs to conduct its business. In addition to the capital of owners and investors, the resources needed by most companies include material and equipment, information and people. Other companies usually supply material and equipment. Suppliers of people might include schools, the professional associations that serve specific occupational groups, state employment agencies, and companies that offer electronic recruiting services.
- *Unions*. Unions may also serve as a supplier of people, but their role is much larger than this. Firms with employees who are represented by a union involve unions in joint discussions on issues such as improving productivity, outsourcing policies, improving safety, compensation and benefits, and various other conditions of work. In recent years, union leaders and their members have moved away from their traditional adversarial relationship with management to a collaborative, problem-solving relationship. Despite this general trend, work slowdowns and strikes remain as major threats to companies in which unions represent the employees. Similar actions may occur to protest a merger or acquisition, particularly when the consequence is loss of jobs and workforce reductions. Early involvement by union officials in merger or acquisition discussions may prove to help ensure the need for the action itself in the short term, and for its ultimate success in the long run.
- *Alliance partners*. Whether a company is seeking a merger partner or a company with which to form an IJV, the characteristics of that partner are critical to the success of the new operation. Companies need to seek out those that are trustworthy, cooperative

and likely to resolve conflicts that arise throughout the existence of the new operation. Because these characteristics are particularly important to companies involved in CBAs, they are developed rather extensively throughout the chapters in this book.

Organizational members

Organizational members are another key stakeholder group. Unlike the other external stakeholders we discussed above, organizational members reside within the organization. Included in this group are all of the people who hold positions within the organization, including the CEO and other top-level executives, other managers and supervisors, professionals and administrative specialists, line employees, part-time employees, and so on. Because they are such a diverse stakeholder group, they have a great variety of concerns. Nevertheless, most members of this stakeholder group share concerns about pay and benefits, quality of work life, and employability. This is particularly true with mergers and acquisitions, where some employees at all levels of a new, combined company are likely to lose their jobs as a consequence of job reduction and restructuring. In fact, mergers can often be differentiated from acquisitions on the basis of which employees remain with the newly combined company.

Finding synergy

Clearly, the primary concerns of the stakeholder groups differ somewhat, and conflict among stakeholders is common. And this is even more true when multiple companies are involved, as in mergers, acquisitions, or IJVs. When applied to CBAs, these conflicts or synergies become much more complex and significant because several companies and their multiple stakeholders are involved. They are involved in the early stages, as the new combined company is discussed, and they continue to be involved as the new entity becomes operational. Consequently, it is important that they be considered and included in the management of and the evaluation of the CBAs (Jackson and Schuler, 2003; Yan and Luo, 2001).

Theoretical perspectives for understanding HRM in IJVs

Throughout this book we draw upon several theoretical perspectives. These perspectives serve as frameworks for our analyses and are the foundation upon which we have developed the guidelines presented in subsequent chapters. For readers who are not familiar with them, we summarize them briefly here. These theoretical perspectives, which are based in sociology, economics, management, and psychology, have also been summarized by Jackson and Schuler (1995), Barkema *et al.* (1997), and Evans *et al.* (2002).

General systems theory

In general systems theory, the unit of analysis is understood as a complex of interdependent parts (von Bertalanffy, 1950). An open (as opposed to a closed) system is dependent on the environment for inputs, which are transformed during throughput to produce outputs that are exchanged in the environment. Open systems models seldom address organizations or large units within organizations. Katz and Kahn's (1978) *The Social Psychology of Organizations* is an exception in that it treats HRM as a subsystem embedded in a larger organizational system. The open systems view of HRM has been developed further by Wright and Snell (1991), who used it to describe a competence management model of organizations. Skills and abilities are treated as inputs from the environment; employee behaviors are treated as throughput; and employee satisfaction and performance are treated as outputs. In this model, the HRM subsystem functions to acquire, utilize, retain, and displace competencies.

Role behavior perspective

Katz and Kahn (1978) focused on roles as the interdependent components that make up an organization system. Instead of using specific behaviors and job performances as the fundamental components, this perspective shifts the focus from individuals to social systems characterized by multiple roles, multiple role senders, and multiple role evaluators. Katz and Kahn defined role behaviors as "the recurring actions of an individual, appropriately interrelated with the repetitive activities of others so as to yield a predictable outcome." HRM is the organization's primary means for sending role information through the organization, supporting desired behaviors, and evaluating role performances. It is effective, therefore, when it communicates internally consistent expectations and evaluates performances in ways that are congruent with the system's behavioral requirements (e.g., see Frederiksen, 1986). This view is consistent with motivational theories such as expectancy theory and reinforcement theory, which assert that individuals demonstrate behaviors and attitudes that are desired and rewarded. Role requirements are, in turn, presumed to depend on contextual factors such as business strategies, the culture of the country, and the nature of the industry. By implication, effective HRM helps employees meet the expectations of role partners within the organization (i.e., supervisors, peers, and subordinates), at organizational boundaries (i.e., customers and clients), and beyond (i.e, joint venture partner and society).

Institutional theory

A role theory perspective assumes that individuals respond to normative pressures as they seek approval for their performance in socially defined roles. Similarly, institutional theory views organizations as social entities that seek approval for their performances in socially constructed environments. Organizations conform to gain legitimacy and acceptance, which facilitate survival (Meyer and Rowan, 1977; Zucker, 1977). Because multiple constituencies control needed resources, legitimacy and acceptance are sought from many stakeholders. Research on institutionalization (Scott, 1987; Zucker, 1987) focuses on pressures emanating from the internal and external environments. Internally, institutionalization arises out of formalized structures and processes, as well as informal emergent group and organization processes. Forces in the external environment include those related to the country (e.g., laws and regulations), the professions (e.g., licensure and certification), and other organizations – especially those within the same industrial sector.

Resource dependence theory

Like institutional theory, resource dependence theory focuses on the relationship between an organization and its constituencies. However, resource dependence theory emphasizes resource exchanges as the central feature of these relationships, rather than concerns about social acceptability and legitimacy (Pfeffer and Cohen, 1984). According to this perspective, groups and organizations gain power over each other by controlling valued resources. Furthermore, HRM activities and processes are assumed to reflect the distribution of power within a system (Conner and Prahalad, 1996). In the case of the two partners of our IJV, the one with the greater bargaining power is the one more likely to shape the HRM activities of the IJV (Martinez and Ricks, 1989). Similar reasoning applies *vis-à-vis* the larger merger partner or the acquiring firm.

Human capital theory

In the economics literature, human capital refers to the productive capabilities of people (Becker, 1964). Skills, experience, and knowledge have economic value to organizations because they enable it to be productive and adaptable; thus, people constitute the organization's human capital. Like other assets, human capital has value in the marketplace, but unlike other assets, its potential value can be fully realized only with the cooperation of the person. Therefore, all costs related to eliciting productive behaviors from employees – including those related to motivating, monitoring, and retaining them – constitute human capital investments made in anticipation of future returns (Flamholtz and Lacey, 1981).

Organizations can use HRM in a variety of ways to increase their human capital (Cascio, 1991; Flamholtz and Lacey, 1981). For example, they can "buy" human capital in the market (e.g., by offering desirable compensation packages) or "make" it internally (e.g., by offering extensive training and development opportunities). In human capital theory, contextual factors such as market conditions, unions, business strategies, and country culture are important because they can affect the costs associated with alternative approaches to using HRM to increase the value of the organization's human capital and the value of the anticipated returns, such as productivity gains (e.g., see Boudreau and Berger, 1985; Russell *et al.*, 1993).

Transaction costs theory

Transaction cost economics assumes that business enterprises choose governance structures that economize transaction costs associated with establishing, monitoring, evaluating, and enforcing agreed-upon exchanges (Williamson, 1979, 1981). Predictions about the nature of the governance structure of an organization will incorporate two behavioral assumptions: bounded rationality and opportunism (i.e., the avoidance of forbearance). These assumptions mean that the central problem to be solved by organizations is how to design governance structures that take advantage of bounded rationality while safeguarding against opportunism. To solve this problem, implicit and explicit contracts are established, monitored, enforced, and revised. The theory has direct implications for understanding how HRM activities are used to achieve a governance structure for managing the myriad implicit and explicit contracts between employers and employees (Chi and McGuire, 1996; Wright and McMahan, 1992). Partners try to establish contractual relationships with each other to reduce their transaction costs. They find this process, however, easier to do *vis-à-vis* explicit, visible resources, than with invisible assets like competencies and knowledge.

Agency theory

Agency theory focuses attention on the contracts between a party (i.e., the principal) who delegates work to another (i.e., the agent) (Jensen and Meckling, 1976). Agency relations are problematic to the degree that (a) the principal and agent have conflicting goals and (b) it is difficult or expensive for the principal to monitor the agent's performance (Eisenhardt, 1988). Contracts are used to govern such relations. Efficient contracts align the goals of principals and agents at the lowest possible cost. Costs can arise from providing incentives and obtaining information (e.g., about the agent's behavior and/or the agent's performance outcomes). Agency theory appears to be particularly useful for understanding executive and managerial compensation practices, which are viewed as a means for aligning the interests of the owners of a firm (i.e., principals) with the managers in whom they vest control (Reuer and Miller, 1997). It is also useful in gaining insights into how venture partners can control the behaviors of the general manager of the IJV, or how the acquiring firm can control the behaviors of the managers in the acquired firm.

Resource-based theory

The resource-based theory of the firm blends concepts from organizational economics, strategic management, and strategic human resource management (Schuler and Jackson, 1999). A fundamental assumption of this view is that organizations can be successful if they gain and maintain competitive advantage (see Porter, 1985). Competitive advantage is gained by implementing a value-creating strategy that competitors cannot easily copy and sustain (Barney, 1991) and for which there are no ready substitutes. For competitive advantage to be gained, two conditions are needed: first, the resources available to competing firms must be variable among competitors; and second, these resources must be immobile (i.e., not easily obtained). Three types of resources associated with organizations are (a) physical (plant; technology and equipment; geographic location); (b) human (employees' experience and knowledge); and (c) organizational (structure; systems for planning, learning, and monitoring; controlling activities; and social relations within the organization and between the organization and external constituencies). HRM greatly influences an organization's human and organizational resources that are associated with organizational learning and the acquisition of the "intangibles" in joint venture relationships, and therefore can be used to gain competitive advantage (Pucik, 1988; Schuler and MacMillan, 1984).

Organizational learning theory

According to the organizational learning theory perspective (Kogut, 1988; Teece, 1987), prior learning facilitates the learning and application of new, related knowledge (Cohen and Levinthal, 1990). This idea can be extended to include the case in which the knowledge in question is itself a set of learning and knowledge management skills. This capacity increases as a function of the previous experience, its learning processes, and the need for information the firm considers lacking in order to attain its strategic objectives (Lane *et al.*, 2001; Steensma and Lyles, 2000). As regards entry to a foreign market, advocates of the internationalization process school have argued that firms expand slowly from their domestic bases into progressively distant areas. Learning from previous expansions is the driving force behind new investments whether in IJVs or IM&As (Barkema *et al.*, 1997).

Information processing perspective

The information processing perspective is based on the premise that organizations are created to facilitate the flow of information for effective individual and organizational decision making (Egelhoff, 1991; Morgan, 1986). The focus is on the capacity and facilitation characteristics of organizational structure and practices that support, encourage, and reward transfer of information both within the organization and across its boundaries to IJV partners and the IJV itself, and that enable the organization to acquire knowledge to transform the data and information. Learning theory then enters to address how the organization can use this information in a creative way to better deal with and learn from the environment and its own experiences (Daft and Weick, 1984; Garvin, 1993; Makhija and Ganesh, 1997).

Selection theory

The selection theory perspective is referenced here with respect to the selection of potential IJV partners, new business managers, the head of the IJV itself or the staff of the IJV, and even potential merger or acquisition targets. Consistent with statistical propositions, this perspective suggests that the probability of more effective (successful) selection decisions increases as the total number of choices (e.g., applicants) increases (Boudreau and Rynes, 1985). Other things being equal, it behooves an organization to increase the number of choices it has in order to improve the likelihood of a positive selection decision.

Drawing from these theoretical frameworks and perspectives, we offer several guidelines for effectively managing HR issues in CBAs. These guidelines appear throughout the remaining chapters.

Overview of chapters

Chapter 2 – "International joint ventures." After describing the importance of IJVs, their characteristics, and reasons for IJV successes and failures, we provide a four-stage model of HR issues in IJVs. This model provides the foundation for Chapter 3.

Chapter 3 – "Managing human resources in international joint ventures." In this chapter we develop the implications of IJVs for human resource management. Basing the chapter upon the experiences of IJVs and limited systematic research on IJVs, we offer several guidelines for effectively using HRM policies and practices to manage the HR issues that arise in the process of IJV formation and implementation.

Chapter 4 – "International mergers and acquisitions." Chapter 4 describes the nature of international mergers and acquisitions, their importance, the reasons for their use (and nonuse), their success and failure rates, and the assumptions made about them. A three-stage model of HR issues in international mergers and acquisitions is developed, and serves as a foundation for the discussion in Chapter 5.

Chapter 5 – "Managing human resources in international mergers and acquisitions." In this chapter we develop the implications of IM&As for human resource management. As in Chapter 3, we offer guidelines for how to use HRM practices and policies to increase the chances for successfully managing IM&As. These guidelines are suggested by the experiences of IM&As, limited systematic research, and the theoretical perspectives described in Chapter 3.

Chapter 6 – "Managing cultural diversity in cross-border alliances." Within cross-border alliances there are a few major topics and phenomena that warrant greater treatment. One of them is the understanding and management of cultural diversity. Chapter 6 describes the many forms of cultural diversity that must be managed in CBAs and offers several guidelines for managing cultural diversity effectively in such alliances.

Chapter 7 – "Managing cooperation, control, structure, and exit in cross-border alliances." Like Chapter 6, Chapter 7 presents detailed discussions of several phenomena that impact on the quality and success of many types of cross-border alliances. Guidelines are offered for building trust, managing cooperation, balancing control, and planning for exits from alliances.

Chapter 8 – "Cross-border alliances and the HRM profession." The final chapter addresses the roles of HR departments and HR professionals in CBAs. While it is suggested that there are many roles and competencies required, the effectiveness of dealing with the HR issues in IJVs and IM&As is likely to be enhanced if HR professionals work in partnership with all the other multiple stakeholders.

Additional learning aids

To provide a broad-based illustration of the topics, stages, and HR issues and HRM activities discussed throughout the chapters, two case studies are provided in the Appendixes. The case of Davidson-Marley BV is a four-part example of an IJV between a US and a British company, located in the Netherlands. In this case, the focus is on the process of establishing the IJV as viewed from the perspectives of the two parents and the IJV itself. The Precision Measurement Instrument company is an example of an established IJV between a US and a Japanese company, located in Japan. This case focuses on the operation of a mature IJV.

In addition, at the end of each chapter a case example illustrates some of the issues presented in the chapter. Finally, a set of references and Internet resources is provided at the end of the book, for readers who wish to continue to build and enrich their understanding of HRM in CBAs.

Conclusion

Cross-border alliances (CBAs) are important phenomena in the business world today, but their success is far from assured. When firms enter into such alliances, much is at stake. Successful CBAs create new jobs, improve the economic conditions of a community, and produce wealth for share-owners. Conversely, failed CBAs may mean lost jobs, loss of tax revenue, declining share values, and even the eventual demise of companies. By developing a better understanding of the reasons for success and failure in CBAs, managers may be able to increase their ability to negotiate and implement more successful alliances.

This book focuses on the possible human resources-related reasons for CBA success and failure. After identifying the human resource issues that arise in CBAs, we discuss their implications for a variety of human resource management activities. Within each chapter, the discussion illustrates the role of human resource policies and practices in developing and implementing successful CBAs.

2 International joint ventures

> To be a real winner in financial services, you have to be a global company.
>
> Christopher "Kip" Condran
> Head, AXA, U.S. Operations

Many companies enter the global economy by first entering into various nonequity cross-border alliances. Eventually, however, the evolution from domestic to global company is likely to involve the formation of equity-based cross-border alliances (CBAs), such as international joint ventures.

International joint ventures (IJVs) are legally and economically separate organizational entities created by two or more parent organizations that collectively invest financial as well as other resources to pursue certain objectives. Although an overwhelming majority of IJVs involve only two parent firms (one from a foreign country and the other from the home country), some ventures may consist of multiple participants. For example, Xerox Shenzhen is a joint venture (JV) formed between Xerox China Ltd., Xerox's wholly owned holding company in China, and Fuji Xerox, which itself is a U.S.–Japanese JV in Japan. Although there is no single agreed-on definition of an IJV, a typical definition is:

> A separate legal organizational entity representing the partial holdings of two or more parent firms, in which the headquarters of at least one is located outside the country of operation of the joint venture. This entity is subject to the joint control of its parent firms, each of which is economically and legally independent of the other.
>
> (Shenkar and Zeira, 1987a)

There are other forms of JVs including those established between affiliated home country-based firms, between unaffiliated home country-based firms, or between home country- and third country-based firms. Nevertheless, joint ventures that are launched by home country-based (foreign) and host country-based (local) firms are the dominant form of joint venture partnership.

To set up an IJV, each partner contributes cash, facilities, equipment, materials, intellectual property rights, labor, or land-use rights. According to joint venture laws in most countries, a foreign investor's share must be over a certain percentage of the total equity (e.g., 25 percent in China). Generally, there is no upward limit in deregulated industries in most countries, whether developed and developing. However, in governmentally controlled or institutionally restricted sectors, foreign investors are often confined with respect to equity arrangements.

One way to structure IJVs is for each parent to have equal ownership. For example, Prudential-Mitsui is an IJV in which Prudential Insurance and Mitsui Trust & Banking each have 50 percent ownership. Another alternative is for one firm to have majority ownership, and thus also have greater control. In the equity joint venture between America's Corning and Mexico's Vitro, Corning assumed majority ownership (51 percent) while Vitro owned a minority stake (49 percent).

Although international alliances and joint ventures are particularly difficult to manage (Killing, 1983), it appears that as the necessity for rapid response becomes greater, as business risks and costs soar, and competition becomes more severe, firms are relying on international joint ventures with increasing frequency (Cascio and Bailey 1995; Doz and Hamel, 1998; Evans *et al.*, 2002; Harrigan, 1987a; Hopkins, 1999; Lei *et al.*, 1997; Schuler, 2001; Sparks, 1999). While some international joint ventures are short-term in nature, others can aim for longer-term synergies and benefits between partners (Cyr, 1995; Pucik, 1988; Sparks, 1999).

In this chapter and the next, we focus on IJVs for several reasons (Inkpen and Beamish, 1997). First, developing an understanding of the HR issues associated with IJVs requires a depth of analysis not necessary for other types of alliances (Cascio and Bailey, 1995; Child and Faulkner, 1998; Cyr, 1995; Evans *et al.*, 2002). IJVs are typically used when the required degree of integration between the partners is high and the venture business is characterized by uncertainty and decision-making urgency (Doz and Hamel, 1998). Second, because the creation of an IJV involves establishing an independent organization, the HR issues are particularly evident. For example, it is obvious that a new organization cannot function until reporting relationships are established and JV managers are recruited. Thus, it is easy to see why managing HR issues effectively is essential to the success of this type of cross-border alliance (Luo, 1999; Muson, 2002; Newburry and Zeira, 1997; Pucik, 1988). Finally, most of the conceptual and empirical research on the cross-border alliances area has focused on IJVs. Thus, the lessons learned about managing HR issues in IJVs provide a basis for understanding the issues that arise in other forms of cross-border alliances.

Ownership structures

When an IJV is being formed, one of the key strategic decisions is how to arrange the *ownership structure*. The ownership structure is generally defined by the percentage of equity held by each parent. It is particularly important because it determines the levels of control and profit sharing during the IJV's subsequent operation. In the presence of two partners, the joint venture is named a majority-owned joint venture when a foreign investor has greater than 50 percent equity stakes, and a *minority-owned joint venture* if the investor owns less than 50 percent equity stakes. If ownership is exactly 50 percent, the joint venture is considered *co-owned* or *split-owned*.

A partner with majority equity holding has more at stake in the alliance than the other partners. Normally, the equity position will be associated with an equivalent level of management control in the venture. In other words, control based upon equity ownership is often direct and effective. Nevertheless, the correspondence between holding equity and managerial control is not always exact. It is possible for a partner to have a small equity holding but exercise decisive control. Usually, however, management control in general reflects ownership, especially in the international context.

The ownership structure often ends up equally split when both partners want to be majority equity holders. A fifty-fifty percent ownership split ensures that neither partner's interests will be quashed, other things being constant. It best captures the spirit of partnership and is particularly desirable in high-technology JVs as insurance that both partners will remain involved with the venture's technological development. Equally distributed ownership is the only way that top management from each parent firm will stay interested enough to avert problems in the venture. In fact, the use of equal ownership accounts for 50 percent or more of joint ventures in developed countries (Beamish, 1985). Co-owned ownership structure can ensure equal commitment from each partner. Decision making must therefore be based on consensus, which often means a prolonged decision process that can lead to deadlocks. The success of fifty-fifty equity ventures relies strongly on the synergy between partners over issues ranging from strategic analyses to daily management of the venture. It is important that partners speak a common language, have similar background knowledge, and share a set of short-term and long-term objectives. By contrast, partners coming from diverse market environments, with different business backgrounds and conflicting goals, often have a harder time making a fifty-fifty venture a success.

In a minority position, the partner risks opportunism and giving away expertise to the local partner without sufficient returns. More importantly, the ability to control alliance operations is weakened. When dominant, however, the foreign partner risks losing the local partner's access to land, labor, raw materials, production facilities, and expertise in dealing with the bureaucracy of the developing country. As noted earlier, the fifty-fifty option presents its own difficulties when differences between the two partners result in managerial problems and impasses.

Firms attach varying importance to equity ownership levels in JVs depending upon their strategic goals, global control requirements, resource dependence, firm experience, and alternatives for bargaining power, to name just a few factors. A firm may not care much about the equity arrangement if it has many other alternatives for gaining bargaining power and thus controlling the JV's activities. A firm without these alternatives, however, has to rely more on equity arrangement for the control purpose. Of course, high-equity ownership itself cannot ensure a party's satisfaction with JV performance. Venture performance depends more on successful management, especially human resource management, by both parties. We discuss this in Chapter 3.

The importance of international joint ventures

Using an IJV as a mode of international business operation is not new (Ohmae, 1989a, b, c, 1995). But economic growth in the past decade of global competition, coupled with shifts in trade dominance and the emergence of new markets, has contributed to the increase in the use of IJVs (Cyr, 1995). According to Peter Drucker, IJVs are likely to grow in importance:

> Multinationals now tend to be organized globally along product or service lines. But like the multinationals of 1913, they are held together and controlled by ownership. By contrast, the multinationals of 2025 are likely to be held together and controlled by strategy. There will still be ownership, of course. But alliances, joint ventures, minority stakes, know-how agreements and contracts will increasingly be the building blocks of a confederation.
>
> (Drucker, 2001: 5)

Types of international joint ventures

While the concept of the IJV may imply cooperation and partnership between two firms, this is not always be the case (Child and Faulkner, 1998; Perlmutter and Heenan, 1986; Sparks, 1999):

> The change from competitive to collaborative strategies is often merely a tactical adjustment aimed at specific market conditions. Many of these new partnerships should be viewed as a hidden substitute of market competition, not its dissipation. The objective is similar: attaining the position of global market leadership through internalization of key value-added competencies. The potential competitive relationship between partners distinguishes strategic alliances that involve competitive collaboration from more traditional cooperative ventures.
>
> (Pucik, 1988: 78)

Pucik suggests that relations in IJVs that are motivated by cooperation such as the Davidson-Marley IJV, are different from those in IJVs motivated by competition:

> In a truly cooperative relationship the underlying assumption is the feasibility (and desirability) of long-term win/win outcomes. In the partnerships that involve competitive collaboration, the strategic intent of achieving dominance makes the long-term win/win outcome highly unlikely. This does not imply that all partnerships between multinational

firms are always competitive in nature. However, many of them are, especially when seen in a long-term dynamic context. Partnerships that involve competitive collaboration are dynamic in nature. The relative endowment of resources, skills, and competencies and the sources of bargaining power can change over time. For one firm to be able to sustain its long-term competitive advantage, the organization and control of the partnership has to reflect its competitive context.

(Pucik, 1988:79)

IJVs can differ according to the resources they are attempting to leverage. On the one hand, they may be leveraging *tangible resources*, including land, equipment, labor, money, or patents. On the other hand, they may be leveraging *intangible resources*, especially competencies such as management and organizational skill, knowledge of the market, or technological capability (Contractor and Lorange, 1988). These assets are typically unseen and embodied in people within the organization. They represent tacit knowledge that may be difficult to understand and only appropriated over time (Teece, 1987).

Regardless of the motivation for the IJV or the resources involved, firms can structure their relationships so that they are bringing together either: (a) different structural or functional specializations that complement each other, e.g., production and marketing functions; or (b) similar structural or organizational characteristics that build upon or add shared value, e.g., two banks combining their functional assets to build a greater asset base to enter new markets (Porter and Fuller, 1986; Slocum and Lei, 1993). A recent case study (described in Appendix A) conducted by the authors between a U.S. firm (Davidson) and a U.K. firm (Marley) and their IJV, Davidson-Marley in the Netherlands, provides an illustration of the functional specializations that complement each other:

> Located in Europe, Marley gave Davidson knowledge of the market. Far more than this, it gave them functional fit and personal contacts. While Marley understood the marketplace, Davidson had expertise in manufacturing and administrative systems. Thus, while Davidson supplied the technology and the systems, Marley supplied knowledge of the markets and the contacts needed to get the IJV built.
>
> (Schuler *et al.*, 1991: 56)

Thus IJVs can be differentiated on the basis of:

- Cooperative versus competitive motivations: Fuji and Xerox, and Davidson and Marley had cooperative motivations.
- Source of leverage: visible, physical resources such as physical location or plant and equipment versus invisible resources such as competencies.
- The nature of their structure or organizational characteristics such as functional specialization (e.g., distribution vs. manufacturing as in the IJV between TEC in Japan and Precision Measurement called Precision Measurement of Japan (PMJ), as described in Appendix B) vs shared value-added.

- Location; for example, the parents may be in two different countries, such as Davidson and Marley, and the IJV in a third, or the IJV may be in the country of one parent, as with PMJ and TEC. Alternatively, the two parents can be located in developed countries and the IJV in a developing country.

The IJVs between partners with competitive motives attempting to leverage competencies and using a functional specialization structure appear to be the most challenging (Evans, *et al.*, 2002; Pucik, 1988; Schuler, 2001; Slocum and Lei, 1993). Here the relationship tends to be more unstable: one partner wants to gain at the expense of the other, and the methods of defending against one of the attacks on the other partner's competencies are problematic. Although it is easy to develop these conceptual categories of the types of IJVs,

> in all cases, it is important to remember that alliances do not always fit neatly into conceptual boxes. Some partnerships are complementary in parts of the value chain and competitive in others, and a nuanced approach to HRM may be needed. The character of alliances also may change over time. Some alliances are born competitive, while others migrate into a competitive alliance zone over time, an indication that the original need to collaborate may be vanished, primarily because the partners have learned so much from each other that their respective knowledge gaps may have disappeared.
>
> (Child and Faulkner, 1998: 211)

International joint ventures in different contexts

The logic of building IJVs in developed countries may differ from that in developing countries. To most multinational enterprises (MNEs), establishing IJVs in developing countries is mainly designed for gaining access to markets that they cannot penetrate, or cannot penetrate quickly enough to obtain a competitive advantage. Forming IJVs in developed countries, however, often emphasizes co-option, co-specialization, or knowledge internalization (Doz and Hamel, 1998). *Co-option* is the process of neutralizing the competitors' threats and turning potential competitors into allies or providers of the complementary goods and services that allow new businesses to develop. *Co-specialization* is the synergistic value creation that results from the combining of previously separate resources, positions, skills, and knowledge sources. As MNEs refocus on a narrower range of core skills and activities, co-specialization becomes increasingly fundamental. IJVs in developed countries also often serve as a forum for learning and internalizing new skills, in particular those which are tacit, collective, and organizationally embedded. *Knowledge internalization* is hence the process of integrating acquired knowledge from the partner with the firm's own existing knowledge system. When these skills are learned from a global partner, internalized, and exploited beyond the boundaries of the alliance itself, they become more valuable.

Challenges and risks associated with building IJVs

Not every firm should build IJVs to expand globally, and building IJVs is not necessarily a superior strategy to other investment choices in all circumstances. According to a survey by McKinsey & Co. and Coopers and Lybrand, about 70 percent of IJVs fall short of expectations (Doz, 1996). As legally and economically independent organizations, IJVs operate like stand-alone firms and have to engage in all the different types of regular business activity that any independent firm has to undertake. However, IJVs are more complex than the single organization: they involve multiple interorganizational relationships: the relationship between the partner firms, the alliance management's relationship with the foreign parent and with the local parent, and the relationship between the alliance's managers nominated by different partners. Each of these relationships can be extremely difficult to manage. IJVs represent an intercultural and interorganizational linkage between two separate parent companies that join force with different strategic interests and objectives. Inter-partner conflict may arise from sources such as cross-cultural differences, diverging strategic expectations, and incongruent organizational structures. These conflicts in turn can lead to instability and poor performance of the alliance.

Similarly, it is quite a challenging task for the alliance management to effectively create and maintain a healthy relationship with each of the parent firms. In addition to the complex inter- and intraorganizational relationships that a IJV has to manage, the external institutional environments in which the alliance operates can also be quite complex and difficult to manage. On the one hand, like a single, stand-alone organization, an IJV has to interact with the different components of the institutional environment in a local country. On the other hand, as it is the joint child, the alliance's operations are heavily influenced by the institutional environments faced by its parents. Moreover, the cultural environments are different. An alliance has to hire local employees, including both managers and workers. In many cases, taking advantage of the cheap local labor is a major objective of companies from developed economies in forming alliances in developing countries. As a result, cultural and intercultural issues become a challenging task for IJVs.

The above complexities generate problems or risks for using IJVs. First, *loss of autonomy and control* often causes inter-partner conflicts and alliance instability. Each partner may want to control the alliance's operations with its own, and members often have not created adequate mechanisms to resolve such conflicts in decision making. For that reason, coordination and governance costs are generally heightened in IJVs. Cross-cultural partners may differ from each other in terms of long-term objectives, time horizons, operating styles, and expectations for the alliance.

Second, the *risk of possible leakage* of critical technologies may be sizable and often difficult to avoid. Committing distinctive resources is often necessary for gaining a competitive edge in a foreign market. This, however, may engage leakage of valuable intellectual property (known as "*appropriability hazard*"). As distinctive resources are relatively difficult to specify, contract, and monitor, hazards associated with limited protection of such rights are particularly high for these resources, especially in developing countries where intellectual property rights systems have not yet been well established. In the absence of strong control over alliance activities and self-protection mechanisms, local partners may disseminate the foreign investors critical knowledge to third parties.

Third, inter-partner *differences in strategic goals* of alliance formation often lead to cumbersome decision-making processes, which may in turn cause strategic inflexibility. This may be compounded when the alliance managers do not share strategic directions and goals set by parent firms. In the absence of sufficient organizational control over alliance activities, IJVs might even be considered impediments to the flexibility of an MNE's global strategy. The MNE may need to maintain global integration and manipulation of all parts of its global network (outside the IJV) for strategic or financial purposes, but because of the inflexibility of the IJV, global optimization may not be possible for sourcing, capital flows, tax reduction, transfer pricing, and rationalization of production.

Fourth, local partners may *become global competitors* in the future, after developing skills and technology via the alliance. Japanese firms, for example, often plan ahead to increase the benefits they extract from an IJV, leaving the European or American partners in a worse strategic position. In other words, they may look upon partnerships as a cynical competitive move based on tactical expediency (Contractor and Lorange, 1988; Hamel, 1991). Reflecting on its IJV with NEC, one senior executive in Varian Associates (a U.S. producer of advanced electronics including semiconductors) concluded that "all NEC had wanted to do was to suck out Varian's technology, not sell Varian's equipment (Hamel and Prahalad, 1994).

Finally, IJVs may be more *susceptible to governmental regulations* and interventions than local firms in a host country. The host government, especially in less developed countries, may impose restrictions over the level of ownership, location choice, material procurement, distribution arrangement, compulsory export, or profit repatriation. In addition, some countries may have strict antitrust laws that prohibit certain forms of business cooperation among firms. Failure to consider this hazard when forming a global alliance may result in costly and unnecessary litigation, wasteful use of the firm's resources, and setbacks to its competitive position.

Because of the above drawbacks, international managers should make a strategic assessment about the necessity of building IJVs in the course of a feasibility study. This strategic assessment should emphasize value creation and thus is more than a cost–benefit analysis. This is especially true when the alliance is used to learn about a new environment and thereby reduce the uncertainties present in a new territory, when a strategic, rather than financial, view is necessary to capture value creation. Along with the increasing competition and technological development, an IJV is increasingly engaging multiple sophisticated businesses, calling for distinctive resources from multiple partners. This makes value creation analysis for building IJVs more important and more difficult at the same time.

Reasons for forming an IJV

International joint ventures have become a major form of entry into global markets (Barkema *et al.*, 1997; Evans et al., 2002). Harrigan (1986, 1987a) argued that since a joint venture draws on the strengths of its owners, it should possess superior competitive abilities that allow its sponsors to enjoy synergies. If the venture's owners cannot cope with the demands of managing the joint venture successfully, Harrigan advised the owners to use nonequity forms of CBAs such as cross-marketing and/or cross-production, licensing, and research-and-development consortia. Some companies shun joint ventures, preferring 100 percent ownership to the drawbacks of loss of control and profits that can accompany shared ownership (Gomes-Casseres, 1989). Some companies prefer the versatility of an alliance to a joint venture (Muson, 2002). However, many firms, regardless of previous international experience, enter into IJV arrangements. The most common reasons cited in the literature are:

- to gain technical and administrative knowledge, to learn, and to transfer that knowledge (Cyr, 1995; Inkpen and Dinur, 1997; Mudambi, 2002; Lei, Slocum, and Pitts, 1997);
- host government insistence (Datta, 1988; Gomes-Casseres, 1989; Inkper and Dinur, 1997; Shenkar and Zeira, 1987b);
- to gain rapid market entry and catch more customers (Berlew, 1984; Harbison, 1996; Morris and Hergert, 1987; Shenkar and Zeira, 1987b; Sparks, 1999; Tichy, 1988);
- to capture increased economies of scale (Datta, 1988; Newburry and Zeira, 1997);
- to gain local knowledge (Datta, 1988; Lasserre, 1983; O'Reilly, 1988) and local market image and channel access (Gomes-Casseres, 1989; Harbison, 1996);
- to obtain vital raw materials (Shenkar and Zeira, 1987a) or technology (Gomes-Casseres, 1989);
- to spread the risks (Morris and Hergert, 1987; Pucik, 1988; Shenkar and Zeira, 1987b);
- to improve competitive advantage in the face of increasing global competition (Porter, 1980);
- to support company strategies for internationalization (Evans *et al.*, 2002).

The importance of learning

Of these, the reasons that appear to be gaining substantial momentum are learning and knowledge sharing and transfer (Child and Faulkner, 1998; Foss and Pedersen, 2002; Shenkar and Li, 1999). According to Lei *et al.* (1997: 203):

Alliances have emerged as organization designs that enable organizations to deal with the increasing complexity of building and learning new sources of competitive advantage to compete in the global economy. In principle, all strategic alliances may be thought of as coalignments between two or more firms in which the partners seek to learn and acquire from each other products, skills, technologies, and knowledge that are not available to other competitors.

Opportunities. In many industries, increasing global competition and unabated technological advancement have resulted in a wide range of cross-border collaborative partnerships intended to access knowledge, skills, and resources that cannot be internally produced by organizations in a timely or cost-effective fashion. Organizational learning has long been considered a key building block and major source of competitive advantage (Badaracco, 1991). A global alliance is not only a means by which partners trade access to each other's skills but also a mechanism for actually acquiring a partner's skills. In bringing together firms with different skills, knowledge bases, and organizational cultures, IJVs create unique *learning opportunities* for the partner firms. By definition, alliances involve sharing of resources. This access can be a powerful source of new knowledge that, in most cases, would not have been possible without the formal structure of an IJV. As such, IJVs are no longer peripheral but a mainstay of competitive strategy. IJVs forge new knowledge transfer pathways across both technologically and traditionally linked positions.

Learning opportunities are manifested in two areas: *operational* and *managerial*. *Operational knowledge* that one firm can acquire from the partner firm includes knowledge about technology, processes (including quality control), production, marketing skills, and operational expertise (e.g., relationship-building expertise). *Managerial knowledge* that one firm can acquire from the partner firm comprises organizational and managerial skills (e.g., leadership, human resource management, skills related to organizational structure, managerial efficiency, and employee participation), market skills (international and host country), industrial and collaborative experience, and financial management skills (e.g., skills related to cost control, tax reduction, capital utilization, financing, risk reduction, resource deployment, and asset management).

Challenges. Using and relying on external learning and knowledge transfer is challenging and complex (Barkema *et al.*, 1997; Mudambi, 2002). A major source of instability and potential gain to one partner is its greater *learning capacity*.

> The asymmetric appropriation of invisible benefits – such as the acquisition of product or market know-how for use outside of the partnership framework, or even to support a competitive strategy targeted at the partner – cannot be easily protected. The asymmetry results from the internal dynamics of the strategic alliance. Benefits are appropriated asymmetrically due to differences in the *organizational learning capacity* of the partners. The shifts in relative power in a competitive partnership are related to the speed at which the partners can learn from each other. Not providing a firm strategy for the control of invisible assets in the partnership, and delegating responsibility for them to operating managers concerned with short-term results, is a sure formula for failure.
>
> (Pucik, 1988: 81)

Not surprisingly, then, firms considering IJVs have become more concerned about learning, and the capacity for learning as reasons for forming an IJV with another firm (Kamoche, 1997). A fundamental impediment to inter-partner learning and knowledge transfer originates from the nature of knowledge involved. Codified *explicit* knowledge is generally transparent and readily accessible and transferable; but many elements of knowledge transferred between IJV partners are tacit. *Tacit* means that the knowledge is deeply embedded in organizational routines (e.g., structure, rules, and policies) and difficult to codify and teach. In organizations, tacit knowledge involves intangible factors embedded in personal beliefs, experiences, and values. It is also stored organically in team relationships. If two firms seek transfer of the knowledge that is explicitly codifiable (e.g., patents), they normally choose international licensing instead of the IJV. When the knowledge is tacit, and thus uncodifiable in the license contract, the IJV becomes a better device for transferring or sharing this type of knowledge. CBA-In-Action 1 provides an example showing how Chrysler and Mitsubishi used the IJV for acquiring each other's tacit knowledge.

Learning through an alliance: Chrysler's experience

CBA-In-Action 1

When Chrysler joined forces with Mitsubishi Motors Corp. in 1986 to create Diamond Star Motors (DSM), Chrysler's major objective was to gain first-hand knowledge about Japanese management and manufacturing principles. Chrysler deliberately ceded management control for daily operations to Mitsubishi to learn how that firm handled the complex engineering, functional, and operational tasks involved in launching and manufacturing a new range of mid-sized models. Chrysler aimed to do the following:

1 *Adopt a top-down commitment.* Top management clearly conveyed to venture employees why learning is a key objective and how to obtain good information.
2 *Encourage company-wide visits.* Chrysler senior management asked managers at all levels and all functions to make an effort to visit, and learn from, DSM.
3 *Identify high-potential managers.* One of the first trainees at DSM was a very promising engineer who secured a high-level position within manufacturing after training at DSM.
4 *Seek individuals with open minds.* Learning success largely depends on how willing and open the individuals are to learning new ideas and skills. Alliance managers' individual curiosity is an important success factor.

Naturally, each party wants to protect its knowledge from uncompensated leakage to the other. Because of inter-partner asymmetry of knowledge demand and supply, partner protectiveness and accessibility to its knowledge will be correspondingly asymmetrical. In general, partners are likely to be more protective of their knowledge resources when their competitive advantages rely more on them. In a situation of high competitive overlap between partners, one or all firms may be very reluctant to share knowledge and will strive to prevent knowledge leakage to partners because of the risk of knowledge spillover. If IJV partners are rivals or potential rivals, a firm would have a limited incentive to share knowledge.

The extent to which one partner's knowledge is accessible to the other depends on interfirm trust, knowledge complementarity, and reciprocal needs. Increasing trust between partners may reduce partner protectiveness. Knowledge complementarity stimulates inter-partner learning and leads to knowledge transfer. A reciprocal need for each other's knowledge resources provides a solid basis for collaboration and trust. High complementarity increases both incentives for knowledge transfer and accessibility to partner knowledge. Similarly, a reciprocal need for each other's proprietary knowledge boosts knowledge exchange between partners and ensures resource accessibility (Inkpen, 1995; Kogut and Zander, 1996).

Certainly, behaviors and styles of managers in organizations have a significant impact on the ability and willingness of a firm to learn (Frayne and Geringer, 2000). For example, learning requires managers to be open and willing to suspend their need for control. McGill *et al.* suggest that learning-oriented managers need to demonstrate cultural awareness and "humility" which respects the values and customs of others: "cultural-functional narrowness and/or ethnocentricity results in an educated incapacity that reduces the ability of organizations and managers to learn" (1991: 11). Learning can be facilitated by flexibility and a willingness to take risks. Human resource management policies and practices can play a role supporting this knowledge flow, sharing and transfer; for example, by supporting and rewarding risk taking and flexibility (Cyr, 1995; Lei *et al.*, 1997; Pucik, 1988).

While firms and individuals need the ability and willingness to learn as they enter into the IJV formation process, they also need to be transparent so that others may learn as well (Child and Faulkner, 1998; Hamel, 1991). Thus both partners need to have similar qualities that support learning if the partnership is to have a longer-term success (Doz and Hamel, 1998; Hamel, 1991; Lyles, 1987; Parkhe, 1991; Pucik, 1988). Because learning capability can quickly lead to attaining competitive advantage (Prahalad and Hamel, 1990), asymmetry in learning capability can soon lead to partnership instability and dissolution. Although potentially providing a short-term success for one partner, it may also preclude future beneficial IJV partnerships from even being established (Hamel, 1991). Thus while IJV partnerships can produce significant advantages, these can be maximized more effectively in the context of a longer-term, cooperative relationship between the partners (Doz and Hamel, 1998; Makhija and Ganesh, 1997).

Thus learning is critical to today's IJVs, and this begins with the very nature of the design of JVs. Learning also continues as the parents learn more about each other and more from each other (Inkpen and Dinur, 1997). This continues with the parents learning from the IJV itself, which they in turn can use for other units and other JVs. Knowledge and learning sharing and transfer can be seen permeating several levels or stages of the IJV process (Makhija and Ganesh, 1997). Consequently, human resource issues and activities permeate several stages of that process (Child and Faulkner, 1998; Pucik, 1988). The importance of learning and knowledge flow, sharing and transfer is further highlighted by the assumptions made about IJVs.

Basic assumptions made about IJVs

The following set of assumptions underlie a great deal of the IJV activity today (Evans *et al.*, 2002; Schuler, 2001; Sparks, 1999). These assumptions reflect the importance of learning and knowledge as reasons for IJVs. They also suggest the role and importance of HR issues and HRM activities in IJVs. The assumptions include the following:

- IJVs are difficult to run successfully.
- The partners in an IJV learn from each other.
- Ability, motivation, and capacity for learning at the individual, group, and organizational levels are critical to the success of the venture.
- Knowledge and learning can result in instability of the venture.
- Different types of knowledge are transferred by different types of methods.
- A venture with two foreign parents experiences different learning dynamics from a venture with only one foreign parent.
- Ventures in developing countries have different dynamics from those in developed countries.
- Sources of learning include the parents and the IJV itself.
- Learning and transfer of knowledge are essential for success of the venture.
- There are unique issues and stages in the evolution of the IJV.
- There will be conflicts at some time in the life of the IJV.
- There will be changing desire for control by the partners during the life of the IJV.
- Staffing is critical issue for success.
- Organizational structure is critical for success.

As shown in these assumptions about the IJV process, as well as in the reasons for using IJVs – particularly when there is an emphasis on learning – HR issues abound in IJVs. Clearly, the success of IJVs does not depend solely on their ability to manage these HR issues. However, failure to deal effectively with these issues may contribute to the eventual failure of an IJV.

Failure rates of IJVs

Giving further support to the importance of human resource management in IJVs is analysis of the reasons for their failure. IJV failure rates (up to 70 percent) reflect the difficulty of *establishing* a successful IJV (Beamish, 1985; Evans *et al.*, 2002; Harrigan, 1986; Levine and Byrne, 1986; Sparks, 1999). Reasons for failure include the following:

- Partners do not clarify their respective goals and objectives.
- Negotiating teams lack IJV experience,
- A realistic feasibility study is lacking.
- There is lack of clarity about the capabilities of the partner.
- Partners fail to learn *about* each other.
- The impact of the venture on the parent organization is misjudged (Harbison, 1996).

IJV failure rates also reflect the difficulty of *developing* and *implementing* an IJV; for example:

- One partner learns faster than the other, thus reducing its dependency on the other partner.
- Managers from different partners within the venture cannot work together.
- Managers within the venture cannot work with the owners' managers.
- Partners simply renege on their promises.
- Partners fail to trust each other.
- Partners fail to learn *from* the other.
- Markets disappear.
- The technology involved does not prove as good as expected.
- Competitive forces change.

IJV failure can also be associated with the longer term, with how well either parent is able to benefit from the IJV itself. The difficulties at this *advancement* stage of benefiting from IJV itself include:

- unwillingness or inability of the parent to learn from the IJV;
- lack of appropriate organizational structure, managerial roles, and leadership;
- lack of adjustment to the stages of IJV development;
- unwillingness or inability to learn from the parents;
- unwillingness or inability to transfer knowledge from the IJV to the parents, or share it with the parents (Beamish and Inkpen, 1995; Evans *et al*., 2002; Harbison, 1996).

Criteria for success and failure

Clearly, IJV success or failure can occur at several points in time, making it easy to claim success prematurely. Furthermore, the meaning of success or failure is difficult to define. The criteria for defining success or failure depend on the parent companies' expectations and motives for establishing the joint venture. "Joint ventures can be deemed successful in spite of poor financial performance, and conversely, they can be considered unsuccessful in spite of good financial performance" (Schaan, 1988). For example, financial performance may take second place to profits from management fees or royalties from technology transfer. With the emphasis on learning in the current literature, criteria for success are increasingly seen in the longer-term perspective and from the viewpoints of multiple stakeholders, including customers, employees, and society, as presented in Chapter 1 (Child and Faulkner, 1998; Evans *et al*., 2002). A case in point is the method used by Du Pont in its ventures, as described in the CBA-in-Action 2 (Yan and Luo, 2001).

Regardless of how failure rates are measured or determined, many of the reasons are associated with HR issues. And because IJV success rates are still far less than 80 percent, it appears that all IJVs might benefit from increased awareness of how effective HRM can help address such issues.

Performance assessment in Du Pont's ventures

Du Pont first engaged in joint ventures near the beginning of the twentieth century and has pursued more than forty joint ventures since 1950, in a broad array of businesses. Annually, the venture head and a representative from the most closely related worldwide business center set profit goals and evaluated performance. In addition to financial measures, mostly relating to return per resource committed, other criteria are used. These include:

- how safely and ethically the venture operates;
- environmental impact of the venture;
- the venture's innovativeness;
- degree to which the venture satisfied the other partner (this is to forestall discontent);
- degree to which the venture fills the need of its host country (this is to forestall government interference);
- degree of learning about industries, technologies, management techniques, the partner's skills, or countries;
- how smoothly the venture runs (personnel and coordination issues);
- ability to repatriate profits;
- how well the venture meets goals based on the reasons it was created.

Actual performance criteria vary by venture and strongly reflect the reasons the venture was created. Du Pont considers that flexibility is necessary because each venture is unique. One constant exists: safety, health, and environmental dimensions (what Du Pont personnel call "the SHE issues") are always a must. As ventures mature and markets change, criteria change. In particular, once a project is authorized, it has a "proof period." After year 3 (proof year for established products) or year 5 (proof year for ventures involving new product categories), much greater emphasis is placed on financial measures, reflecting the maturing of the venture and the parent's correspondingly appropriate shift from input to output measures.

Four-stage model of IJVs

As introduced earlier, the organizational and human resource issues in IJVs are clearly very extensive (Child and Faulkner, 1998). However, they can be further refined and categorized into several stages, stages that begin with the development of the IJV itself (Evans *et al.*, 2002; Lei *et al.*, 1997; Makhija and Ganesh, 1997; Pucik, 1988; Schuler, 2001). The four stages of the IJV process include:

1 formation: the partnership stage;
2 development: the IJV itself;
3 implementation: the IJV itself; and
4 advancement: the IJV and beyond.

These four stages include activities that begin even before the IJV itself is formed and concludes with the relationship among the three entities: two partners and one IJV. While the literature generally treats one partner as being in the same country as the IJV, as is the case with the Precision Measurement of Japan case, this need not be so. A three-country IJV, however, makes the entire process more complex, and the human resource issues more extensive and important, as illustrated in the four case studies of the Davidson-Marley IJV (Appendix A). The HR issues in each stage of the IJV process are numerous, as illustrated in Box 2.1.

These HR issues and their implications for human resource management policies and practices are more fully developed in Chapter 3. Suffice it to say at this point, however, that there are a multitude of human resource issues at each stage. Here we describe the stages in more detail.

Box 2.1 Four stage model of HR issues in international joint ventures

Stage 1: Formation: the partnership

a Identifying the reasons for forming the IJV
b Planning for the utilization of its potential benefits
c Selecting a manager for new business development
d Finding potential partners
e Selecting the partner(s)
f Understanding control, building trust, managing conflict
g Negotiating the arrangement

Stage 2: Development: the IJV itself

h Locating the IJV and dealing with the local community
i Establishing the appropriate structure
j Getting the IJV management team

Stage 3: Implementation: the IJV itself

k Establishing the vision, mission, values, culture and strategy
l Developing the HRM policies and practices
m Dealing with unfolding issues
n Staffing the IJV

Stage 4: Advancement: the IJV and beyond

o Learning between partners
p Transferring the new knowledge to the parents
q Transferring the new knowledge to other locations

Stage 1: Formation: the partnership

Many writers compare IJVs to a marriage (Child and Faulkner, 1998; Sparks, 1999; Tichy, 1988). The analogy seems to spring from those factors necessary for success, and problems inherent in IJVs owing to their contractual nature. To manage an IJV for success, it is important to understand joint venture formation as including:

- identifying the reasons for forming an IJV;
- planning for the utilization of its potential benefits;
- selecting and retaining a manager for new business development;
- finding potential partners;
- selecting the partner(s);
- understanding control, building trust and managing conflict; and
- negotiating the arrangement.

Identifying reasons for forming the IJV

Potential partners in an IJV need to separately determine their purposes for using an IJV as part of their business strategy. Also noted above, these reasons may include (a) minimizing the sum of production and transactions costs (Hennart, 1988); (b) improving one's competitive position (Gomes-Casseres, 1989); (c) acquiring knowledge (Child and Faulkner, 1998; Kogut, 1988); (d) increasing one's acceptance and legitimacy (Pfeffer and Cohen, 1984); and (e) gaining a new source of skills to improve one's human capital (Cascio, 1991). To maximize success, the objectives of the potential partners should be complementary; that is, the objectives of each should mesh with those of the other firm.

In addition, the success of an IJV is more likely when the parents have *absorptive capacity*. Absorptive capacity refers to capabilities that affect a firm's (here, the parents') ability to learn (Ghoshal, 1987; Shenkar and Li, 1999) and which make them effective repositories of embedded knowledge (Badaracco, 1991; Inkpen and Crossan 1995; Luo, 1998). The firm's ability to monitor, process, integrate, and deploy new flows of knowledge will depend, among other things, on its ability to link this knowledge to its existing knowledge base. A firm must already have knowledge and understanding in a given area if it is to learn from its venture partner in that area (Hamel, 1991; Shenkar and Li, 1999).

Planning for the utilization of potential benefits

The HR issues in an IJV are extremely complex. As trust building, learning, communicating, and selecting are so critical to IJV success, they need to be planned. Early planning in JVs is especially important in order that differences in cultural and management styles between the parents and the venture are considered. Without planning, the likelihood of reaping the gains from the IJV is diminished

(Cyr, 1995; Evans, *et al.*, 2002; Pucik, 1988). Assessing the differences in partners on such qualities as culture, managerial styles, intentions, and absorptive capacity can be part of an HR audit that is conducted prior to formation of the IJV (Pucik, 1988). HR planning can also include an analysis of such external factors as labor market conditions, the nature of legal and cultural conditions, and political and economic conditions in the country or countries of the potential partner and the IJV itself (Florkowski, unpublished, forthcoming 2004; Florkowski and Schuler, 1994).

Selecting the manager for new business development

Although CEOs or COOs may spot IJV opportunities, the managers for new business development are usually responsible for making the IJV happen. Together with a counterpart in the other parent, the manager for new business development carry out the activities remaining in Stage 1. Consequently, the selection of these managers is critical. The more knowledge and experience these managers have, the more likely it is that the IJV will be a success. Consequently, CEOs and former CEOs like Jack Welch of General Electric think that the selection of these managers is one of their most important responsibilities (Stewart, 1999). Because they play such an important role, the parents and the JV will be very dependent on these managers. Thus, the parents may need to offer incentives to increase the chances that these managers will remain with the JV (Lei *et al.*, 1997).

Finding potential partners

Potential partners can come from past JVs, suppliers, competitors, and other firms. Partners from past alliances or JVs make good potential partners for new IJVs because more information about these firms is available, which reduces uncertainty (Child and Faulkner, 1998). Past experience enables the organization to learn not only about the IJV process itself but also about the styles, operations, goals, and practices of the other potential partner. Similar patterns of familiarity may exist with suppliers, but in those relationships the amount of control over the supplier has often been substantially greater than over another past partner. Thus there is likely to be a lesser amount of IJV-relevant knowledge about suppliers.

Increasingly, competitors are a major source of potential partners (Cyr, 1995; Lei *et al.*, 1997; Pucik, 1988). These potential partners are likely to offer knowledge complementarily (one may have a core competency the other does not have): thus, the potential for learning may be greater. IJVs formed with competitors may be less stable, however, particularly if the motivation of the partners is competitive rather than collaborative (Doz and Hamel, 1998).

During the process of IJV formation, foreign companies must identify a potential pool of companies from which to select. The mid-range linkage between partner selection and alliance success rests in inter-partner fit. Thus, the principal consideration for identifying a potential pool of partners is about the inter-partner fit or the mix of skills and resources in alliances. This fit is composed of three important elements: *strategic fit*, *organizational fit*, and *financial fit*.

Strategic fit is defined as the degree to which an IJV partner would augment or complement another's strategies and capabilities in light of industry, market, product, customer, capital or technology-related issues. This, in turn, involves a configuration comprising the inter-partner arrangements, the external environment, and the JV's effectiveness. The successful configuration of these elements requires not only an appropriate alignment of an IJV's organizational capabilities to the external environments, but also a proper match between two partner firms' competitive advantages in such areas as market power, competitive position, industrial experience, and innovation capability.

Organizational fit can be defined as the match between each partner's administrative practices, control mechanisms, cultural practices, and HR characteristics, and may directly affect the efficiency and effectiveness of inter-partner cooperation. It may be useful to conceive of strategic fit (or its source of variance: operation-related partner attributes) as a necessary, but not sufficient, condition for alliance success and organizational fit. Thus, one cannot merely address strategic fit, or operation-related attributes, without understanding that the organizational integration between partners may also be a prerequisite of synergy creation.

Finally, *financial fit* concerns the degree of match in cash flow position and capital structure between partners. Reducing uncertainty in operational cash flow is usually one of the major reasons behind the formation of a joint venture. The reduction of default risk depends on the correlation of the pre-venture cash flows of the two partners. A larger firm, as a result of an alliance, will have better access to capital markets and lower financing costs. This cost advantage implies a reduction in the firm's risk from the lender's viewpoint, which can be achieved by corporate diversification or a conglomerate merger. Tax savings on interest payments or transfer pricing are additional benefits from financial fit. Other than capital structure optimization, financial issues such as foreign exchange earnings, risk hedging, foreign currency financing, and currency swap are major concerns of managers when forming IJVs. Because of this complexity, financial clauses in JV and financial management during JV operations are key to joint venture success.

Each of the above fits is vital in creating a good IJV. Accepting a partner with superior strategic traits but lacking strong organizational and financial attributes may result in an unstable alliance. The possession of desirable organizational attributes without corresponding strategic and financial competence may leave the alliance unprofitable. A partner with superior financial strengths but without strategic and organizational competencies can lead to an unsustainable alliance.

Selecting the partner(s)

Once a pool of potential partners is identified, there are criteria that should be considered in partner selection:

- compatibility of goals;
- complementarity of resources;
- a cooperative culture;
- commitment; and
- capability.

Figure 2.1 schematically highlights these criteria, the five Cs, for selecting appropriate partners.

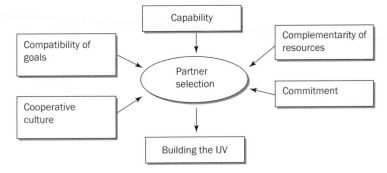

Figure 2.1 The five Cs scheme of partner selection

Goal compatibility. IJV performance flourishes within an atmosphere of inter-partner cooperation and trust but is hindered by opportunism and conflict. Goals behind individual parents can be different, but goals set for the alliance must be compatible (congruent). This is because objectives set for an alliance are collective or common gains for all parents involved. When an IJV's collective goals set by different parents are incongruent, inter-partner conflicts are inevitable in the subsequent phase of operations. In this case, firms are more likely to use opportunistic rather than cooperative strategies during joint venture operations. For instance, many Japanese firms seek Western partners' product innovation via IJVs whereas their counterparts pursue market expansion and/or process innovation in Japan. Similarly, while foreign parents want joint ventures in China as vehicles for accessing that huge market, Chinese parents see IJVs as channels by which to acquire foreign technologies and organizational skills. In contrast, goal congruence reduces a player's uncertainty about what another player will do and propels organizational and strategic fit between foreign and local parents. It may generate more financial or operational synergies because every party is highly motivated to move in the same strategic direction. Additionally, goal compatibility stimulates the commitment of resources by each party.

The situation that holds the most promise for compatibility is one in which strategic goals converge while competitive goals diverge. For example, Du Pont and Philips have a strategic alliance in which both manufacture compact discs, yet respect each other's market boundaries. Unfortunately, not all IJV goals are as compatible. Large companies sometimes send a string of employees to smaller partners for the sole purpose of gaining knowledge. To avoid the pitfall of ambiguous or different goals, participants should make sure they synchronize to begin with, then review what has been accomplished in terms of their original goals at least every three to six months. The success of a consortium between Boeing and three Japanese heavy industry companies to design and build the 767 and future Boeing aircraft is partially attributable to goal compatibility. Boeing sought foreign partners to ease its financial burden and operational risks while the Japanese tried to expand their role in the aerospace industry. The Japanese are now increasing their participation in the industry significantly, providing an ever-increasing portion of production parts and assembly. Boeing has reduced the risks of development by adding a large potential customer and by lowering the financial commitment required for production.

Resource complementarity. It is well recognized that the greater the resource complementarity between foreign and local parents, the greater the operational and financial synergies due to a superior integration of complementary resources pooled by different parents. Resource complementarity also reduces governance and coordination costs and stimulates information exchange during diversification. More importantly, inter-partner complementarity improves the learning curve, thus providing additional benefits to the IJV. In essence, an IJV is a special mechanism for pooling complementary assets. Embedded in the complementary skills approach is the assumption that a firm will seek skills it perceives as lacking but considers vital for the fulfillment of its strategic objectives.

Cooperative culture. Every company has its own unique corporate culture. Companies need to ascertain how well they can manage their differences. Management needs to weigh the pros and cons of cultural differences and how they will impact the IJV. Cooperative cultural and management styles influence mutual trust, which in turn affects venture success. Symmetry must exist at the top level of management, and peer relationships between the top executives of the IJV partners should be established. These relationships are especially important in IJVs that are dissimilar in size.

Normally, maintaining cooperation can become difficult when partners come from different countries. Americans tend to be individualistic. They are not, generally, group oriented. Compared with that of Europeans, their business culture is not as responsive in its approach to IJVs involving firms from other countries. This individualistic attitude is in sharp contrast to that of the Japanese, for example, whose entire cultural direction is oriented toward participation within the group context. Such differences can be complementary, however. The mix of Toyota's team approach and General Motors' corporate style contributed significantly to doubling productivity at NUMMI (New United Motor Manufacturing Company), an IJV between the two companies.

A great danger that exists when cooperative culture is maintained is that one firm may inadvertently relinquish its unique core technology, expertise, or knowledge to the other firm. For example, U.S. companies are generally not as skillful at learning from their venture partners as the Japanese. Many foreign firms view IJVs as an easy way to gain access to U.S. markets and learn U.S. technologies at the expense of U.S. firms. Not only do many foreign companies seek optimal benefit from their venture partners in the United States, but the culture they originate from (especially Japanese culture) is better equipped to accomplish this task.

A company needs to take a close look at compatibility in organizational and management practices with a potential partner. For instance, it should ask: Are both companies centralized or decentralized? If not, are both management teams flexible and committed enough to overcome potential conflict? Do prospective partners use line or matrix organizations, international departments, or global product groups?

Commitment. Finding a partner with an equal sense of commitment to the IJV is the keystone to success. It is also crucial to the realization of the other four Cs. Even if partners appear capable and compatible, the chances of the venture weathering changing market conditions are slim unless they are both willing to invest time, energy, and resources in the alliance. Without this commitment, a partner's resources, complementary or not, cannot help the venture realize its strategic objectives. Without commitment, compatible goals and commensurate risks remain uncultivated. A partner's commitment also affects ongoing trust building and maintenance. Commitment counters opportunism and fosters cooperation. For instance, in HP Medical Product Co. Ltd. Qingdao, China, the eighteen-month R&D project on a new electrocardiogram has been extremely successful, reducing product costs from $10,000 to only $3,000. The Chinese engineers contributed their knowledge of production that fits the demands of Chinese consumers in the most cost-effective way with the maximum local content.

When IJVs face unexpected environmental changes and market dynamics, commitment serves as a stabilizing device offsetting contextual uncertainties. Commitment is therefore even more critical in a volatile environment and/or over a longer term. Inter-partner conflict is more or less inevitable as IJVs evolve. If commitment from both partners is reasonably high, such conflicts may not seriously impair the profitability and stability of the IJV. If low, however, these conflicts will become a primary source of instability and even lead to termination of the venture. For example, the two partners of an IJV in South Korea, Daewoo and GM, each blamed the other for the lackluster performance of the Pontiac LeMans in the United States. Daewoo accused GM of failing to market the LeMans aggressively in the United States, while GM maintained that the initial poor quality of the LeMans and the unreliable supplies soured dealers on the car. Lack of commitment ended this IJV in 1992.

Capability. Capabilities of the potential candidates are of prime importance. IJV architects need to determine which capability to seek from each partner. While the ideal contribution is highly situational, the value-creating logic should guide the assessment of capability contribution. In general, it is critical for IJVs to have the ability to tilt the competitive balance in favor of the coalition and to allow members to gain competitive strength. For instance, in its battle against Sony for leadership of the video cassette recorder (VCR) market, JVC brought a new standard, new products, and the Japanese manufacturing advantage to its coalition. In Europe, the partners were sufficiently strong to provide market access, but sufficiently weak that they could not go it alone. Thus, JVC avoided Philips while co-opting that company's weaker, but not minuscule, European competitors: Thomson, Thorn, Nokia, and others. While each was relatively weak, they collectively provided large-scale access to European markets and the ability to lobby their respective governments and the European Community.

In the case of the Davidson-Marley joint venture (Schuler *et al.*, 1991), Davidson (in the United States) was selecting a partner from among four different licensees with which it had experience in Western Europe. From these potential partners it chose the one (Marley in the United Kingdom) with which it had the most in common. This commonality included the following:

- Both used consensus-style management.
- Both were part of a larger organization that is relatively decentralized.
- Both desired to move to the Continent with a manufacturing presence.
- Both had similar views on how to grow the business.
- Both had similar philosophies on how to run a business and how to manage human resources.
- Both desired a fair and open relationship (Schuler *et al.*, 1991).

It appears that the selection produced a relatively good match using the five Cs (Schuler *et al.*, 1991). Certainly both partners were interested in a long-term, cooperative relationship.

Understanding control, building trust and managing conflict

Consensus has it that the very nature of JVs contributes to their failure: they are a difficult and complex form of enterprise (Shenkar and Zeira, 1987b), and many companies initiate IJVs without fully recognizing and addressing the major issues they are likely to confront (Morris and Hergert, 1987). Success requires adept handling of three key issues: *control*, *trust*, and *conflict*.

Control. Control, along with trust and learning, is one of the most important and most studied topics in the IJV literature (Geringer and Hebert, 1989; Inkpen and Currall, 1997; Yan and Gray, 1994). As a consequence, it is introduced here, but more fully developed in Chapter 7. Control is basically a purposeful and goal-oriented activity that influences the acquisition, interpretation, and dissemination of information within an organizational setting.

Control issues in an IJV often arise in decisions about:

- hiring and training of JV managers;
- sources of raw materials;
- product design;
- the production process;
- quality standards;
- product pricing;
- sales strategies;
- budgeting of sales and cost targets;
- capital expenditures; and
- finance.

Who actually controls the operation can depend on who is responsible for the day-to-day management of the IJV. Ownership distribution may matter less than how operating control and participation in decision making actually is apportioned (Harrigan, 1986). For a parent with minority ownership, for example, the right to appoint key personnel can be used as a control mechanism (Schaan, 1988).

Control can be achieved by appointing managers loyal to the parent company and its organizational ethos (Killing, 1983). Of course, loyalty to the parent cannot be guaranteed: "The ability to appoint the joint venture general manager increases the chances that the parent's interests will be observed, but it is no guarantee that the joint venture general manager will always accommodate that parent's preferences" (Schaan, 1988: 14).

Top managers of the IJV will be expected to make decisions that deal with the simultaneous demands of the parents and their employees in the enterprise. At times, such decisions will by necessity meet the demands of some parties better than those of other parties. If the partners do not anticipate such decisions, they may fail to build in control mechanisms to protect their interests. Weak control also can result if parent company managers spend too little time on the IJV, responding to problems only on an ad hoc basis. Finally, control-related failures are likely to occur if control practices are not reevaluated and modified in response to changing circumstances (Doz and Hamel, 1998; Inkpen and Currall, 1997).

Trust. Inkpen and Currall (1997) define trust as a reliance on another partner under a condition of risk. Four dimensions of trust include (a) communication and information exchange; (b) task coordination; (c) informal agreements; and (d) surveillance and monitoring, indicating the absence of trust. Trust is positive because it strengthens interorganizational ties, speeds contract negotiations (Reve, 1990), and reduces transactions costs (Bromiley and Cummings, 1993).

It appears that learning and trust are positively related while trust and the use of informal and formal controls are negatively related (Dyer, 1997; Nooteboom *et al.* 1997; Yan, 1998). Since learning is a critical component of an IJV's longevity, establishing mechanisms to ensure that trust increases benefits the relationship between IJV partners

(Child and Faulkner, 1998; Doz and Hamel, 1998). Thus a partner needs to reduce the likelihood of engaging in opportunistic behavior when the balance of power shifts in its favor (Inkpen and Currall, 1997). Partners need to resist the "race to learn" at differential rates because this will shift the balance of power and the focus of dependencies.

Because joint ventures are inherently unstable relationships, they require a delicate set of organizational and management processes to create trust and the ongoing capacity to collaborate (Johnson *et al.*, 1996). This means that executives in the two parents must be involved in designing management processes that (a) provide effective ways to handle joint strategy formulation; (b) create structural linkages; (c) provide adequate day-to-day coordination and communication; and (d) establish a win–win culture (Child and Faulkner, 1998; Tichy, 1988). More discussion on trust development is provided in Chapter 7.

Conflict. Differences in such parent qualities as relative power, levels of commitment, experience with IJVs, goals, size, location of parents, and cultural similarity can lead to conflict (Killing, 1983; Lin and Germain, 1998; Parkhe, 1991). Many misunderstandings and problems in IJVs are rooted in managerial differences (Datta, 1988). Differing approaches to managerial style are one area that can create problems. For example, one party may favor a participative managerial style while the other may believe in a more autocratic style of management. Another area that can be problematic is acceptance of risk taking when one parent is prepared to take more risks than the other. Such differences often make the process of decision making slow and frustrating. The resulting conflict can be dysfunctional, if not destructive.

Parents need to develop strategies to resolve potential conflicts in order to increase the likelihood of success (Lin and Germain, 1998). Sometimes the partners in an IJV have differing goals. This is especially likely when an IJV is formed as a solution for reconciling incongruent national interests. For example, a parent may be obliged to share ownership with a host government despite its preference for complete ownership and control. In such a case, the two partners are likely to be concerned with different stakeholder constituencies: business strategies may differ as a result. For example, the local partner may evaluate strategic choices on the basis of how effective they are likely to be in the local market, while the multinational parent would favor strategies that maintain image and reputation in the global market (Gomes-Casseres, 1989). Cultural differences also may impact strategy; for example, Americans are alleged to have a shorter-term focus than the Japanese or the Chinese (Hofstede, 1993; Webster, 1989).

Differing levels of commitment from the two parents provide yet another source of conflict (Bere, 1987; Datta, 1988). When an imbalance exists, the more committed partner may feel frustrated by the other partner's apparent lack of concern; or the less committed partner may feel frustrated by demands and time pressures exerted by the other, more committed partner.

In resolving conflicts, Lin and Germain (1998) found that a problem-solving strategy seems to be more effective than strategies involving compromise, force, or legalisms.

They also found that parents with more experience with each other tended to have fewer understandings and relied less on codification than on their knowledge of and trust in each other. With experience, the IJV parents get to know each other better and develop ways of resolving differences (Inkpen and Crossan, 1995).

Negotiating the arrangement

According to Luo,

> Negotiating IJV formation is difficult and costly. . . . Normative specifications and stipulations are necessary for all parties to ensure control of their respective strategic resources while benefiting from possible financial or operational synergies generated from the venture.
>
> (1999: 143)

Major terms stipulated in a joint venture agreement normally include:

- the JV's name and its legal nature (e.g., whether it is to be a limited liability company or not);
- the scope and scale of production or operations;
- the amount of investment, the unit of currency, and equity (ownership) distribution;
- forms of contribution (e.g., cash, technology, land, or equipment);
- the responsibilities of each party;
- technology or knowledge transfer;
- marketing issues (e.g., whether focusing on the export market or the local market);
- composition of the board of directors;
- nomination and responsibilities of high-level managers;
- joint venture project preparation and construction;
- labor management (e.g., various HR issues);
- accounting, finance, and tax issues (e.g., the currency unit of accounting);
- duration of the joint venture (i.e., how many years is the venture planned to last);
- disposal of assets after expiration;
- amendments, alterations, and discharge of the agreement;
- liabilities for breach of contract or agreement;
- *force majeure* (i.e., force or power that cannot be acted or fought against);
- settlement of disputes (e.g., by litigation or arbitration); and
- the effectiveness of the contract and miscellaneous concerns.

Negotiating strategies affect the bargaining process as well as outcomes. Assembling the negotiating team is a critical element in creating a workable alliance. Qualified negotiators must be able to convey effectively what their parents expect to achieve from the IJV, the plans for structuring and managing the alliance, the value of the contributions each partner brings to the table, and useful solutions to potential problem areas. Good negotiators also need to be aware of the culturally rooted negotiating styles of the parties.

Negotiations about forming an IJV become much easier when the discussions involve negotiators with rich experience dealing with diverse cultures.

MNEs often include alliance manager candidates in the negotiating teams. For example, in the alliance activities of ICL, Fujitsu, Westinghouse, Glaxo, Tanabe, Philips, Montedison, and Hercules, the companies usually bring their alliance executive candidates to the negotiating table. This kind of inclusion offers several benefits. First, it provides the executives with an opportunity to see whether they are compatible with their potential partners. Second, it provides continuity. An IJV manager involved in structuring the deal will be aware of its objectives, its limitations, and the partner's strengths and weaknesses. Third, the expertise of the individuals who will manage the alliance can be valuable to the structuring of a workable contract. Lastly, an alliance manager who takes part in creating the alliance is more apt to be committed to its success than one who has had the responsibility thrust upon him or her.

Another successful strategy for negotiating large, sophisticated alliance projects is to have two levels of negotiations (see CBA-in-Action 3). On one level, senior executives meet to define the general goals and form of cooperation. The negotiations concern broad strategy and establishing whether the partners not only want to but can work together. At the second tier, operational managers or experts gather to thrash out the details of the alliance contract. At this level, it is important to include executives who are experienced with negotiating and managing partnerships. Siemens, Toshiba, and IBM followed this strategy when they negotiated an R&D alliance to develop the 256-megabit DRAM chip. Senior executives at the three companies met and agreed on the principal objectives of the alliance contract. The three partners then organized a team to address many structural and managerial issues. Engineers and lower-level managers from each partner formed a single team to iron out the specifics of the development project and map out the work schedule and goals for the project.

Ciba–Corning negotiations

In 1985, Ciba-Geigy of Switzerland and Corning of the United States formed an equally owned strategic alliance called Ciba Corning Diagnostics. Negotiations were facilitated first by the strategic match between the partners. Ciba-Geigy, which is now Novartis, is a global pharmaceutical and chemical company; Corning is a world leader in the application of glass and ceramics technology. The two firms planned to add Ciba's know-how in therapeutics and body mechanisms to Corning's medical technology in order to develop innovative medical diagnostic tests. Negotiations were also facilitated when each partner appointed its R&D director as a member of the alliance's board. This action not only sent a strong signal to the other partner, but also mobilized internal support for transferring technology to the alliance. Lead representatives were also assigned on each side to help build consensus, improve the dialogue and obtain parent support. Moreover, Corning board members often held debates before attending meetings, both to build internal support and to prepare for discussions with Ciba board members.

While each alliance has its own unique needs in terms of negotiators, companies must at least start with a multifunctional team to cover all of the basics. The following individuals are often involved or included in a negotiating team:

- a business or divisional head;
- a member of the future management team for the venture;
- a technical adviser;
- a marketing expert;
- a legal expert;
- a regional or country liaison/translator;
- a financial analyst;
- a human resource expert; and
- a production expert.

Moreover, management needs to check whether both local and corporate headquarters input is needed. Many companies, such as Ford, rely on their different regional operations to handle negotiations directly. Once companies have identified the suitable negotiators for a deal, the executives should be well prepared to sit down and flesh out an agreement.

Not surprisingly, the quality of IJV contract negotiations during the IJV formation can have an impact upon overall performance (Lei *et al.*, 1997; Luo, 1999). Central to the quality of the contract negotiations are the bargaining processes and strategies used by each of the partners (Aldrich, 1979; Green and Walsh, 1988; Yan and Gray, 1994). For partners interested in learning, approaching the negotiations with a problem-solving strategy would appear to be effective. Establishing trust and mutual understanding, perhaps through previous experience, would aid in establishing the culture for the problem-solving strategy.

The characteristics of the contract negotiator(s) can also have an impact on the success of the IJV. These characteristics include cultural similarities, personality and skills, and loyalty. Selecting on the basis of these characteristics and ensuring that they are supported and rewarded are important HRM contributions.

Stage 2: Development: the IJV itself

Once the IJV has been agreed to and formed, there are several important activities that must be addressed in the development of the IJV itself (Child and Faulkner, 1998). These include:

- locating the IJV;
- designing the appropriate structure; and
- getting the IJV management team.

Locating the IJV and dealing with the community

Where to locate the IJV is an important decision. Should it be located in a third country or in the country of one of the partners? Locating in a third country may diminish "the home field advantage" for either partner; however, it may also increase the need for information gathering and broader expertise because several of the local stakeholders, such as union, political officials, culture, and laws, may be unknown to both partners. This was the case with Davidson and Marley. Locating in the country of one partner, however, may give that partner a "local knowledge" advantage. If, however, this knowledge is shared with the other partner, the advantage moves to the partnership and the IJV itself rather than one partner. The same can be accomplished if the IJV is located in a third country of familiarity to one of the partners (Schuler *et al.*, 1991). In either scenario, the organizational and HR implications are significant, as local labor market conditions must be assessed and stakeholder objectives must be identified.

The appropriate structure

In developing the IJV, a major consideration is providing an appropriate organizational structure. One aspect of structure that is particularly important is the extent to which the IJV is given autonomy to make its own decisions, adapt to the local environment, and operate on its own. There are many decisions for which autonomy may be given or withheld by the parents *vis-à-vis* the IJV; for example:

- general administration;
- production technology;
- operations management;
- research and development;
- marketing sales;
- distribution/logistics;
- finance management;
- human resource management; and
- public relations; and relations with the government.

The second structural decision concerns the methods or processes by which the IJV will be attached or integrated into the parents in order to provide a transfer of knowledge, learning and other resources (Doz and Hamel, 1998; Doz and Prahalad, 1981). A key issue to be addressed by the IJV structure is how to ensure that the IJV itself can be locally effective and also that the parents can be globally effective.

Conditions that may be favorable for giving the IJV considerable autonomy over HR, marketing and other decisions include:

- dissimilar operating environments (Prahalad and Doz, 1987);
- lack of industry knowledge by the parents; and

- high quality of the IJV top management team (Beamish, 1985; Zeira and Shenkar, 1990).

Conditions that may indicate that the IJV should have less autonomy over these and other decisions include:

- a need for global coordination (Bartlett and Ghoshal, 1986);
- the fact that the hierarchical nature of the parents requires a control structure over the IJV system (Root, 1988);
- a concern that the JVs may become too strong to control (Harrigan, 1985);
- limited local management ability in the IJV (Child and Markoczy, 1993).

If the structure grants a great deal of autonomy to the IJV, then the parents confront the question of how to integrate the IJV with the parents in order to provide the parents the opportunity to learn and transfer information and knowledge from the IJV. Such information and knowledge flow can be facilitated by formal methods such as detailed documents of conduct and agreed-upon exchanges of specific information; and/or by informal means such as the selection processes used by the IJV and/or personnel transfers and assignments between the IJV and the parents (Makhija and Ganesh, 1997). Used in combination, the formal and informal methods may facilitate the transfer of both explicit and tacit knowledge. With the information and knowledge flowing in both directions, absorptive capacity in the partners and the IJV may be increased, thus furthering the success of all three companies in the IJV process (Egelhoff, 1991).

Getting the IJV management team

The members of the IJV management team include:

- the board of directors;
- the managing director (general manager);
- the HR leader; and
- the COO.

Broadly speaking, the selection criteria for these members include:

- knowledge of the business (Schuler *et al.*, 1992);
- knowledge of the parents' strategy, structure, and values;
- knowledge of local culture, politics, laws, companies (Adler and Bartholomew, 1992; Schuler and van Sluijs, 1992);
- ability and willingness to learn; cognitive complexity (Hamel, 1991; Inkpen and Crossan, 1995);
- ability and willingness to encourage and transfer learning (Hamel, 1991);
- loyalty to the parent;
- ability to negotiate;
- ability to be a boundary spanner (Schuler *et al.*, 1992);

- understanding of cultural differences (Hofstede, 1970);
- tolerance for conflict and ambiguity (Schuler *et al.*, 1992); and
- entrepreneurial spirit and energy, particularly for the managing director.

In addition to using the right criteria, the selection process is critical. To facilitate the objectives of the partnership and the IJV, the managing director and the HR manager may need to be sourced locally, with criteria agreed upon by both parents. In the case of the Davidson-Marley joint venture, both parents got involved in the selection of the general manager: Recognizing the importance of key personnel appointments, the parents agreed to collaborate in the selection of the general manager. They agreed on the search firm that helped them identify candidates, and jointly decided upon the final criteria used in the selection process. Davidson expressed some desire to have a person with manufacturing experience in plastics from the Netherlands. One selected individual went to Davidson's headquarters in New Hampshire for several months. During that time, the individual concerned became familiar with Davidson's technology, manufacturing systems, and HR practices and philosophies (Schuler *et al.*, 1992).

When both parents are interested in the IJV and want it to succeed, they appear to get involved in all the key decisions made early on. Under these conditions, the board of directors is likely to be composed equally of representatives of the parents and the IJV (internal and external to these entities). The COO, if not the managing director, may be selected from the source providing the most experience with the operation of the IJV.

Stage 3: Implementation: the IJV itself

The implementation stage of the IJV process involves:

- establishing the vision, mission, values, and culture;
- developing the HR policies and practices of the IJV;
- dealing with unfolding issues; and
- staffing the IJV.

Establishing the vision, mission, values, culture, and strategy of the IJV

By establishing these, the IJV begins to:

- provide cohesion;
- provide meaning;
- provide direction;
- specify guidelines;
- provide motivation; and
- provide opportunities (Thompson and Strickland, 1998).

The vision, mission, values, culture, and strategy need to support, encourage, and reward learning and the sharing of knowledge (Slocum and Lei, 1993). They also need to support the other needs of the business, the needs of the parents, and the needs of the other multiple stakeholders. With a high-quality top management team in the IJV, the vision, mission, values, and strategy are more likely to be crafted to fit the local needs as well as those of the parents. At this point, it is clearly not in the interest of the IJV to ignore the linkages with the parents. For the parents, willingness to trust the IJV's top management team to act in their interests and at the same time the interests of the IJV is critical (Child and Faulkner, 1998; Inkpen and Dinur, 1997; Schuler and van Sluijs, 1992; Schuler *et al.*, 1992).

Developing the HRM policies and practices

The entire set of HRM policies and practices for the IJV need to reflect the IJV's: (a) vision, mission, values, culture, and strategy; (b) labor market; (c) need for global integration with parent(s); and (d) differences between the country cultures of the parent and the IJV. As shown in Table 2.1, acceptable human resource management policies and practice may vary substantially based upon the cultural dimensions of the countries (Hofstede, 1993).

The more that the development of HRM policies and practices is left with the IJV, the greater the likelihood that the practices will be effective for local adaptation, but not as effective for global integration and learning transfer (Child and Faulkner, 1998). High-quality top managers are more likely to develop locally responsive HRM policies and practices with sensitivity to the parents' considerations. In the IJV between Marley and Davidson,

> [s]pecific selection, performance appraisal, and compensation practices [were] left to the discretion of the new general manager, but it [was] expected that this individual [would] adopt the Davidson-Marley philosophy of employee involvement, participation, job flexibility, egalitarianism, and teamwork. These [were] practices both parents adopted in their own operations to facilitate high quality. Davidson and Marley [felt] that local labor councils [were] flexible and open to these practices, but the task of actually negotiating specifics [was] done by the IJV's management staff.
>
> (Schuler *et al.*, 1991: 57)

Dealing with unfolding issues

There are many HR issues that unfold as the IJV gets set up, including:

● the assignment of managers;
● management training;
● managers' time-spending patterns;

Table 2.1 Likely HR policies and practices in different cultural dimensions

HR practices	Power distance		Individualism		Uncertainty avoidance		Masculinity	
	Low	*High*	*Low*	*High*	*Low*	*High*	*Low*	*High*
Staffing	Select for career progression Joint placement and career decisions	Select for specific job and level Boss places and plans employees' careers	Selection for team players and Willingness to contribute to firm	Selection for individual contributions Desire to develop own career	No job descriptions General career guidelines	Clear job descriptions Clear career paths Specific rules and policies	Fit into group Fit with organization	Take personal responsibility Ability to do job
Appraising	Joint problem solving Personal initiative in planning execution 360% feedback	Assign goals One-way communication	Not focus on task accomplishment as much as group membership and loyalty	Individual task accomplishments Set personal goals	Set of difficult and specific goals that involve high risk-taking	Set easy goals with low risk-taking	Use social benefit, quality of work life and equality	Job tasks and goals Work action plans Performance feedback
Compensating	Employee participation and involvement in reward techniques Profit sharing; gain sharing	No employee participation Status distinctions accepted	Group-based contingent rewards Noneconomic rewards that satisfy recognition needs	Individual-based contingent rewards Individual praise and recognition	Link pay to performance External equity Flexibility Broad banding	Limited use of performance based (at risk) pay; Predictability: pay consistency	Use of social benefits, quality of work life, non-zero sum, job security	Use performance pay; competitive pay, promotion, and recognition
Training and leadership	Skills for advancement	Skills for present job Direction	Skill improvement to contribute to organization Group skills Consideration	Skill improvement for self improvement Autonomy	General application Participative General directions	Task specific Structure; direction	Develop social skills	Develop task skills Initiating structure
Work design	Provides freedom, discretion, and participation	Job structure, feedback and direction by boss	Facilitates work design that includes team work, task significance, feedback from others	Use of task identity, autonomy, feedback from job	Challenge Job enrichment; personal intrinsic gain	Simple job design Limited scope of responsibility Enable group interaction	Job context important Colleagues, security and safety	Job content important Challenge, task accomplishment

Source: Adapted from R. Schuler, "Human Resource Activities in IJVs," *International Journal of Human Resource Management* (February 2001) © R. Schuler, 2001

- management evaluation; and
- career and benefits planning (Shenkar and Zeira, 1990; Dowling *et al.*, 1999).

The substance of these issues needs to be addressed explicitly by any IJV (Lorange, 1986).

Assignment of managers. Each partner may place differing priorities on the joint venture; therefore, a partner may assign relatively weak management resources to the venture. To be successful, not only should the assigned managerial resources have relevant capabilities and be of adequate quality, but the overall blend of these managerial resources should reflect a balance of the interests of both parents and of the IJV. These managerial assignments should reflect equal quality, particularly on the attribute of absorptive capacity, to help ensure an equal capacity to learn and transfer knowledge to the parents. Balance should also be evident in the number and importance of the managerial assignments made by both parents. This balance should also reflect the input and views of the IJV's top management team (Child and Faulkner, 1998).

Because these assignments could be perceived as attempts to control the IJV (Pucik, 1988), it could be argued that the IJV's top management should have the final say in the staffing of any positions within the IJV itself. Where trust needs are high, however, and the parents have the needed competencies, the parents may be able to dictate initial and temporary staffing needs. In the Davidson-Marley IJV case, because of the skills of the two partners, Davidson supplied the human resources relevant to the manufacturing systems and the administrative systems. Marley actually built the plant, but Davidson designed the interior of the facility to fit its technology. In addition, Davidson assigned three design engineers from its facility in the United States to be expatriates in Europe. These engineers worked with fourteen contract designers recruited in Europe to design the component that was to be manufactured in the plant. Marley located a sales manager in the Netherlands, and supplied sales and marketing support to the company. These were all temporary managerial assignments that were removed once the facility was up and running and the local personnel were trained.

As in less formalized cooperative venture organizations, such as project-based cooperative networks and renegotiated networks, the critical management assignment issue is employing people who can communicate and interact with one another effectively in such settings. Overall, assigning personnel to the project should be accomplished according to at least three general criteria:

1 Assigned managers must reflect the necessary specialized skills that each partner has agreed to contribute to the joint venture. These skills must be of adequate quality; thus, second or third stringers should normally not be assigned to the project.
2 The managers assigned must be sufficiently compatible in style to communicate and work together in effecting the cooperative venture. This requires teamwork and cooperation across functions, not isolation within each specialized camp.
3 The assigned managers must have the ability to provide adequate feedback to their respective parent organizations, giving continuous ad hoc support for unforeseen backup activities within a reasonable amount of time.

Management training. It is important to make managers aware of the special nature of IJVs, and then to enroll them in a systematic training program. Such a program should explain the structure of IJVs, identify the various employee groups in such ventures – and the human resource problems they typically create – and offer possible solutions for these problems. *It is important that both parent-company executives and managers assigned to IJVs receive such training*, ideally before they begin their assignment. Such training can do much to help the IJV succeed. For example, executives of the IJV who were involved in selecting partner firms for the venture are likely to negotiate a successful contract, manage the IJV effectively, and make more successful decisions. In short, training can improve the odds that the partner will have a successful "marriage."

Training is generally most effective if it is provided before the venture is under way. However, even IJVs that are already operational can significantly benefit from an organization training and development effort. These efforts are designed to make employees aware of the complexity of the system, and to sensitize them to the needs and constraints of employees in other groups. A role-based intervention is particularly recommended because it allows for an analysis of each party's expectations but avoids deep emotional involvement by the participants. In a role-based intervention, participants learn to understand the constraints faced by other "players" in the venture; this understanding can lead to better communication and deeper trust among the groups. Ideally, such an effort should begin early in the life of the venture, and should be tailor-made to fit the needs of the particular IJV.

Training in partners' national cultures and languages can be a most important step towards breaking down internal cultural barriers and blocks to mutual understanding. It is particularly important that the partners' staff who have to work together receive language instruction (where relevant) and training designed to promote their understanding of the partner's culture, national institutions, mindsets, and codes of behavior. This preparation will not compensate for errors in selection that result in people who are intolerant, inflexible, or otherwise ill-suited to working with other organizational or national cultures. It will, however, enable those who are well chosen to avoid some of the pitfalls that can otherwise jeopardize the effectiveness of cross-partner teams and meetings. The facility and willingness to converse, at least to some degree, in the partner's language expresses goodwill and opens the psychological door to further communication.

An appreciation of the likely cultural or political sensitivities of a partner's staff can avoid unnecessary conflict and mistrust. For example, in collective meetings with East Asian staff, it is vital not to place individuals in a position where they are shamed before their colleagues; this is an extreme cultural sensitivity. This does not mean, however, that opinions and evidence should not be challenged in the management meetings held by, say, a Sino-Western joint venture. It means, rather, that care and time have to be taken over the course of several meetings to move toward a shared understanding that everyone present, especially the senior foreign manager, can be questioned in a courteous way without any face being lost, and that this amounts to a "testing of reality" that is of benefit to everyone in carrying out their work. The aim, in this case, is to blend the personal courtesy of the East with the open inquiry of the West. It is much more difficult to achieve this if the partners' HRM routines do not include suitable briefings and role plays to prepare staff for these situations.

Managers' time-spending patterns. The IJV has to carry out a set of operating duties simultaneously with its development of new strategies. This raises the issue of the appropriate emphasis to give to operating tasks and strategic tasks; sufficient human resources must be allocated for both. The situation is similar to that of an independent business organization: the IJV must be able to draw sufficient human resources from the operating mode to further develop its strategy. If the parent organizations place strong demands for short-term results on the IJV, this may leave it with insufficient resources to staff for strategic self-renewal. This problem is likely to be intensified if the IJV has to look for a customer base to support its existence. Over time, the balance between focus on operations versus strategic planning may shift as the IJV becomes more independent and the short-term operating tasks become more manageable.

Management evaluation. Assessing managerial performance and competency is also necessary. The partners must cooperate in assessing their performance of one another's functional specialists. Doing so helps prevent the inadvertent buildup of second-string functional specialists. For this reason, managerial performance and competency judgments issues should involve all of the partners (the parents and the IJV itself) in cooperation. In these situations, it may be appropriate to use joint performance review committees to make judgments and give feedback. CBA-in-Action 2 (p. 36) furnishes an example (Du Pont) of how the alliance performance could be appraised to reflect concern for multiple stakeholders (Jackson and Schuler, 2003).

The long-term relationship and shared objectives of Davidson and Marley made inappropriate staffing decisions less likely. Also, early decisions to limit reliance on expatriates to the controller and three design engineers helped to minimize the potential problems arising from off-loading surplus managers. Thus in the case of Davidson-Marley, the concern by the parents of monitoring and evaluating the IJV itself was minimal (Schuler and van Sluijs, 1992). This was also true at PMJ.

Career and benefits planning. It has been reported that more than 50 percent of expatriates felt that their overseas assignments were either immaterial or detrimental to their careers (Schuler *et al.*, 1991) – a finding that indicates potential motivational problems any IJV may encounter. The motivation of executives assigned to an IJV can be enhanced by the creation of a clear linkage between the assignment and an assignee's future career. Some assurance of job security may be needed to offset perceived risks. As with any overseas assignment, assignment to a joint venture may make the manager's future career appear uncertain. If the parent company has not thought through this issue, this uncertainty may be justified. Thus, parent organizations should offer career planning to counter the ambiguity and risks associated with an IJV assignment, and to limit the potential for unsatisfying repatriation experiences (Black *et al.*, 1999; Brewster and Harris, 1999; Caligiuri and Lazarova, 2000; Shenkar, 1995).

Apart from career-path disturbances, the assignment to an IJV post usually requires relocation to a foreign country, with all the disruption to family and social life that such a posting entails. Benefits packages must be designed to maintain the economic and social lifestyle of the manager so that the individual does not lose through the IJV assignment (Dowling *et al.*, 1999).

Staffing the IJV

Success of the IJV rests upon getting the right people at the right place at the right time. Cyr (1995: 120) recommended the following guidelines for staffing all IJV positions:

1 Use extensive screening procedures for employees at all levels.
2 Exchange staff from the parents who are strong contributors with appropriate skill sets (not "deadwood" that the parent firms wanted to relocate).
3 Allocate sufficient numbers of staff to the joint venture to maximize the benefits of continuous improvement through high employee involvement.
4 Hire managers for the JV with special skills beyond those of traditional managers (e.g., possessing cultural and political expertise as well as knowledge of management techniques).
5 Staffing "the top" (e.g., the JV's board) with managers who have exemplary personal skills, the ability to communicate effectively, and flexibility.
6 Develop HR policies that protect the interests of the joint venture (e.g., retain key JV personnel) but at the same time allow flexibility in order that staff do not feel trapped in the venture.

Sources of staff members for the IJV include:

- parents;
- local country nationals;
- third country nationals;
- competitors;
- suppliers;
- customers;
- schools.

Certainly, most employees of an IJV have to be recruited locally. Recruiters from the host country are familiar with the host environment, and sensitive to the needs and expectations of the host country employees – as well as those of the venture's major domestic customers. Thus they can hire local employees who are well suited to the venture's needs and mission. The human resource managers from the parents, on the other hand, need to be familiar with the concerns of the transferees and expatriate workforce, so that problems resulting from unfamiliarity and split loyalty can be minimized. Most countries allow foreign companies, including IJVs, to regulate a probationary period for local employees. Those having an unsatisfactory record can be either released or put on a new probationary period. Subject to advance notice, IJVs may lay off employees for poor performances.

For IJVs in general, the selection criteria include:

- ability to perform the job;
- acceptance of the mission, values, strategy, structure, policies, and practices of the IJV; and
- motivation and ability to learn and share knowledge (Child and Faulkner, 1998; Harvey *et al.*, 1999)

Stage 4: Advancement: the IJV and beyond

The advancement stage of the IJV involves:

- learning between the partners;
- transferring new knowledge and learning to the parents; and
- transferring new knowledge and learning to other locations.

Learning between the partners

Organizational learning is a collective learning process that involves all members of an organization. It includes all the processes that lead organizations to question and alter existing procedures. In general, there are three forms of inter-partner learning and knowledge transfer that can occur as a consequence of IJV involvement: (a) the IJV learns from the parents; (b) the parents learn from the IJV; and (c) the parents learn from each other.

Initially, much of the learning involves the flow of knowledge from the parents to the IJV. For example, the product and market know-how of the parents is transferred to the JV in order to establish a viable organization. Staff employed in the IJV then gain experience and they may extract additional knowledge from the parents as necessary. The parents, in turn, may be learning from each other – either directly, or indirectly as knowledge from one parent flows into the IJV and then is extracted by the other parent. Ideally, the parents benefit further from their knowledge investments as the IJV itself begins to generate new knowledge, which can be transferred back to the parents. If there is no transfer of new knowledge back to the parents, the parents may fail to realize any knowledge gains from the alliance.

In all of these forms of learning, the partners actively extract and transfer knowledge – either overtly or covertly. Each firm seizes knowledge that is available within the organizational boundaries of the other alliance partners. For example, in its five joint ventures in Japan, Bosch, a German automaker, established "strategy meetings" focusing on directing the regional flow of knowledge. These promoted an intense exchange of technicians, which helped establish a worldwide "Bosch standard." Bosch sends trained German technicians to the Japanese JVs to guarantee an effective transfer of technology and the company's internal quality standards. Bosch also gains deep cultural knowledge, which is created in the JVs and then transferred to German headquarters. The resulting knowledge benefits all members of the Bosch group that seek to gain access to Japanese clients worldwide.

After successful knowledge transfer, pragmatic changes can be effected and internal knowledge continues to be transformed. Management processes may be reorganized to reflect the tacit knowledge that has been gained. The corporation may even alter the internal procedures for collecting and analyzing tangible knowledge and thereby improve its internal capability for knowledge generation. For example, by becoming familiar with the culture of learning in its Japanese partners, Bosch is able to anticipate technological and organizational developments and react accordingly. Its Japanese alliances help it monitor changes in the Japanese market. Thus, Japan functions as a training ground for learning abstract knowledge processes. Bosch internalizes Japanese knowledge and learns to anticipate competitor moves.

Inter-partner learning and knowledge transfer can provide a significant payoff. However, without active management of the learning process, many of these opportunities will remain unexploited. In industries in which know-how is critical, companies must be expert at both in-house and inter-partner learning. CBA-in-Action 1 (p. 32) illustrates how Chrysler improves the inter-partner knowledge transfer through their internal efforts.

Openness is crucial to knowledge sharing or transfer between partners. This is because much of what the parties are trying to learn from each other or create together is so difficult to communicate. It is often embedded in a firm's practices and culture, and it can only be learned through working relationships that are not hampered by constraints.

Lei *et al.* (1997: 208) describe one type of formal communication channel used by partners that recognize the importance of learning and improving in a collaborative relationship:

> Smooth implementation to facilitate learning requires all levels of management to work on developing "alliance protocols" that enable careful knowledge creation and sharing among the partners. In their simplest form, *alliance protocols* represent the communication channels by which the alliance's managers and technical staffs share technologies, skills and managerial acumen. Some alliances (e.g., Motorola–Toshiba in advanced memory chips) use "gatekeepers" or "collaboration departments" that serve as the structural mechanism by which partners can access each other's technologies. Other alliances (e.g., IBM–Siemens in semiconductors) use "forums" by which each partner's advances in new chip designs and manufacturing processes are shared among key technical staffs Jointly developing and agreeing to these protocols early on is important to maintaining a balanced relationship, whereby neither partner feels that their contributions or opportunities to learn from the other are neglected or undervalued.

Transferring the new knowledge to the parents

It is one thing for partners to share knowledge and learn from each other, and quite another for a parent to learn from the IJV itself (Cyr, 1995; Inkpen and Dinur, 1997; van Sluijs and Schuler, 1994). Topics of learning symmetry, trust, and control may play out differently, and perhaps with a greater degree of complexity (Child and Faulkner, 1998). In the scenario with the IJV itself, partner A can learn from and about partner B, and the IJV itself. For the sake of learning symmetry, partner A may want to ensure that partner B also learns from the IJV itself. Thus the need to set up mechanisms to transfer new knowledge from the IJV to both parents is essential, although this may be more difficult with one local and one foreign parent.

Parents, however, may still find that building trust with the IJV itself is important. Without trust, the IJV may try to avoid transferring learning and knowledge to the parent. What is transferred instead is merely information. This may be more likely as the IJV grows and establishes its own identity and seeks independence from the parents. Notable U.S. firms doing well at transferring knowledge from the IJV to the parent use two different techniques. Corning, one of the largest users of joint ventures, transfers learning through communication, largely oral communication. Its culture supports this process. Hewlett-Packard, by contrast, uses a disciplined, written approach. While different, both companies are long-experienced veterans of JV learning and knowledge sharing.

According to Harbison (1996), most U.S. firms are still at an ad hoc stage of JV learning and knowledge sharing. The evidence seems to suggest that Asian and European parent firms do a better job of this than do U.S. firms.

> Overseas companies believe Americans are not passing along the lessons learned throughout the organization to the extent that Europeans have. Although capturing learning and institutionalizing skills is key, in most companies the learning is unstructured and the transfer of skills inefficient. Even some companies with more alliances experience – particularly large, decentralized companies – still behave like the least experienced because they do not capture and transfer information.
>
> (Harbison, 1996: 7)

Essentially, parents and the JV need the right people who are willing and able to learn trust and transfer or share knowledge between them. Moreover, they need to have communication systems that are as complex as the IJV process itself (Cyr, 1995). They also need to repatriate the IJV managers effectively. Human resource management decisions will gradually be handled by the JV organization. Within the JV, human resources will have to be regenerated and developed and reallocated to new jobs therein, as in an independent business organization. Given the opportunity, however, the parent organizations should attempt to "welcome back" relevant human resources from the joint venture, and not automatically release them so that they might "accidentally" end up with competing organizations.

Transferring the new knowledge to other locations

Thus far, learning and knowledge transfer have occurred from one partner to another and from the IJV itself to the parent. In both cases, the parent organization is gaining new learning and knowledge that can be used for its internal operations or for its next IJV process (Child and Faulkner, 1998; Doz and Hamel, 1998; Hakim, 2002). While consideration for transferring this learning and knowledge to future IJVs will enter into the complexities of partner selection described in the first stage, transferring learning to other units within the organization is more straightforward and more under the control of the organization. Nonetheless, managers are involved, and need to be encouraged to behave in ways that facilitate learning and knowledge transfer, such as by adopting cooperative, team-oriented behaviors. To continue to get these needed behaviors, reward systems need to be aligned with those behaviors.

Conclusion

The international joint venture is one of many forms of cross-border alliances. While other CBAs are important and used frequently by companies, the IJV poses the most numerous and apparent human resources issues. For example, there are both organizational-level and individual- or group-level HR issues in transferring learning and knowledge to and from other locations. Associated with just this one HR issue are numerous implications for HRM policies and practices in the parent companies and the IJV itself. The four-stage model of international joint ventures described in this chapter provides a framework for understanding the HR issues that arise in each stage of IJV development and implementation.

Fujitsu in Spain: barriers to alliance management

Fujitsu established a majority joint venture, SECOINSA (Sociedad Española de Comunicaciones e Informática, SA), partnering with the National Telephone Company of Spain and various Spanish banks. Fujitsu was not able to prevent conflict arising in the real world of joint ventures. Communication proved to be a difficulty: both firms had to rely on English as the common tongue although it is the second language for both. The Japanese felt they could not disclose their true feelings in written English. They favored a more interpersonal and fluid rapport that adapted to issues as they arose. Moreover, the Spanish believed the Japanese were too business focused and hidden behind a barrage of company talk that prevented friendships or rapport from developing. They also felt that the Japanese were not well rounded because their at-work and after-work personas merged into one; Spanish people favor a distinct separation between job and leisure. The Japanese rarely adapted to the ways of the Spanish, and this in turn made the Spanish believe that the Japanese looked down on local ways. Such misunderstandings on both sides undoubtedly hindered rapport.

Disharmony also existed in management. Decision making at Fujitsu was through the *ringi-sho* system, in which an idea is documented and distributed to all relevant parties for approval. *Ringi-sho* is thus a conservative approach that can minimize risks but takes too long in a decision-making process. Further, the Spanish are inclined to assume that authority is earned through ability and merit, and that authority automatically leads to power, whereas the Japanese treat age as the determining factor in earning power and authority.

Finally, Fujitsu wanted to maintain stringent control over its products and prevent imitation. It wanted all the components to be tested in Japan at its facilities, but since manufacturing was done in Spain, SECOINSA favored Spanish-made components. SECOINSA suggested that the work could be done in Europe if Fujitsu would supply the specifications, testing, and quality control methods. Fujitsu was willing to provide the needed information, but refused to reveal it to any outside parties, and would not pass along any information in writing. This made quality control difficult to ensure.

Managing human resources
in international joint ventures

3

Davidson-Marley BV was built using participative management processes and using human resource management practices that supported employee development, teamwork and full skill utilization.

Jean Theuns
HR Manager, Davidson-Marley BV

Analyzed within the multiple stakeholder perspective described in Chapter 1, human resource management has a significant impact on the profitability and survival of the organization itself, and it also has consequences for customers, suppliers, society, and employees (Becker and Huselid, 1998; Donaldson and Preston, 1995; Harrison and St. John, 1996). It can impact virtually all the stakeholders of a company (Becker and Huselid, 1998; Becker *et al.*, 1997; Freeman and Liedtka, 1997; Handy, 1998; Kaplan and Norton, 1996; Useem, 1996; Wood, 1991). Human resource management in IJVs has the potential to be even more important, for it affects several organizations, not just one, and these may be located in several communities (Cascio and Serapio, 1991; Dowling *et al.*, 1999).

In IJVs, business issues and HR issues are often one and the same (Child and Faulkner, 1998; Pucik, 1988). For example, the need to build trust and establish cooperation has implications for the selection and assignment of managers for the IJV. Developing and utilizing an organizational learning capability also has implications for HRM:

An organization has many tools to manage the process of learning (Hedberg, 1981), but in principle, the learning ability of an organization depends on its ability to accumulate invisible assets. As invisible assets are embodied in people, policies regarding human resources are critical to organizational learning. The objective of the HRM activities is to complement line management in providing a supporting climate and appropriate systems to guide the process of learning. Organizational learning results from a combination of hard and soft organizational practices anchored in specific HRM activities.

(Pucik, 1988: 81)

For individuals as well as teams, the importance of learning, sharing, and transferring knowledge has implications for the competencies (knowledge, skills, abilities, personality, and habits) to perform their organizational roles. Ineffective HR policies and practices may produce a workforce that is incompetent and unmotivated, poorly matched with job requirements, inadequately socialized and uncommitted to the IJV itself, and/or unable to manage their dual loyalties to the IJV and its parents.

In this chapter, we offer several guidelines for effectively addressing the HR issues that arise in the development and operation of IJVs. Although most of these guidelines have not yet been subjected to rigorous empirical tests, they are consistent both with the existing literature on IJVs and with a broader theoretical literature on effective human resource management.

Guidelines for managing human resources in IJVs

As summarized in Box 2.1 (see p. 37), the formation and operation of an IJV raises many HR issues that have implications for how the partners (the IJV parents and the IJV itself) manage their human resources. Many of these implications are grounded in the assumption that IJV parents and the IJV itself are all interested in learning (Parkhe, 1991). As we suggested in Chapter 2, organizations can provide a context for effective learning. Watkins and Marsick (1993: 8–9) put it this way:

> The learning organization is one that learns continuously and transforms itself. Learning takes place in individuals, teams, the organization, and even the communities with which the organization interacts. Learning is a continuous, strategically used process – integrated with and running parallel to – work. . . . The learning organization has embedded systems to capture and share learning.

With these structural elements in place, organizations can further support knowledge flow, sharing, and transfer by ensuring that their employees possess and exhibit:

- openness;
- systemic thinking;
- creativity;
- self-confidence; and
- empathy.

The parent and the IJV benefit from HRM practices that support and reinforce these role behaviors (Jackson and Schuler, 2000, 2003; McGill et al., 1992). The HRM practices that are most appropriate will be described in more detail throughout this chapter.

In addition to putting in place HR policies and practices that support learning, there may also be a need to provide some activities for *un*learning. Unlearning is especially important when the IJV is located in a country outside the home countries of the parents. At the same time that the parents are developing information processing and control capabilities that enable them to coordinate their activities across diverse environments, they may need to unlearn practices typical of their home countries (Barkema *et al.*, 1997: 427; McGill *et al.*, 1992). Thus firms entering into an IJV should be prepared to examine their current ways of managing and be willing to discard practices that create obstacles to learning and to the long-term success of an IJV (McGill *et al.*, 1992). Pucik (1988) identified several HR policies and practices that should be *avoided* when learning is desired. These are shown in Table 3.1.

Table 3.1 Human resource management: obstacles to organizational learning in cross-border alliances

HRM activities	HRM practices to avoid
HR planning	● Strategic intent not communicated ● Short-term and static planning horizon ● Low priority of learning activities ● Lack of involvement by the HR department
Staffing	● Insufficient lead-time for staffing decision ● Resource-poor staffing strategy ● Low quality of staff assigned to the IJV ● Staffing dependence on the partner
Training and development	● Lack of cross-cultural competence ● Unidirectional training programs ● Career structure not conducive to learning ● Poor culture for transfer of learning
Appraisal and rewards	● Appraisal focused on short-term goals ● No encouragement of learning ● Limited incentives for transfer of know-how ● Rewards not tied to global strategy
Organizational design and control	● Responsibility for learning not clear ● Fragmentation of the learning process ● Control over the HR department given away ● No insight into partner's HR strategy

Source: Adapted from V. Pucik, "HRM in International Joint Ventures," *Human Resource Management* (Spring 1988): 83

Guidelines for managing human resources in Stage 1

Guideline: When learning is important to the IJV parents, HRM activities should identify and develop the absorptive capacity of the parents.

Learning theory suggests that to learn efficiently requires ability, a knowledge base. Cohen and Levinthal (1990) describe an organization's ability to learn in terms of its *absorptive capacity*. Absorptive capacity is the ability to acquire, assimilate, integrate, and exploit new knowledge, skills, culture, and ideas (Beamish, 1987; Buckley and Casson, 1998; Inkpen and Crossan, 1995; Luo, 1998). Absorptive capacity results from organizational experience and insight and from individual skills, knowledge, and ability (Shenkar and Li, 1999). Human resource management activities that support these qualities include relevant training and development and systematic selection practices (Barkema *et al.*, 1997; Cyr, 1995; Pucik, 1988).

Learning theory suggests that IJV relationships are more likely to be stable if the partner's absorptive capacity is similar. As Inkpen and Beamish (1997), Shenkar and Li (1999), and Badaracco (1991) have suggested, with equal absorptive capacity, partners are able to learn at equal rates. Unequal rates of learning create instability in the relationship, threatening the long-term viability and success of the IJV. Consequently, capacity analysis and development needs to be planned for early on – that is, during the formation stage of the IJV process (Evans *et al.*, 2002; Pucik, 1988).

Guideline: HRM activities should contribute to ensuring that there is a high degree of fit between potential partners.

Luo (1998) suggests that input into the initial screening of partner candidates and into the final selection decision in partner determination be made on the basis of *strategic*, *organizational*, and *financial* criteria and the five clusters of criteria (five Cs) set out in Chapter 2. Basing his arguments on the work of Hamel (1991) and Yan and Gray (1994), he proposes that partner selection on these criteria is necessary for a more stable, and thus longer-term, relationship. Certainly one of the dimensions of fit that highlights this is that on absorptive capacity. If partners differ in their ability to learn, asymmetry in learning occurs, which leads to an imbalance in bargaining power, distrust, and potential for opportunism, and hence increased control and therefore termination of the IJV process (Doz and Hamel, 1998; Inkpen and Beamish, 1997).

One way that HR professionals can improve the degree of fit between IJV partners is to participate in assessing organizational fit, but this is not their only contribution. Even when the degree of fit is found to be suboptimal, a potential relationship may not be shelved forever. HRM activities may play a critical role in increasing some aspects of the fits, particularly those associated with organizational criteria. For example, HRM activities can play a significant part in increasing a firm's absorptive capacity (Pucik, 1988) and thereby improve a partner's organizational criteria.

Guideline: HRM activities should be designed to build trust between the partners. This will increase the ability of potential partners to address and resolve the potentially divisive issues related to control.

Finding a satisfactory solution to the problem of control is a major challenge for potential IJV partners (Inkpen and Currall, 1997). Partners who know little about each other are likely to exhibit lower trust toward each other and each is likely to seek ways to remain in control. As potential partners learn more about each other, they can begin to establish a relationship based more on trust. In other words, trust can become the mechanism (or substitute) for control. Trust diminishes the transaction costs associated with monitoring a partner's behaviors. Thus, by facilitating learning between potential partners, HRM activities can promote the development of trust and thereby diminish the divisiveness and the transaction costs associated with formal control mechanisms (Frayne and Geringer, 1990). For example, the HR professionals in the potential parent firms might collaborate to conduct formal assessments and evaluations of their cultures and workforce capabilities. Another means by which HR professionals can promote the development of trust between potential partners is by ensuring that the manager for new business development (who often plays a key role during Stage 1 of the IJV process) is capable and appropriately motivated.

Guideline: The use of HRM activities that promote effective conflict resolution should be used to enhance the likelihood of IJV success.

Because of the nature of the IJV process, conflicts or disagreements are almost inevitable, even among the most compatible partners. Learning about and developing trust in the partner may reduce conflict, but it will not eliminate it completely. Thus, potential IJV partners must be able to manage and resolve conflict productively to ensure that it does not create a divisiveness that eventually destroys the partnership (Child and Faulkner, 1998). During contract negotiations between the potential IJV partners, an integrative, problem-solving approach establishes an open dialogue. This in turn facilitates the discussion and resolution of issues that arise in later stages of the IJV process. HRM activities that help establish a context for effective conflict resolution include participating in the selection and training of people involved in IJV negotiations and promoting effective communications among other managers and professional working within the potential partner firms.

Selection and training

Applicants for the position of lead negotiator should be evaluated against the criteria identified as consistent with the role behaviors and expertise for an integrative bargaining strategy (Delaney, 1996). Selecting on the basis of fit with the position and the characteristics of the organization will assist in obtaining an individual who is both skilled and committed to the organization and the long-term interests of the joint venture process (Child and Faulkner, 1998). Once the lead negotiator has been chosen, performance appraisal criteria for this person should be consistent with the role behaviors required by a problem-solving bargaining strategy. For other managers and professionals who are more tangentially involved in the negotiations, training programs may be helpful to ensure that everyone understands the importance of adopting a problem-solving approach and to develop their skills in problem solving and conflict resolution.

Communications among other managers and professionals

The formal negotiations that occur between potential partners as they attempt to specify the details of their partnership often receive considerable attention, but these are not the only discussions that deserve attention. Throughout Stage 1, there are likely to be many less formal but equally important discussions among managers and professionals who would eventually be affected by the formation of the IJV. HRM practices that encourage and support effective communications among these other players can also contribute to the eventual success of the IJV. Thus, frequent appraisals and feedback, training for cross-cultural communications, and offering rewards and recognition for developing effective communication skills are all activities that can be used to improve communications among the various managers and professionals who participate in Stage 1 of the IJV process.

Guidelines for managing human resources in Stage 2

Guideline: When deciding where to locate the IJV, a key HRM activity should be assessing the needs of all primary stakeholders.

Making a decision about where to locate the IJV is likely to be one of the major objectives during Stage 1 of the IJV. Regardless of where the IJV is eventually located, the establishment of this new business will have implications for many constituencies (stakeholders). In order to ensure that the concerns of these stakeholders are addressed satisfactorily, their concerns must be identified and considered in the day-to-day operations of the IJV. Support or resistance from any major stakeholder group may determine the location decision and the IJV's longer-term operating success. Understanding the concerns of various stakeholders was important in the decision about where to locate the Davidson-Marley IJV. Local government support and laws, labor market conditions and employee expectations, and the general tone of management–labor relations were all considered, in addition to nearness of supplies and customers. In this entire process of stakeholder characteristics identification and assessment, the HRM department can play a vital role, as described further in Chapter 8 (Evans *et al.*, 2002; Jackson and Schuler, 2003).

Guideline: In order to ensure the long-term success of an IJV, state-of-the-art HR policies and practices should be used to ensure that a high-quality IJV management team is recruited and retained.

The relationship between the parents and the IJV provides the context for learning among the partners (Child and Faulkner, 1998; Doz and Hamel, 1998). When this relationship is characterized by a high degree of autonomy for the IJV, the stage is set for the IJV to learn. Conversely, when control over the IJV is great, there is less opportunity for the IJV to learn the most effective means of operating within the local situation. Unless the parents feel confident that the IJV management team can achieve success on its own, they will be reluctant to provide the management team with the autonomy it needs to try new things, make mistakes, and learn from its experiences. Subsequently, the parents also will reap fewer benefits, as their own ability to learn to be effective in the local conditions of the IJV is constrained. Several HRM activities can help to ensure that the IJV management team is a top-quality team. These include management job design, selection, development, and retention.

Management job design

When evaluating the attractiveness of the management jobs associated with a new IJV, potential applicants will evaluate the attractiveness of the job – including the degree of autonomy and control they can expect to exercise day in and day out. The most qualified managerial talent will be seeking significant freedom, responsibility, and challenge in the IJV management jobs. The applicants will be looking for a job that offers personal learning and development opportunities, which will enable them to continue to increase their own value in the labor market. Alternatively, less talented applicants – especially those who are risk-averse and uncomfortable with uncertainty – will accept jobs that provide less autonomy and greater protection from failure. Management jobs that are designed to fit the latter type of applicant would be counterproductive to learning within the IJV and among all IJV partners. They would also diminish the likelihood of long-term success for the IJV and the parents (Cyr, 1995).

Selection of IJV managers

Observers (Cyr, 1995; Gomes-Casseres, 1987; Harrigan, 1986; Lyles, 1987; Pucik, 1988) have suggested that the effective use of joint ventures requires managers to develop special liaison skills to cope with the mixed loyalties and conflicting goals that characterize shared ownership and shared decision making. Managers of JVs also need to have and to instill team-building values, and be receptive to ideas generated outside the organization. Thus using these criteria when selecting IJV managers promotes the hiring of a high-quality IJV management team (Child and Faulkner, 1998).

Other criteria to consider when selecting IJV managers are suggested by the following description of Huub Cilissen, the first general manager for Davidson-Marley BV. Mr. Cilissen was selected by the parent firms from three Dutch short-listed candidates who had been identified by a search firm. One important consideration in the final selection appears to have been that he was from the local region. The IJV was located in the southern province of Limburg, which is an area that has distinctive social customs and dialect. While the selection of a Dutch person from outside this region might not have been detrimental to the IJV's operation, the IJV parents believed that hiring a local manager would offer many advantages in a small facility with a participative, egalitarian management style. In selecting Cilissen, the parents also gave significant weight to experience in manufacturing. They also conducted numerous interviews to evaluate how well he was likely to fit with the operating styles and management philosophies of the parents (Schuler and van Sluijs, 1992).

Developing the IJV managers

Of course, sometimes conditions make it difficult to acquire a top-quality top management team, as Toyota knows. Toyota produces about 30 percent of its cars overseas, in twenty-five countries. But observers say that none of its overseas operations works as well as those in Japan. For example, its U.S. plants are the best in North America, but these assembly lines are only about 50 percent as efficient as the Japanese ones. A lack of well-trained local managers seems to be one of Toyota's major problems. Whereas Toyota's Japanese plant managers typically have twenty years' experience with the firm's production systems, local managers often start with almost no experience (Hakim with Maynard, 2002). Under circumstances such as these, the selection criteria must be relaxed and HR activities should be designed to train and develop the IJV managers.

Retaining the IJV managers

As the members of the IJV management team gain in experience, their value increases, as does the importance of retaining them. Loss of team members would diminish a core competence for the parents – a competence in joint venture management. To ensure that team members remain loyal to the parents, which facilitates information flow and learning, agency theory suggests that appraisal and compensation practices should evaluate and reward learning, market penetration, and customer acceptance.

Guidelines for managing human resources in Stage 3

Guideline: In order to ensure the IJV's long-term success, the IJV should develop its own vision, mission, values, culture, and strategy.

The success of the IJV depends upon its being locally responsive and yet globally linked with its parents. Institutional theory suggests the importance of attending to the objectives of the IJV's multiple stakeholders. On this point, who better to know the local stakeholders than the IJV itself, even within the same country as one of the parents? Indeed, who needs to be more concerned and responsive to the needs of the multiple stakeholders other than the IJV itself? With a well-selected IJV top management team, there is a good likelihood that the vision, mission, values, culture, and strategy will be crafted to fit the IJV's local circumstances (Thompson and Strickland, 1998).

While having the ability to do this is important, it is not a sufficient condition; the top team members need to be motivated as well. The parents' demonstration of trust via minimal control in the top managers will be an important incentive to motivate these IJV managers. Performance evaluations that highlight and reward the intents of both parental and IJV criteria will further the enhance the motivation of the top team to establish local responsiveness while at the same time linking the IJV to the vision, mission, values, culture, and strategy of the parents (Schuler *et al.*, 1992). Thus, establishing a vision, mission, value, culture, and strategy that support, encourage, and recognize learning and sharing will be in the interests of both the IJV and the parents (Evans *et al.*, 2002; Pucik, 1988), as more of these behaviors will occur both within the IJV and between the IJV and its parents.

Whenever a firm establishes operations in more than one country, it raises the question of how to strike the right balance between globalization and local action. All operations need to be locally effective, yet the firm as a whole also needs to be globally effective. The resource dependence and institutional perspectives emphasize the importance of adopting a strategy that is responsive to local conditions. This appears to be particularly true when it comes to HRM acitvities. Whereas technological and financial issues may be addressed globally, issues associated with the managing of people need to reflect the local culture, labor market conditions, religion, laws, local politics, and local competitive pressures (Adler, 2001; Hofstede, 1993; Porter, 1980; Schneider and Barsoux, 1997). Locally developed human resource activities are more apt to incorporate these local conditions and thus be more effective in managing human resources. Indeed, this was the case at Davidson-Marley BV (Schuler and van Sluijs, 1992; Schuler *et al.*, 1992). For example, staffing is one of the important human resource management activities essential to an IJV. Recruitment and selection practices designed to reflect local conditions have a greater likelihood of attracting the largest pool of potentially qualified job applicants (Dowling *et al.*, 1999). According to selection theory, this situation is more likely to produce candidates who will perform their jobs effectively and have a long-term relationship with the organization (Boudreau and Rynes, 1985).

Guideline: If tacit *knowledge is to be learned and transferred, HRM activities should reflect a long-term orientation. Conversely, if* explicit *knowledge is of primary concern, HRM activities that reflect a short-term orientation may be more effective.*

Tacit knowledge is invisible; it resides in the minds of the people and the processes they have created (Child and Faulkner, 1998; Inkpen and Beamish, 1997). According to the human capital perspective, this knowledge can be more effectively retained and transferred through human resource activities that foster loyalty and commitment to the organization (Cyr, 1995; Lei *et al.*, 1997; Pucik, 1988). Such activities include values that emphasize loyalty, commitment, and the importance of long-term relationships; extensive socialization and career development programs; performance appraisal criteria that emphasize the process through which results are achieved, as well as output; and compensation that rewards longer-term success and team-based activities (Lei *et al.*, 1997). Parents may attempt to maintain expatriates in the IJV for longer assignments in order to help transfer the tacit knowledge back to the parent. So here the parents and the IJV may have to recognize and reward the individual for developing a dual loyalty.

Explicit knowledge is that which can be modified, stored in data files, and seen by others (Lei *et al.*, 1997; Pucik, 1988). Explicit knowledge is less dependent upon the capabilities and motivations of specific individuals, and it is easily conveyed and transferred between units and individuals (Inkpen and Dinur, 1997). Consequently, long-term relationships become less important and human resource management activities may appropriately focus on supporting behaviors that are instrumental in the shorter term. Less investment in career development programs is required, and appraisal criteria and compensation practices can reflect immediate results and individual output. Expatriates from the parents or even project managers may be sent by the parents for short-term assignments with the express purpose of gathering explicit knowledge. One benefit of this approach may be that it is less costly. But the downside is that it fails to establish a relationship based on trust. Thus, it should be used only when the parents do not intend to maintain a long-term relationship with the IJV (cf. Doz and Hamel, 1998).

Guideline: Career planning and benefits should be offered to managers assigned to the IJV in order to ensure a successful IJV process.

Career planning and benefits provide managers an understanding of and assurance in their relationships with the parents and the IJV itself. This is provided through pre-assignment posting activities for the expatriate and his or her family, specific terms and conditions of the assignment itself, educational and housing benefits for the expatriate and family, and, finally, repatriation plans (Caliguiri and Lazarova, 2000). Done effectively, all of these can help ensure that the expatriate will perform as anticipated and that premature recall will be unnecessary (Black *et al.*, 1999). The effect will be to help ensure the likelihood of the IJV success.

Guidelines for managing human resources in Stage 4

Guideline: Partners should continually assess and calibrate their learning capabilities to ensure that learning symmetry is maintained.

According to learning theory, learning capabilities, or absorptive capacity (Cohen and Levinthal, 1990), influence the rate of learning. Because learning symmetry is critical to the stability of the partners' relationship, it needs to remain in balance. Such a condition can be facilitated by assessment of each partner. As the IJV matures, adjustments may be needed to reduce any differentials. Because learning capability is influenced by HRM activities, it is reasonable to regard this process of assessing and recalibrating the partner's absorptive capacity to ensure learning symmetry as an important human resource management activity.

As part of the process of assessment and calibration of the partner's learning capabilities, other HRM activities such as appraisal, compensation, and development need to be examined, because these support and encourage the continued use and enhancement of existing learning capabilities (Child and Faulkner, 1998). It remains, however, to ensure that channels of communications exist to facilitate knowledge flow.

Guideline: As the IJV matures, investments in improving formal and informal communication should be made to increase the likelihood of knowledge flow and learning among partners.

As partners learn more about and from each other, they develop more trust and willingness to share, and become less protective of their knowledge (Inkpen and Currall, 1997). Trust alone does not ensure learning, however. Also needed are appropriate channels for formal and informal communication among the partners (Makhija and Ganesh, 1997). Utilization of joint task forces, temporary assignments of employees from one partner to another, and investments in improved cross-cultural communication all assist in formal and informal transmission of communication and information:

> Communication systems which are open, and which operate both horizontally and vertically in the venture, contribute to the degree employees know about JV goals and objectives, and about management's intentions regarding products, processes, and policies.

> In joint ventures involving multiple cultural groups, communication presents special challenges. Across cultures, information exchange is enhanced by the use of illustrations and interpreters, and through an understanding of the cultural norms for communication of different cultural groups.

(Cyr, 1995)

*Guideline: Continuous evaluation and adjustment of all HRM activities is required
to ensure the IJV's long-term success.*

Like any organizational system, an HRM system that is static will soon outlive its
usefulness. Because conditions in the environment and within the organization are
constantly changing, managing people effectively demands vigilance and flexibility.
Reviewing and reevaluating HR policies and practices begins with understanding the
objectives of the existing HR system – for example, was it designed to support long-term
relationships or short-term relationships? Was it intended to promote learning between
the parents or only between the IJV and the parents? A complete review and evaluation
consider all major stakeholders. Even if they are not formerly included in the evaluation
processes, their voices are likely to be heard one way or the other. The results of the
evaluation process serve as input into decisions about whether to revise the existing
HR system, but may also alert managers to new strategic issues.

Ongoing evaluation and review of the HR system is essential for continuous
organizational learning and improvement. Where deficiencies are found, the HR
professionals must assess whether these are due to poor implementation of a good
HR plan, or whether the original plan was itself flawed. Appropriate HR practices may
be foiled by managers and subordinates who fail to implement them. For example, when
the IJV seems to be struggling for its very survival, managers in the parent organizations
may find it difficult to allow IJV managers the autonomy they initially agreed to.
In response, IJV managers may become suspicious of the parents' intentions and
begin to question their commitment to the parents' objectives. Performance reviews,
compensation decisions, and a variety of monitoring activities can all send signals which
suggest that the relationships among the partners have begun to drift away from the
original intent. An HR review might also detect whether professionals in the organization
feel that learning and knowledge transfer are truly valued and rewarded. Finally, even
if an initial evaluation reveals that HR policies and practices are achieving the intended
results, continuous evaluation should become part of the management routine, because
changes in the parents' and IJV's objectives may require changes in their approaches
to managing their human resources.

Conclusion

As described in Chapter 2, there are many human resource issues in cross-border
alliances, particularly in international joint ventures. This chapter has developed
the implications of these issues for several human resource managerial activities.
Although the relevant body of research on these topics is small, we have stated
our views about how to manage IJVs effectively in the form of guidelines. These
guidelines are not hard-and-fast rules. Rather, they reflect informed judgments that
are consistent with both theory and the experiences of several IJVs. As additional

research and insights accumulate, these general guidelines will surely be modified and refined.

Next, we proceed with a similar discussion focusing on international mergers and acquisitions (IM&As). In Chapter 4 we describe the growing importance of IM&As and develop a three-stage model that highlights the HR issues embedded in this important form of cross-border alliance. Chapter 5 then presents several guidelines for addressing the HR issues that arise in managing IM&As.

HR challenges in the IJVs at Rolls-Royce PLC

Case Example

Background

Rolls-Royce is a U.K.-based multinational with its headquarters in Derby, England. It employs 45,000 staff worldwide of whom 20,000 are employed outside the U.K., with North America accounting for over 10,000 of those.

The core business of Rolls-Royce is the design and manufacture of gas turbine engines, and more recently the provision of repair services. Consequently, it has been called a "power company" as it supplies the power in four main business areas: commercial airplane engines; defense airplane engines; marine; and energy (power station design and installation).

In 1996, Rolls-Royce (RR) set up a new business: the repair and overhaul business, or the "after-market business," to offer clients repair services. Today, this fast-growing business has 6,500 employees, of whom 2,500 are based in the U.K., 2,000 are RR employees worldwide, and 2,000 are employees in ten IJVs.

The IJVs around the world are of various sizes, with North America being the largest region and Asia Pacific the second largest. The IJVs are essentially there to service their major customers, namely, the companies that are buying RR engines.

RR's strategic motivations for setting up IJVs included:

1. *Capability*. The shift toward the repair and after-market services required a different set of capabilities from the traditional RR manufacturing capabilities. The company needed to go outside to find the necessary expertise. A key requirement was the need to respond very quickly to the requirement of the customer. This had not been an RR strength, Rolls-Royce being a proud company traditionally based on long-term research and development (R&D) and engineering excellence. Also, RR required access to external technology not available within the company. So it joint-ventured with small workshops that had the specialist technology and the flexibility to meet customer requirements.
2. *Capacity*. The company also needed to build global capacity to demonstrate that it was a global player. Major customers such as award-winning Singapore Airlines expected to

see an RR presence in their part of the world. RR set out to achieve a presence in all parts of the world where major customers would buy the next family of its leading-edge engines, The Trent engines, which have given the company an edge over two global competitors: GE and Pratt & Whitney.

A key problem for RR was how to implement a strategy based on building up a global network in the repair and overhaul business; for example, "How do you set up in Singapore to service a major Asian-based global carrier when you need 500 highly trained specialist airplane engineers?" It would have been a very difficult option for RR to set up on its own and to recruit a specialist workforce from scratch.

The strategy was to take the IJV route with its major customers (particularly companies buying the new family of large, wide-bodied airplane engines from Rolls-Royce). One example is the IJV between RR and a major Asian-based global carrier (called here, ABGC). ABGC realized that repairing airplane engines was not its core business, and it agreed with RR that the airplane repair was best handled by setting up a new joint venture set up specifically for the purpose. The advantage of the IJV for RR was that it inherited a highly trained workforce from ABGC, which moved some of its workers to the IJV. Also, combining the capabilities of the two companies created the capacity to break into new markets; that is, the new IJV could compete for other repair business from other airlines.

HR challenges in the IJVs

According to a senior Rolls Royce HR Director for RR Airplane Services, a key challenge in the RR–ABGC international joint venture was how to develop a highly trained specialist workforce. Recruitment and retention were also critical challenges. The challenge of attracting staff to the IJV was critical, as many staff initially preferred to stay with their recognized employer, ABGC.

The challenge of influencing developments in the IJV when you do not have full control was significant. Sometimes the local company (the IJV) may do different things from what a parent may want done because of local conditions. Consequently, the HR director in the parent needs to keep others in the parent company away from the IJV and allow the IJV the autonomy it requires to respond to the local environmental pressures it faces and develop the business strategies and HR strategies appropriate to its circumstances. The parent company, however, may want to gain as much knowledge and learning from the IJV (and the other partner) as possible, which may require being closely involved with the IJV. This situation of the desire for parental control and/or desire for knowledge versus local operating autonomy is a major dilemma facing the management of IJVs.

The supply of senior managers with the competencies and experience required is also a major challenge. Often it is very difficult to fill the key posts, and management training is not always in place, but RR has been doing its best.

From the past few years of experience with IJVs, RR has been gaining valuable HR insights in using and managing IVJs successfully. These include:

continued

- the need to understand the cultural issues better;
- the need to develop longer-term career paths for some IJV staff;
- the need to get qualified management talent in place as soon as possible; and
- the need to develop reward systems and build up expertise in compensation systems for IJVs.

Note: This case study was prepared by Hugh Scullion, Strathclyde University, Glasgow.

International mergers and acquisitions

This merger is not only in line with the long-term strategic approach of Nestlé, but the complementary strengths of Nestlé and Ralston Purina will accelerate both the growth and the performance of the Nestlé group.

Rainer Gut
Chairman, Nestlé Corporation

More and more companies worldwide are seeing that merging with or acquiring others is a major way of surviving and becoming more globally competitive (Evans *et al.*, 2002). With the merger of U.S.-based Ralston Purina and Switzerland-based Nestlé, Nestlé expanded its presence in the U.S. pet food market. Prior to the merger, Nestlé was number two behind Ralston Purina. Ralston, on the other hand, gained access to global markets that it had not yet succeeded in leveraging. But international mergers and acquisitions (IM&As) are complex and filled with challenges. Jon Symonds, chief financial officer at AstraZeneca, believes the key to finding the right merger partner comes down to finding a company with a compatible research philosophy and culture. The AstraZeneca deal merged companies based in the United Kingdom and Sweden. Because the Swedes spoke excellent English, language problems were minimal. In addition, the corporate cultures of the two firms were similar. But that did not happen by accident; it was part of the plan:

> Our number one criteria became the cultural fit of the two businesses, and that ruled out most potential partners. In the pharmaceuticals industry you've got to be very careful. You can construct quite compelling mergers on the basis of financial parameters, looking at the value the merger will create. But, because the only thing you've got to be sure of in this industry is the ability to reinvent yourself every 10 years, you cannot translate that into numbers.
>
> (Alexander, 2000: 7)

Companies today need to be efficient, profitable, flexible, adaptable, and future-ready, and to have a dominant market position. Without these qualities, it seems virtually impossible to be competitive in today's global economy. In some industries, such as insurance or banking, firms may use mergers and acquisitions to move into new markets. For example, Merrill Lynch, a U.S. financial services firm, acquired London-based Mercury Asset Management in order to move into the international financial services arena. At other times, consolidation is the major objective. For example, the world's largest steel producer is Arcelor. It was created from a three-way merger of some of Europe's largest steel companies. Those three companies, in turn, had each grown in earlier years through numerous smaller acquisitions, as the global steel industry began slowly to consolidate (Andrews, 2002; Hitt *et al.*, 2001). In industries such as pharmaceuticals or software technology, large firms may work with smaller firms that have developed or are developing new products, which the large firms can manufacture and/or distribute more efficiently (Galpin and Herndon, 1999).

Regardless of industry, however, it appears that it has become all but impossible in our global environment for firms to compete effectively without participating in mergers or acquisitions (Child *et al.*, 2001; Evans, *et al.*, 2002; Lucenko, 2000). The deals between many of the largest global firms attest to this, including AXA–Equitable Life Assurance Society, McKinsey–Envision, UBS–Paine Webber, Crédit Suisse–DLJ, Celltech–Medeva, SKB–Glaxo, Siemens–Westinghouse, Johnson & Johnson–Alza, Pfizer–Warner Lambert, Nestlé–Purina and Deutsche Telekom–Voice Stream (Fairlamb, 2000; Javidan, 2002; Lowry, 2000; Seriver, 2001; Taylor, 2002).

During the past two decades, cross-border acquisitions have exploded. According to W. T. Grimm's Mergerstat Review, there were only 197 cross-border acquisitions in 1985, and by 1999 there were 957. In the United States, for example, cross-border acquisitions of U.S. companies accounted for 19 percent of all takeovers during 1999. This compared to only 6 percent in 1985. Despite all the challenges associated with IM&As, recent studies suggest that the combined firms are often worth more than the uncombined firms would have been (Seth *et al.*, 2002). Thus, longer-term, the future appears to be ripe for a continuation of IM&A activity, even though a temporary cooling off of the economy is also nearly inevitable.

And why not? The factors that have driven the IM&A activity in the past decade are forecast to intensify: the need for large economies of scale, deregulation, globalization, expanding markets, risk spreading, and the need for rapid response to market conditions. Although the pace of IM&A activity slowed in 2001 and 2002, even in the tough financial environment and the falling stock market in 2000, the value of global mergers and acquisition exceeded $3.5 trillion for the first time (*The Economist*, 2001).

As a consequence of these realities, companies have become better at doing deals. Several have trained staff who can facilitate mergers and acquisitions quickly, efficiently, and thoroughly such as Michael Volpi at Cisco Systems (Holson, 2000). However, according to Jack Procity, partner-in-charge of business integration services at KPMG, many companies still have a long way to go when it comes to integrating their businesses effectively (Lucenko, 2000).

Some cite recent mergers and acquisitions as evidence for this, e.g., Conseco and Greentree Financial; Case and New Holland; HRS and CUC International;

DaimlerChrysler; McKession and HBO; Vodafone and Mannesmann; and Mattel and The Learning Company (Arndt, 2001; Sirower, 1997). Evidence beyond these specific examples suggests that they are more the norm than the exception (Charman, 1999; Creswell, 2001a; Krass, 2001).

Many companies seem to be confronted with the need to carry out mergers or make acquisitions, yet the odds of doing so successfully are relatively low. These odds can be increased, however: firms that have gained more experiences and that take a systematic approach to learning from experiences in their deal making are more likely to be successful (Arndt, 2002; Ashkenus *et al.*, 2000). As part of their systematic approach to completing successful IM&As, managers pay attention to HR issues that exist throughout the stages of international mergers and acquisitions.

The purpose of this chapter is to articulate a systematic, people-oriented approach for effectively achieving IM&As from beginning to integration and postintegration. We begin by identifying the types of mergers and acquisitions and the reasons for their successes and failures. Then a simple three-stage model of the IM&A process is used to outline several HR issues that arise during IM&As. This model provides the foundation for Chapter 5, which describes how effective HRM can contribute to IM&A success.

Types of international mergers and acquisitions

International mergers and acquisitions represent the end of the continuum of options companies have in combining with each other. Representing the least intense and complex form of combination is licensing. Next come alliances and partnerships, and then joint ventures. Mergers and then acquisitions conclude the combination options. In a merger, two companies come together and create a new entity. In an acquisition, one company buys another one and manages it in a way that is consistent with the acquirer's needs. Mergers and acquisitions have the greatest implications for size of investment, control, integration requirements, pains of separation, and HR issues (Doz and Hamel, 1998; Schuler and Jackson, 2001).

The key HR issues that arise in IM&As vary somewhat depending on the specific circumstances or type of IM&A under consideration. Some mergers are "mergers of equals." Examples of these include the merger between Citicorp and Travelers, forming Citigroup; and that between Ciba and Sandoz, forming Novartis. Other mergers take place between firms that are clearly unequal – at least in total size and market value. Similarly, there are various types of acquisitions. Examples include those involving acquisition and integration such as those typically made by Siemens and Cisco Systems; and those involving acquisition and separation such as between Unilever and Bestfoods. There are also friendly acquisitions and hostile acquisitions, although cross-border hostile acquisitions are relatively rare (Evans *et al.*, 2002). Acknowledging the different types of mergers and acquisitions is necessary in order to understand the many different HR issues that arise in IM&As. For example, a merger of equals often compels the two companies to share in the staffing implications; whereas a merger of unequals results in the staffing implications being shared unequally (Kay and Shelton, 2000). In this chapter, we only briefly touch on some of the HR issues associated with the different types of IM&As. A more detailed consideration is provided in Chapter 5.

Reasons for international mergers and acquisitions

There are numerous reasons for companies to merge or acquire as highlighted in Box 4.1. Some of the most frequent include:

Box 4.1 Reasons for companies to merge or acquire

To promote growth:

- for market extension abroad;
- because surplus cash is available to invest in faster-growing economies;
- because the domestic market is mature or simply too small to accommodate growth;
- to achieve the size necessary for effective global competition.

To manage technology:

- to exploit the superior technology advantage of the target;
- to transfer technological capacity to a foreign environment.

As a response to government policy:

- to circumvent tariffs, quotas, etc., on imports or exports;
- to take advantage of the tax structure and other policies;
- because some policies penalize foreign firms;
- because some policies encourage foreign investment;
- because denationalization can make merger candidates available.

To take advantage of exchange rates, which can affect:

- the prices of foreign acquisitions;
- the costs of doing business abroad;
- the value of repatriated profit to the parent;

As a response to political and economic conditions:

- seeking low or at least predictable inflation;
- seeking a more positive labor relations climate;
- benefiting from greater depth and breadth of financial markets.

Reduce labor costs and/or increase productivity:

- acquiring a workforce with more skills;
- taking advantage of an equally skilled workforce that costs less.

To follow clients, e.g.:

- banks expanding abroad to retain clients who have expanded abroad;
- consulting firms expanding to serve the needs of global clients.

To diversify and manage risk:

- product diversification;
- diversification of suppliers;
- diversification of operations;
- diversification of customers.

To achieve greater vertical integration:

- forward or downstream integration;
- backward or upstream integration;
- acquiring scarce talent and skills.

As this list shows, IM&As occur for many reasons. In recent years, people-related reasons have become more common. For example, engineers and scientists are in high demand worldwide. In industries where intellectual capital is critical to business success, as it is for semiconductor and optical networking firms, technically skilled employees are seen as more valuable than the company's product. Some banks even make dollar estimates of the value of a firm's employees, for example by applying metrics like price per engineer. When Broadcom bought chipmaker SiByte, it paid $18 million per engineer (Creswell, 2001b). Of course, such deals can be successful only if the employees in the target firm agree to stay after the deal is completed, and retaining talent after any merger or acquisition can be difficult. It may be even more difficult when employees in the target firm are expected to shift from working for a well-regarded domestic firm to working for a foreign-owned company, which may have less status or prestige or is simply unknown.

Track record

Companies that are successful and innovative in managing IM&As create value, and they also develop a core competency in IM&A management. This in turn can give the company an edge over others that have not been successful and/or have not learned from their past efforts. And the more experience a firm gains, the more it can learn from each additional merger or acquisition, thus solidifying its core competency and competitive advantage (Ashkenus *et al.*, 2000; Child *et al.*, 2001). Given that experience with mergers and acquisitions has grown and the base of experience has expanded, it may seem reasonable to assume too that the chances of success compared with failure have expanded (Very and Schweiger, 2001). In fact, the evidence is that even experienced firms cannot be sure of success. Research on M&As within the United States has found that more than half of the companies involved in large M&As in recent years have underperformed in their sector (Habeck *et al.*, 2000).

The picture is not quite as dismal for cross-border deals, however, according to research conducted by the Mercer Consulting Group. It studied 152 U.S.–European deals valued at $500 million or more from 1994 through mid-1999. In these deals, a European company purchased a U.S. business or vice versa. The consultants tracked the share price of the buyer for twenty-five months, beginning one month before the deal was announced, and compared it with the share prices of their competitors. Their analysis revealed that 54 percent of the acquiring companies outperformed their competitors (Arndt, 2002). Nevertheless, even these results indicate that IM&As face significant hurdles, and far too many seem to be financial failures.

It is interesting to speculate why transatlantic IM&As have a better success rate than U.S. domestic mergers and acquisitions. One explanation may be that geographic expansion is a primary reason for these deals, and thus there is less emphasis on cost cutting. It may also be that the acquirers in these deals are more likely to allow the target firm to continue operating more or less autonomously – rather than expecting it to adopt the acquirer's ways of doing business. In addition, of course, IM&As are scrutinized much more carefully by banks, regulators, and union shareholders in Europe. Finally, owing to the international dimension, the acquirers may be much more sensitive to the need to address cultural differences, and this heightened awareness may result in this issue being addressed more effectively throughout all phases of the IM&A process.

Reasons for failure

International mergers and acquisitions fail for a variety of reasons, and often several reasons for failure may operate simultaneously. Among the typical reasons cited (e.g., see Atlas, 2002; Ghemawat and Ghadar, 2000; Hitt *et al.*, 2001; Javidan, 2002; Sparks, 1999) for IM&A failure are these:

- A hastily constructed strategy is put in place, with poor planning and unskilled execution.
- Expectations of possible synergies are unrealistic.
- Either the acquirer or the merger partner fails to exercise due diligence.
- There is a failure to move quickly to meld the two companies; managers take months (and years) trying to integrate the firms and searching for synergies.
- Transition costs are underestimated.
- Debt service siphons funds from internal projects and discourages riskier projects.
- Too much is paid (e.g., because executive egos drive the deal-making process).

- Firms discipline managers with financial controls rather than strategic controls (i.e., what is good for the firm in the long term).
- Acquisitions do not seem to be good substitutes for innovation. Acquirers often kill innovative efforts through financial control.
- Talent is lost or mismanaged.
- Culture clashes between the two entities go unchecked.
- Different languages make effective communication too difficult.
- The focus of executives is distracted from the core business.

Perhaps of these, culture clashes, gaps, or incompatibility and losses of key talent are cited the most frequently, although even these become intertwined with other reasons (Bianco, 2000; Evans *et al.*, 2002; Jackson and Schuler, 2003).

By way of an example, many outsiders believed that a culture gap made DaimlerChrysler's period of adjustment exceptionally difficult (Gibney, 1999). Daimler and Chrysler each had their own agenda, focusing on different aspects of the automobile market, making one vision difficult to see. Given the acknowledged existence of two cultures, how could DaimlerChrysler truly become one company with one vision? (The DaimlerChrysler merger is examined in more detail in the case example at the end of the chapter.)

Loss of key talent and intangible assets is another significant reason given for a failed merger or acquisition. Consistent with NationsBank's (aka Bank of America) strategy of acquisition, CEO Hugh McColl paid a premium price of $1.2 billion for Montgomery Securities in October 1997. Subsequently, according to the Conference Board,

> Most of the best investment bankers walked out after a series of rows with Montgomery's management, and culture clashes with the commercial bankers at headquarters. They are now ensconced in the thriving firm of Thomas Weisel, run by Montgomery's eponymous former boss. Though Bank of America spent a further fortune trying to revive the investment bank, Montgomery is no longer the serious force it once was in Silicon Valley.

Reasons for success

Perhaps not surprisingly, some of the major reasons cited (e.g., Evans *et al.*, 2002; Viscio *et al.*, 1999) for success in mergers and acquisitions include:

- Goals and objectives are well thought out.
- Due diligence addresses both hard and soft issues, including effective communications and cultural integration.
- Acquisition is friendly, which may facilitate a faster and more effective integration and possibly mean the acquirer paid a lower premium.
- The acquiring firm selects target firms carefully, acquiring firms with the strongest complementarities.
- Overpayment is avoided.

- The acquiring firm has financial slack (cash or a favorable debt position. Financing (debt or equity) is easier and less costly to obtain.
- Negotiations are conducted carefully and deliberately.
- Planning for combination and solidification steps is completed early, so that the issues are understood.
- Firms have experience with change and are flexible and adaptable. Faster and more effective integration facilitates achievement of synergy.
- Sustained and consistent emphasis is placed on R&D and innovation.
- A well-developed HRM system makes it easier to retain key talent.
- Communications with all stakeholders are extensive and timely.

This list of reasons is corroborated by the findings of Watson Wyatt's Global M&A Survey. They concluded from their research that the managers should follow these guidelines to improve their chances of success in IM&As (Watson Wyatt, 2000):

1 Develop a more realistic timescale, including allowance for the time required to prepare for an effective due diligence procedure.
2 Start the planning of integration processes sooner and get HRM professionals involved earlier.
3 Work to align expectations in the acquiring and acquired businesses.
4 Confront difficult decisions, including employee and HR issues, earlier in the process.
5 Change managers quickly if they fail to adapt.

Thus, while there are many reasons for success and failure in mergers and acquisitions, whether in North America, Europe, Asia, or elsewhere, one requirement for success is effectively managing the many issues related to people. Next we consider the HR issues that are prominent in each of the three major stages of the IM&A process.

Three-stage model of mergers and acquisitions

Box 4.2 summarizes the HR issues to be addressed in three stages of the IM&A process. The three stages shown are (1) pre-combination; (2) combination and integration of the partners; and (3) solidification and advancement of the new entity (Evans *et al.*, 2002; Habeck *et al.*, 2000). These three stages are applicable to most of a firm's business functions (finance, marketing, distribution, IT, manufacturing, etc.), but we highlight here only the issues that are most closely associated with managing human resources.

Stage 1: Pre-combination

The pre-combination stage includes all of the activities that occur before the IM&A is completely legal. Thus it includes the process of determining the reasons for becoming involved in a merger or acquisition (as a buyer or a target), searching for possible partners (whether domestic or international), evaluating the alternatives, selecting and

Box 4.2 HR issues in three stages of international mergers and acquisitions

Stage 1: Pre-combination

- Identifying reasons for the IM&A
- Forming IM&A team/leader
- Searching for potential partners
- Selecting a partner
- Planning for managing the process of the IM and/or A
- Planning to learn from the process

Stage 2: Combination and integration

- Selecting the integration manager
- Designing/implementing teams
- Creating the new structure/strategies/ leadership
- Retaining key employees
- Motivating the employees
- Managing the change process
- Communicating to and involving stakeholders
- Deciding on the HR policies and practice

Stage 3: Solidification and assessment

- Solidifying leadership and staffing
- Assessing the new strategies and structures
- Assessing the new culture
- Assessing the new HRM policies and practices
- Assessing the concerns of stakeholders
- Revising as needed
- Learning from the process

negotiating with a specific partner, and planning for the eventual implementation of the deal. In many respects, these activities are quite similar to those conducted during the formation stage of an IJV (see Chapter 2).

As highlighted in Box 4.2, an important activity in the pre-combination stage of any IM&A activity is identifying the reasons for a possible IM&A. As described earlier, one possible objective is to gain access to additional talent – either because personnel in the foreign country are more skilled or because they cost less or both. If this is one of the key objectives, retention of key talent is often the number one concern, because unless the employees of the target firm (in the case of an acquisition) or merger partner remain with the new company, the objective may not be met.

Another important HR issue is the installation of a dedicated senior executive and a team to head the IM&A process (Taylor, 2002). As noted earlier, inadequate analysis and lack of adequate planning seem to be one reason that IM&As fail. Appointing a capable leader who can focus completely on all the aspects of the IM&A process and putting a team in place with responsibility for managing the process is one tactic that successful companies use to avoid the problem of inadequate planning. Initially, this team may focus on clarifying the strategic objectives, understanding the firm's own financial capacity, and searching for possible partners. Later in the process, this team may appoint and manage other teams to complete the many activities involved with actually implementing a deal.

After a possible partner is selected, discussions with the partner begin. Regardless of how well the two later stages may be planned and implemented, selection of the wrong partner (or target in an acquisition) is likely to diminish the chances of success for the combination. Alternatively, selection of the right partner without a well-thought plan for managing the rest of the IM&A process is also likely to diminish the likelihood of success for the combination (O'Reilly and Pfeffer, 2000). Recognizing this, GE Capital developed a systematic approach to evaluating the likely difficulty of achieving a cultural fit with possible M&A partners. Its approach is described in CBAs-in-Action 1: GE Capital's Pathfinder Model.

GE Capital's pathfinder model for cultural integration

CBA-In-Action 1

GE Capital Services has made the successful management of acquisitions a cornerstone of its strategy for growth. Every business group has a business development officer whose job is to find potential acquisition targets. During the 1990s, the company made more than 100 acquisitions in just five years, growing by 30 percent in the process. GE Capital's experience has shown that acquisitions are much more likely to be successful if the employees who end up working together share the same values and mindsets. Therefore, conducting a cultural audit and identifying cultural barriers are tasks that GE Capital's managers complete before an acquisition decision is final.

Its cultural audits identify cultural differences at all levels: societal, industry-wide, and organizational. Regarding industry-level similarities and differences, the companies are compared in terms of costs, brands, technologies, and customers. If the differences seem so great that they could cause the acquisition to fail, GE drops the planned acquisition. If the differences seem manageable and an acquisition deal is concluded, a systematic process for integrating the cultures then begins.

One of the first steps is to appoint an integration manager, who is responsible for integrating the cultures and the business and operational systems. As soon as the deal is final, key people from the two businesses are brought together to socialize, exchange information, and share their feelings about the new situation. Managers of the acquired company are quickly informed of GE Capital's twenty-five central policies and practices. Integration goals are developed, a 100-day deadline is set, and managers from the two companies meet for a three-day session devoted to exploring the cultural differences.

Managers tell each other about their companies' histories, folklore, and heroes. Other topics include approaches to market penetration, the amount of focus on cost, and reliance on authority versus shared decision making.

These discussions culminate in a written plan for the next six months or more. Such plans generally include short-term projects that require people from the two companies to work together to achieve some quick results, such as reducing costs. The plans, as well as other information related to the integration process, are posted on the company's intranet, where managers throughout the company can study them and learn from each new acquisition experience.

A final HR issue highlighted in Box 4.2 is planning to learn from the IM&A process. According to a recent global survey conducted by Watson Wyatt, a consulting firm, when companies decide to pursue IM&As as a long-term strategy, they should approach their IM&As with the intention of learning by doing. With experience, a company can begin to build up a pool of talent that can then be redeployed in the organization to share and apply the learning they gained. Companies that plan to learn can turn the knowledge and experience acquired in each deal into comprehensive, streamlined, and pragmatic processes that can be applied to future deals (Watson Wyatt, 2000).

The activities in Stage 1 establish a foundation for Stages 2 and 3. For example, in order for Stage 2 to be effective, it is important that the partners have already carefully planned and prepared for it during Stage 1. According to some estimates, lack of integration planning is found in 80 percent of the IM&As that underperform (Habeck *et al.*, 2000).

Stage 2: Combining and integrating the companies

The stage of combination and integration begins after a merger or an acquisition is announced and pre-combination activities are completed. The general approach used to integrate and combine IM&A firms can be characterized as fitting one of four approaches. These approaches reflect substantially different ways of addressing the many management issues present in the alliance. As illustrated in Figure 4.1, four approaches to integration are portfolio, blending, new creation, and assimilation.

Portfolio

In the portfolio approach, managers in the two companies retain a great deal of autonomy. Although the alliance creates legal and economic interdependencies, the top management team assumes that the two organizations will continue to operate more or less as they had operated prior to the IM&A. This is what Johnson & Johnson does with many of its acquisitions (Taylor, 2002). Presumably, the strategic value of

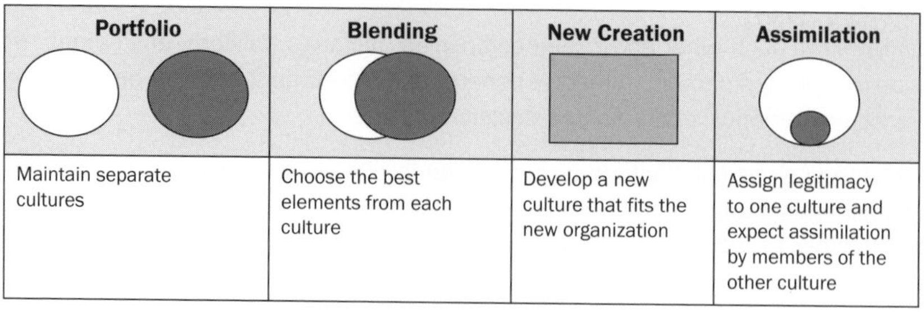

Portfolio	Blending	New Creation	Assimilation
Maintain separate cultures	Choose the best elements from each culture	Develop a new culture that fits the new organization	Assign legitimacy to one culture and expect assimilation by members of the other culture

Figure 4.1 Four approaches to integration in cross-border alliances

© Susan E. Jackson and Randall S. Schuler

the alliance does not require the integration of the separate organizational systems, so differences are "managed" by maintaining segregated organizations. This scenario often occurs when one firm acquires another firm in order to diversify into another business or region and then allows the acquired firm to operate as a relatively autonomous subsidiary. For example, when Nestlé purchased Purina, it expanded into pet foods and did not attempt to merge the Purina operations with other Nestlé units. South African Breweries uses this strategy in its acquisition of local breweries (Kapner, 2002b). The portfolio approach may be especially appropriate when the alliance is between firms in different industries or between firms that contribute to different parts of the value chain (i.e., supplier, manufacturer, distributor).

Blending

The blending scenario arises when top managers expect the two organizations to come together or merge into a new organization that retains the best aspects of the original partners. In this scenario, the intent is to manage diversity through integration, with members of each organization adapting to the procedures and culture of their alliance partner. The blending approach is perhaps most common in IM&As that occur within an industry and between firms that are believed to complement each other's strengths and offset each other's weaknesses.

Presumably, Daimler and Chrysler executives intended to use blending to make that deal a success. At the time, it was the largest industrial merger ever, with two giants agreeing to form a "merger of equals" that would create a global firm employing more than 400,000 employees. Daimler-Benz's strength was in engineering and production of luxury cars, while Chrysler was known for its Jeep and minivan lines and for its innovative marketing (Evans *et al.*, 2002). As we shall see in the case example at the end of the chapter, however, managers from the two companies faced many difficulties as they attempted to blend these two organizations together.

New creation

A third scenario arises when the partners agree to create a new firm that is truly different from either of the original partners. As we have already seen, this is typically what partners agree to do when they enter into a joint venture, especially if the IJV is located in a country other than the countries of the parent firms. The Davidson-Marley IJV is one example of this arrangement. The parent companies established a greenfield plant in a third country. During the formation and development phases of the IJV, managers from the parent firms agreed that they wanted to hire Dutch managers for the IJV and give them great autonomy in making decisions about the plant's design and operation. (In reality, however, managers from the parent firms developed fairly detailed plans before hiring the IJV managers, so approach for the new plant actually fell somewhere between "new creation" and "blending.")

Creating a new organization is the goal of some mergers too, although it seems to be less common. One indication that an IM&A is intended to form a new creation is that the resulting firm takes on a completely new name. Novartis, which was created through a merger of Sandoz and Ciba-Geigy, is one example. Novartis also is an example of a merger that might seem not to involve differences in national culture, because Sandoz and Ciba-Geigy both had their headquarters in Switzerland. In actuality, however, a large portion of Ciba-Geigy's pharmaceutical business was based in the United States, while Sandoz's pharmaceutical base was in Switzerland. Thus, what might have appeared to be a domestic merger in fact required managing significant differences in national cultures.

Assimilation

Finally, in some acquisitions, the buyer clearly intends to take over and control the target. Siemens appears to do this with many of its acquisitions (Javidan, 2002). The target firm may be an attractive candidate for an acquisition because it has some valuable assets, yet for various reasons it is clear that the target firm cannot continue to survive on its own. In this scenario, the expectation is that the target firm will lose its identity and adopt the management practices of the acquiring firm. In other words, the target firm is expected to assimilate into the acquirer, such as happened when Deutsche Bank acquired Bankers Trust (Atlas, 2002). This is also what happened in Pfizer's hostile takeover of Warner-Lambert. When Pfizer acquired Warner-Lambert, it adopted a few of Warner-Lambert's practices, but observers say that little of the Warner-Lambert culture remains today. Not surprisingly, most of Warner-Lambert's top-level managers left the firm.

We assume that each of the four approaches described above can be an effective way to integrate companies in an IM&A. These approaches are more likely to be successful if they have been intentionally adopted by top managers and communicated to employees in the relevant organizations. By making explicit the guiding philosophy that underlies subsequent planning and decision making, managers can more easily align their own actions to be consistent with the philosophy, and employees should be able to interpret managerial actions more accurately.

Regardless of the specific approach, all acquisitions require some degree of integration of systems and processes in order to achieve key synergies. Successful integration is a key challenge in Stage 2 of IM&As. If the firms do not succeed in integrating their activities, the results are predictable. According to recent studies, poor integration accounts for declining productivity, leadership attrition, low employee morale, and failure to meet financial goals (Bobier, 2000). When Pharmacia and Upjohn merged, they faced many of these consequences as they struggled to integrate the cultures of two firms with operations in three countries. Their experiences are described in CBA-in-Action 2: Culture Clash at Pharmacia and Upjohn.

Culture Clash at Pharmacia and Upjohn

CBA-In-Action 2

Shortly after the merger of Pharmacia and Upjohn, the headquarters of the new company was just a stone's throw from England's Windsor Castle. It seemed to be an odd choice for the headquarters of a company created by merging firms whose individual headquarters were in Kalamazoo, Michigan, and Stockholm, Sweden. The decision about where to locate the new headquarters and its 100-person staff is just one example of what happens when two sides distrust each other. For the managers who have to travel from Stockholm, Kalamazoo, and Milan – the locations of the company's main operations and 30,000 employees – the headquarters decision was just one of many sources of stress. Among the others were the following.

- The hard-driving, mission-oriented U.S. approach of the Upjohn managers clashed with the consensus-oriented Swedish approach of the Pharmacia managers. While the Upjohn managers focused on ambitious cost-cutting goals and numerical accountability, the Pharmacia managers kept their employees informed and sought feedback about how to carry out changes.
- The Upjohn managers scheduled meetings throughout the summer and could not comprehend that Pharmacia managers would spend the entire month of August on vacation.
- The internationally experienced Pharmacia managers were surprised by the lack of international savvy and the parochial attitudes of the Upjohn managers. Managers in many European companies are accustomed to working across borders and tend to be more flexible and adaptable than U.S. managers. Upjohn's strict policies subject all workers to drug and alcohol testing and ban smoking. At Pharmacia's Milan location, wine is poured freely in the company dining room, and the boardroom in Stockholm is well stocked with humidors.
- The Upjohn-based CEO put managers on a tight leash, requiring frequent reports, budgets, and staffing updates. The Swedes viewed these tasks as a waste of time and eventually stopped taking them seriously. The Italians felt that the Americans were acting like imperialists and trying to take over.

These conflicts were reflected in the company's bottom line. Everyone had hailed the merger as a wise strategic decision to expand the scale and scope of both firms. The new firm had greater international presence and more products than either firm had alone. But melding the cultures proved more difficult than anticipated, and earnings in the first two years were below expectations, resulting in the resignation of the firm's CEO.

One approach that helped to bridge the cultures among members of the research units was moving the U.S. and European managers back and forth across the Atlantic. According to Research Executive Vice President Goran Ando, doing so helped speed cultural learning and development of mutual respect. But the basic styles of the managers have been slow to change. Ando explained:

> I am a Swede who has lived in both Britain and the United States for a number of years. I see in Americans a more can-do approach to things. They try to overcome problems as they arise. A Swede may be slower on the start-up. He sits down and thinks over all the problems, and once he is reasonably convinced he can tackle them, only then will he start running.

Guy Grindborg, a technical trainer for the Swedish firm Ericsson, Inc., observed similar differences, causing him to adjust the way he conducts training sessions when he's in the United States:

> The Swedish approach is more the engineering approach: "Tell me why and how this thing works." The American approach is much more direct. Their attitude is: "Don't teach me to be an expert, just tell me what I need to know to do my job."

Given the challenges of managing the naturally occurring organizational and national cultures that were present in the new company, the idea of adding even more diversity by locating headquarters in yet another cultural context was a novel one. In the long run, however, it proved to be ineffective; headquarters has since been moved. Where would you locate this company's headquarters, and why?

Because Johnson & Johnson (J&J) engages in so many mergers and acquisitions, it has been able to study its own experiences and learn from the successes and failures. This company's research clearly indicates that a systematic, explicit integration process is at the heart of successful mergers or acquisitions. Furthermore, J&J has learned the importance of tailoring decisions about how to approach the task of integration to take into account the specific strengths and weaknesses of the acquired company. J&J has also learned that Stage 2 should proceed as quickly as possible – the sooner the process begins, the better. Ideally, decisions about the management structure, key roles, reporting relationships, layoffs, and restructuring should be announced within days of signing. Creeping changes, uncertainty, and anxiety that last for months are debilitating and drain value from an acquisition (Bobier, 2000).

Whereas Stage 1 activities set the scene for IM&A activity, those in Stage 2 are the ones that make the activity come to life. Clearly there are differences here between a merger and an acquisition, and there are differences between mergers of equals and those between a clearly dominant acquirer and a subordinate target. Nevertheless, many of the same HR issues arise regardless of such differences.

Stage 3: Solidification and assessment of the new entity

As an IM&A takes shape, it faces issues of readjusting, solidifying, and fine-tuning. These issues take on varying degrees of intensity, although not importance, depending upon the approach to integration that the firms adopt. The intensity can be quite high for an international merger of equals that is intended to lead to the creation of a new entity, and failure to address the HR issues effectively is likely to mean that the intended strategy is never successfully implemented. For DaimlerChrysler, Stage 3 lasted more than two years (Muller *et al.*, 2001). During that time, its managers grappled with all of the HR issues listed under Stage 3 in Box 4.2 (p. 87).

As Stage 3 unfolded for DaimlerChrysler, it became clear that the original description of this deal as a merger between equals was inaccurate. Eventually, Schrempp acknowledged in an interview with the *Financial Times* what everyone had long suspected: that the acquisition was a takeover right from the start and was never supposed to be a merger of equals. "Me being a chess player, I don't normally talk about the second or third move. The structure we have now with Chrysler [as a stand-alone division] was always the structure I wanted," Schrempp told the interviewer (Evans *et al.*, 2002: 250).

When Tyco International was actively making acquisitions, it was especially quick to solidify the leadership and staffing needs of the acquired firm. Mr. Kozlowski (the former CEO) and his in-house team of merger specialists would dismiss incumbent managers and hand-pick their replacements. Generous pay plans were used to retain desired talent. Factories would often be closed quickly, and without any apparent sentimental concern. Despite other problems the firm has faced recently, this sure-footed approach to solidifying the staffing situation quickly is generally recognized as beneficial for any IM&A (*The Economist*, January 26, 2002).

Conclusion

Like IJVs, effectively managing international mergers and acquisitions requires dealing successfully with many significant HR issues. Each stage of the IM&A process presents new challenges as well as new opportunities to create value by managing people effectively. Next, in Chapter 5, we turn to a more detailed discussion of the HR issues that arise in each of the three stages of IM&As.

Strategic partnership at DaimlerChrysler

From the day the merger was first announced, many outsiders believed that the culture differences between Daimler and Chrysler would create major problems during the post-marriage period of adjustment. The quintessential values and attitudes of each company's host country were reflected in everything – from product design to manufacturing, marketing, and approaches to managing human resources. Top executives in the new firm seemed to believe that the two company cultures could simply be put in a blender and poured out as a new, synergistic company. Cultural issues were all but ignored. To many observers, it seemed as if the only time when cultural issues were addressed was when executives made general statements to the media regarding the differences in the two companies. Either top management at Daimler and Chrysler did not fully realize the implication of cultural differences, or they chose to focus on operational and business synergies while simply hoping that cultural differences would resolve themselves.

Recalling his first meeting at the Mercedes-Benz U.S. headquarters in Montvale, NJ, Chrysler marketing chief Jim Holden described the relationship between the two companies this way:

> Many Daimler-Benz executives initially viewed Chrysler as a primped-up matron would regard an earnest young suitor. We felt like we were marrying up, and it was clear that they thought they were marrying down. As the Germans presented their view of the brand hierarchy – Mercedes on top and everything else far, far below – the tension in the room was palpable.

During the initial stages of the merger, Chrysler president Thomas Stallkamp indicated that Daimler intended to adopt Chrysler's product development methods, which emphasized teamwork rather than individual-oriented work procedures. Chrysler in turn would adopt many Daimler operating practices, including rigid adherence to timetables and its methodical approach to problem solving. The required cooperation failed to emerge, however. The battle became public knowledge when Daimler executives refused to use Chrysler parts in Mercedes vehicles.

Despite evident problems, Daimler's chief of passenger cars, Jürgen Hubbert, declared, "We have a clear understanding: one company, one vision, one chairman, two cultures" (*The Economist*, 2000). Since the departure of Robert Eaton (Chrysler's former chairman), it is true that only one chairman (Jürgen Schrempp) runs the company. Hubbert's other assertions are questionable, however. DaimlerChrysler may be "one" company in name, but two separate operational headquarters are maintained, one in Michigan and one in Germany. Business operations continue under separate paradigms, as evidenced by "Daimler's" decision to allow "Chrysler" more leeway in the design and production of its vehicles, which more closely emulated the practices of the "old Chrysler." Daimler and Chrysler each focus on different aspects of the automobile market, making one vision difficult to see. With the acknowledged existence of two cultures, can DaimlerChrysler truly become one company with one vision?

Note: This case example is adapted from Schuler and Jackson (2001).

Managing human resources in international mergers and acquisitions

5

Crossfire is not only a great product, executed in record time, creating lots of excitement and a very satisfying bottom line, but it stands for the almost unlimited opportunity we have from the merger of Daimler-Benz and Chrysler. Crossfire never could have come to fruition without the merger. The merger enables us to do this product in a very unique form – we never did anything like it before – and this will show the world that Chrysler is a very different company.

Dieter Zetsche
CEO Chrysler Group, March 27, 2002

Although the merger between Daimler-Benz and Chrysler has struggled over cross-cultural differences, it appears that the relationship is beginning to pay off. This merger highlighted the human resource management (HRM) challenges that can be a part of international mergers and acquisitions. Like many other executives who have lived through a merger, DaimlerChrysler executives now understand that it is not enough to manage the legal, financial, and operational elements of mergers and acquisitions. Maximizing the value of a deal requires that the human side of organizational change must also be managed well (Kay and Shelton, 2000). Nevertheless, managing the human side of IM&A activity appears to receive less of the top management's attention than is necessary to ensure success (Child *et al.*, 2001; Evans *et al.*, 2002). According to David Kidd, a partner at Egon Zehnder International in Chicago,

Many mergers do not create the shareholder value expected of them. The combination of cultural differences and an ill-conceived human resource integration strategy is one of the most common reasons for that failure. Given the well-publicized war for talent, I am constantly surprised by how little attention is paid to the matter of human capital during mergers.

(Light, 2001: 39)

So if people issues are so critical, why are they neglected? Possible reasons include:

- Executives believe that they are too "soft" and, therefore, too hard to manage.
- Social costs and benefits are regarded as secondary.

- There is a lack of awareness or consensus that people issues are critical.
- There is no spokesperson to articulate these issues.
- There is no model or framework that can serve as a tool for us systematically to understand and manage the people issues.
- Therefore, the focus of attention in IM&A activity is on other business aspects such as finance, accounting, strategy, and manufacturing.

Yet experienced managers readily acknowledge that merger and acquisition success is not possible unless HR issues are dealt with effectively. Among the most important HR issues are (a) retention of key technical talent; (b) communications; (c) retention of key managers; and (d) integration of corporate cultures. In addition, as part of the process of integrating firms, the entire human resource system in each company may be subject to evaluation, revision, or replacement. While these human resource issues are important for IM&As throughout the world, their importance varies according to the type of IM&A combination described in Chapter 4 (Figure 4.1, p. 90). For example, if the portfolio approach is used to manage the acquired firm, there may be less need to evaluate, select, and replace employees than there is in acquisitions that result in complete integration of the two companies. If one firm is to be assimilated into the other, one HR system may be dismantled completely, while the other remains intact. In addition to the HR issues that arise in the *integration* stage of IM&A activity, there are several other HR issues that become evident in the stages of pre-combination and solidification. In this chapter, we build upon the three-stage model presented in Chapter 4 to discuss these HR issues in more detail. We also develop guidelines for effectively managing HR issues throughout the IM&A process.

Managing HR issues during Stage 1 (pre-combination) of IM&As

Guideline: Determine whether or not a key objective is developing the organization's IM&A capabilities. If yes, adopt HR practices to support organizational learning.

Building upon the learning theory perspective, it becomes apparent that HR issues will be particularly important for firms that want to build their IM&A capabilities. Used singly, but increasingly in bundles, HRM practices such as recruiting, work systems design, or training and development can help the new alliance be more competitive (Pfeffer, 1996). If learning about the IM&A process is among the objectives that managers have articulated, the role of managing human resources is more likely to be recognized as central to a successful IM&A process. Firms with little IM&A experience that anticipate using IM&As as a long-term strategy may recognize that their early IM&A activities will be learning experiences, but this does not guarantee that managers will make learning a key objective against which their success will be evaluated.

To ensure that learning is *intentional and directed*, as a starting point everyone in the organization needs to understand that learning about how to manage IM&As is a key objective for the organization. As is true for other business objectives, the learning objective will become salient to the extent that the organization develops measures for assessing learning and adopts practices intended to facilitate learning. In addition to encouraging managers to adopt a long-term learning mindset, adjustments in the current HR policies and practices may be needed in order to encourage employees to share and disseminate what they have learned.

In knowledge creation as well as knowledge transfer, HRM practices play a vital role (Evans *et al.*, 2002; Jackson and Schuler, 2003; Pucik, 1988). For example, if developing the firm's IM&A capabilities is an important long-term objective, managers with prior IM&A experience (e.g., in a previous job) should be identified early in Stage 1 and then encouraged to participate on the various planning teams and task forces that are created at this stage. In addition, training programs for employees throughout the company should begin to incorporate basic educational modules to inform employees about the legal, financial, operational, and human issues associated with IM&A activity. Employees who understand the legal and financial constraints that managers face in the early stages of the IM&A process will be less likely to impute negative motives to executives who have not been completely open and forthcoming about their intentions to engage in an IM&A. Later, when the nature of the deal becomes public, educated employees will be in a better position to understand the implications of the deal for them. When a merger or acquisition is announced, uncertainty about the implications of the deal is one of the greatest sources of stress among employees. Although uncertainty cannot be completely eliminated, it can be reduced. For example, employees who understand the different reasons for IM&A activity will be less likely simply to assume that layoffs are certain to follow the announcement of a deal. Instead, they can understand that some deals may have almost no consequences for their own job security, while other types of deals are almost certain to result in layoffs. In either scenario, uncertainty is reduced and employees are empowered by their improved understanding of the situation.

Guideline: Make retention of key talent a top priority.

According to the human capital and resource dependence theories, having capable senior management in place for IM&As is as important as it is for IJVs. Effective leadership increases the possibilities of a successful international merger and acquisition. The successful combinations of Ciba and Sandoz or SKB and Glaxo or Nestlé and Purina reflect the priorities and competencies of senior management. In the best firms, HR policies and practices that support the development of excellent leaders will already be in place long before Stage 1 of a particular IM&A deal. When strong leadership talent is already available, effective retention practices can help ensure that qualified existing managers remain after the merger or acquisition is completed (Atlas, 2002).

Conversely, it is best to identify the managers who will be let go as soon as possible and begin to plan for their exit. Sometimes, compensating for a lack of leadership talent is one of the motivations for engaging in IM&A activity. Under this scenario, the expectation may be that weaker players should and will be let go after the merger. When managers are to be let go, a natural tendency is to delay making the difficult decisions as long as possible. But this approach can create several undesirable consequences for those who must eventually leave, as well as those who stay.

Guideline: Identify employees who will serve as team leaders in Stage 2 (integration) and involve them in as many Stage 1 activities as possible.

Except perhaps in IM&As that will be managed using the portfolio approach, teamwork will be essential to successful integration. Furthermore, the work of the integration teams is likely to be facilitated by early involvement of those team leaders in the IM&A process. Therefore, Stage 1 is the appropriate time to select and begin developing the team leaders who will be essential to success in Stage 2.

Guideline: The due diligence process should include an analysis of the cultures of the partners, the HR policies and practices of the two firms, the financial liabilities associated with HR policies and practices, and the financial risk associated with potential loss of key talent.

When two firms are seriously interested in pursuing an IM&A, they typically sign an agreement that outlines the information that each party will be allowed to gain access to prior to the deal's close and provides a time frame for completing the review. Experienced firms realize the importance of gaining access to information about a wide variety of HR issues during this review process. Conducting a thorough due diligence process in the IM&A requires a complete assessment of the HR environment of the partner firms.

The term "soft due diligence" is sometimes used to refer to assessment of the HR issues associated with IM&As, and perhaps this is why HR issues often receive too little attention during the due diligence process. Receiving more attention in due diligence are such functions as strategic business development, finance, operations, marketing, and sales (Watson Wyatt, 2000). According to Mitchell Lee Marks, a San Francisco-based management consultant who has worked on more than sixty mergers over the past fifteen years, "Many CEOs gloss over softer HR issues, including potential cultural problems, only to realize later that they've made a huge mistake" (Greengard, 2000). Although widely used, the term "soft due diligence" is misleading. Assessing the cultures of the two firms is the softest element of a complete HR due diligence process, but appropriate analyses of the many other HR issues that are important to IM&A success are anything but "soft." To capture the importance of both hard and soft due diligence, Johnson & Johnson executives prefer to use a single concept that incorporates both terms: discovery process (Bobier, 2000).

Cultural assessments

In cultural audits and assessments, perceptions and opinions are the primary source of "data." Being dependent on soft data does not mean that assessments of culture are unsystematic, however. Cultural assessments for IM&As are especially complex, owing to the interplay between corporate culture, country culture, and industry culture (Jackson and Schuler, 2003; Shenkar and Yan, 2002). On the other hand, the importance of conducting a cultural assessment seems to be more easily grasped when a CBA is involved and thus may receive more attention in IM&As than in some domestic IM&As (cf. Numerof and Abrams, 1998).

Cultural assessments involve describing and evaluating the two companies' philosophies and values regarding such issues as: leadership styles; time horizons; relative value of stakeholders; risk tolerance; and the value of teamwork versus individual performance and recognition (Numerof and Abrams, 1999). In the DaimlerChrysler combination, the importance of company cultural differences, initially downplayed, became the reason for allowing the business units to function as they wished as long as they achieved their goals (Andrews and Bradsher, 2000; Tierney, 2000). In addition to company cultural assessments, firms entering into IM&As may need to assess differences in industry cultures and country cultures. Because of the significance of understanding and managing cultural diversity in CBAs, Chapter 6 is devoted to this topic.

HR policies and the financial liabilities associated with them

Ideally, the due diligence process includes a complete assessment of the commonalities and differences in between the HR policies in the firms entering into an IM&A. In other words, approaches to staffing, performance measurement, career development, training, compensation, and provisions to ensure due process should all be assessed. In actuality, however, the elements of HRM that are most likely to receive attention are those with clear financial or legal implications.

Financial risks associated with loss of talent

As explained in Chapter 4, acquiring scarce talent may be one of the primary objectives driving an IM&A. Clearly, when acquiring talent is a key objective, the deal will not be successful if most of the talent chooses to leave after the deal is announced. Even when talent acquisition is not a major objective, however, too much loss of talent can reduce the chances of an IM&A's success. Departures and early retirement of key executives can be financially costly, depending on the terms and conditions of their employment or retirement contracts. Executive departures may also have other costs, however. In addition to losing its managerial expertise, the firm may also lose a valuable source of social and political connections. In industries that depend heavily on "star" talent for

Cooper Industries

Cooper Industries is a Houston-based manufacturer of electrical products, tools, and hardware that regularly evaluates potential acquisition targets, including both domestic and foreign firms. Each year, it pulls out of as many as ten to fifteen deals based on information uncovered during the due diligence process. Helping to make such decisions are three or four HR experts (out of a due diligence team of seven to twenty people). For example, an expert in pension design typically spends several days examining pension agreements and records using a detailed checklist. Among other things on the checklist are the day-to-day costs of managing the pension, retiree medical benefits, severance pay obligations, and employment contracts for executives. For IM&As, this analysis is likely to include conducting several hours of interviews with senior executives of the targeted firm. Usually the process takes about ten days, but more complex deals can take four weeks. The goal is the same for everyone on the team: to find out exactly what they are buying. Although it is probably rare for HR information to be the basis for not going ahead with a deal, it is quite likely that HR information will result in revaluing or repricing the deal (Greengard, 2000: 69).

Because employee benefits plans can have significant long-term financial consequences, they are quite likely to receive scrutiny. When employees are represented by unions, labor contracts also are likely to receive scrutiny. In fact, union representatives may participate in the due diligence process to ensure that issues associated with possible job loss, retraining and outplacement are fully anticipated.

success (such as entertainment), the loss of star talent may diminish the firm's stock. Loss of key technical talent may mean that important and irreplaceable knowledge is lost. If this talent and knowledge migrates to competitors, the firm's competitive advantage may be significantly damaged. Thus, in addition to making plans for retaining key talent, it also becomes necessary to assess the probability of losing key talent and assess the costs associated with such losses. Unfortunately, the science of assigning value to intangibles, including human capital, is still in its infancy. Nevertheless, in recent years some progress has been made in this area (e.g., see Becker *et al.*, 2001). Firms that are serious about assessing the financial risks associated with talent loss recognize the value of systematically estimating such risks even if they know their estimates are fallible.

Box 5.1 summarizes the many elements of the HR system that should be assessed during an IM&A due diligence process. In addition to assessing the managerial implications of these HR elements, legal counsel would also be sought to evaluate any formal contracts that the partners had previously committed to.

Box 5.1 Outline of a due diligence report describing the HR system of a potential international merger or acquisition partner

HR Audits for Mergers & Acquisitions

Conducted by Human Resources. Serves as a framework for collecting and bringing forward information about the organizational capabilities of a target company and its suitability for purchase, and subsequent integration, by X Corporation.

Executive summary:
- Concise overview of HR audit
- Recommendations and integration risks

Company profile:
- Company name, headquarters, site locations
- Number and type of employees at each site
- Date and history of company founding

Culture audit:
- Assess work environment
- Stated or implied values of company
- Employee morale
- Degree of shared vision among leaders and employees
- Frequency and results of employee surveys
- Communication style favored
- Executive team effectiveness
- Use of teams
- Degree of customer focus
- Degree to which the organization applies internal learning
- Attractiveness to potential new hires
- How and when the company celebrates success
- Comparison to X Corporation's culture

Management audit:
- Management style
- Decision-making process used
- Importance of values in managing the company
- Management experience/ capability
- Management development experiences
- Management development experiences
- Likelihood of key managers remaining post-acquisition
- Comparison to X Corporation's management's strengths

Employee audit:
- Overall talent of the employee base
- Strength of technical talent
- Strength of marketing talent
- Strength of functional talent
- Key employees' company origin
- Ability to recruit/retain employees
- Ratio of regular vs. contract employees
- Headcount growth plan through fiscal year
- Likelihood of key employees remaining post-acquisition
- Comparison to X Corporation's employee strengths

Compensation audit:
- Compensation philosophy
- Compensation components
- Grading system
- Job titles/families
- Performance evaluation system
- Investors' perceptions of compensation alignment
- Salary review process/ frequency
- Stock option distribution/ holdings
- Comparison to X Corporation's compensation

Benefits audit:
- Benefits philosophy
- Benefits components
- Trend of benefits development
- Potential savings with merged benefits plans
- Comparison to X Corporation's benefits

Integration issues:
- Compensation plan blending
- Benefits plan blending
- Employee communications plan
- Geographic considerations
- Likelihood of employees to relocate
- Willingness of company to be integrated into X Corporation

Used with the permission of R.W. Beatty, Rutgers University

Managing HR issues during Stage 2 (combination and integration) of IM&As

Of all the HR issues that arise during the IM&A process, perhaps the most critical HR issue for the success of Stage 2 is selection of the integration manager and the leader(s) for the new business (Ashkenas and Francis, 2000).

The integration manager

When Johnson & Johnson analyzed its experiences with mergers and acquisitions, it found that successful combinations were guided by an effective integration manager. The most effective integration managers were able to retained a higher percentage of the acquired companies' leaders, retain a higher percentage of the total employees, and achieve business goals earlier. Furthermore, its research indicated that effective integration managers were more likely to have the following characteristics:

- Successful integration managers focused exclusively on the particular acquisition or merger. This task was not one of many others for which they were responsible.
- Successful integration managers were *not* the same people who were running the business. Presumably, this made it easier for the integration manager to be, and to be perceived as, capable of fairly assessing the strengths and weaknesses of both partners involved in the deal.
- Successful integration managers provided continuity between the deal team and management of the new company. They understood the company, felt a sense of ownership, and were passionate about making the new organization work.
- Successful integration managers participated as members of a steering committee that included other top executives. The steering committee shared responsibility for defining the integration manager's role, establishing the objectives and process of the integration, and overseeing the progress of the various teams involved in all related projects (Bobier, 2000).

Guideline: Create a position dedicated to managing the integration process and clearly define the duties of this position.

For deals that are clearly acquisitions, the job of an integration manager should be managing the integration process, *not* the business. His or her duties include assisting *both* partners as they move through the integration process.

The integration manager can assist the acquired firm by:

- working closely with managers of the acquired firm to create consistency between the acquirer's and the acquiree's standards;
- developing communication strategies to disseminate important information about the integration effort to employees quickly;

- helping the acquired company adopt business initiatives that may not have existed before (e.g. risk management or six sigma) but which are standard practice in the acquiring firm;
- helping managers in the acquired business understand its new parent and learn to navigate through the acquirer's systems;
- translating and explaining the parent's various abbreviations and jargon;
- educating the new management team about the acquirer's business cycle, reviews, and other processes, such as strategic planning, budgeting, and HR assessments;
- helping the acquired firm's managers understand the parent's culture and business customs;
- helping the acquired firm's managers understand both fundamental and minor changes in their jobs; and
- managing the number of requests for information made by the parent, to avoid swamping managers with administrative report preparation.

Effective integration managers do not merely serve as agents of the acquirer, however. They should also represent the interests of everyone in the acquired firm. A perceptive integration manager can sense when tensions in the acquired unit are rising to levels that may prove debilitating, and intervene before the damage is done. They can also help members of the acquiring firm understand the perspective of those in the acquired firm, and appreciate the acquired firm's strengths.

Guideline: Select an integration manager with the competencies needed for this unique position, and develop performance management practices that are aligned with the performance expectations for the position.

As the preceding discussion makes clear, an integration manager must have a variety of skills to be effective. Among the roles that he or she will step into are these:

- project manager;
- communicator; information gatherer;
- adviser;
- advocate;
- relationship builder;
- facilitator;
- ombudsperson;
- negotiator.

Because the job of IM&A integration manager is in some respects unique, it is not one that is likely to be understood by employees who may have the required competencies. Even if the job duties are understood, the position may not be viewed as a highly desirable one, as it is clearly a temporary position. As a consequence, filling this position with the best available talent may require making a significant investment in the recruitment and selection process. Prior to choosing from among a set of candidates, the position itself must first be "sold" as desirable. In firms with a history of IM&A activity, the rewards associated with serving as an integration manager may already be recognized by employees (of course, the risks will also be more apparent). For firms with little prior experience, however, this position is likely to be perceived as a risky one – and indeed that perception may be accurate. Thus, to convince the best talent to sign on to this job, the firm may need to offer appropriate support and assurances of the value the firm places on developing competencies to support future IM&A activity. Certainly, plans for continued utilization of this integration competency and knowledge are imperative for further deals and for knowledge sharing. Having such plans in place may also be essential to convincing the best people to consider taking the position of integration manager.

The new business manager

Another critical task is selecting the leader(s) who will manage the new business combination, particularly if the current top-level managers are likely to depart. If an acquired business has unclear or absent leadership, the result will be crippling uncertainty, lack of direction, stalled new product development, and the postponement of important decisions. According to some experts, strong leadership going forward is essential to acquisition success – it is perhaps the single most important success factor (Taylor, 2002). The essential roles and tasks of the new business leader include developing the appropriate organizational structure, leading the change process, retaining and motivating key employees, and communicating with all relevant stakeholders.

In addition to understanding the business itself, some of the qualities that successful leaders of the newly combined businesses seem to have are these:

- sensitivity to cultural differences;
- open-mindedness;
- flexibility;
- ability to recognize the relative strengths and weaknesses of both companies;
- committment to retaining key employees;
- ability to be a good listener;
- vision; and
- ability to filter out distractions and focus on integrating key business drivers such as R&D and customer interfaces (Bobier, 2000).

Integration teams

Assisting the integration manager are integration teams (Marks and Mirvis, 2000; Taylor, 2002). DaimlerChrysler created over 100 integration teams. Specific teams were assigned to various functional areas and organizational levels within the two companies (Charman, 2000). In almost every IM&A, there are numerous systems and processes that must be integrated in order to support efforts to attain synergies. Examples are sales reporting systems, certain IT systems, the global e-mail network, and the distribution chain. Until these are integrated, day-to-day functioning may seem all but impossible.

Guideline: Establish an integration team to address each system or process that is key to creating value in the new business.

While there may be an endless number of differences in the systems and processes being merged together, the Johnson & Johnson study found that the most effective integration teams focused their attention on those that were essential to creating value. Not all forms of synergy are equally important. As one J&J executive stated, "We only attacked things that would bring benefits to the business. We did not integrate just for the sake of integrating." Once key value drivers are identified, a team should be assigned to creating synergy and tracking the progress of integration (Bobier, 2000).

Of course, the need for integration teams and the tasks that are most important for them to tackle differs according to the integration approach used. If the portfolio approach is adopted, the "integration" teams may focus primarily on developing shared understandings about the systems and processes in use at the various locations and establishing communication practices for people in the different facilities to use when coordination is required. If the blending approach is adopted, the integration teams will need to do much more than help the units develop an understanding of each other. They also will assess the strengths and weaknesses of the alternative systems and make choices about which to retain, which to discard, and where to make modifications. The new creation approach to integration may present an even greater challenge for the integration teams, for with this approach the expectation is that the best elements of systems in both firms will be reflected in new systems designed specifically to meet the needs of the new organization.

Restructuring/downsizing

When an IM&A plan includes significant restructuring and downsizing, the process of integration can be especially painful. Historically, the problem has been that executives tend to restructure slowly and to rely heavily on downsizing rather than on redesigning structures and processes. GE Capital has learned that a swift and definitive approach is best:

> Decisions about management structure, key roles, reporting relationships, layoffs, restructuring, and other career-affecting aspects of the integration should be made, announced, and implemented as soon as possible after the deal is signed – within days, if possible. Creeping changes, uncertainty, and anxiety that last for months are debilitating and immediately start to drain value from an acquisition.
>
> (Ashkenas *et al.*, 2000)

The experiences of Johnson & Johnson affirm the lessons at GE Capital, but its results caution against being too hasty. J&J has learned not dismantle anything until its use is understood and there is something to replace it. In other words, the following guideline appears prudent:

Guideline: Restructuring should be carefully planned and then done early, fast, and only once.

Following this guideline can help reduce the stress created when everyone senses the impending changes but knows not what, when, or how.

> There is no doubting the pressure of work caused by the need to manage integration as well as "doing the day job." Add to that the tendency for people to resist change and the shortage of appropriately qualified management talent and you have a recipe for an over-stressed, under-performing work environment.
>
> (Metha, 2000: 31)

As with other major organizational change efforts, the planning phase of a restructuring or layoff should involve the staff who will be affected by the change to help ensure their understanding and cooperation. A schedule for the change process should be developed and the changes should be conducted according to the plan. Given the importance of managing such changes, expertise in change management is an essential competency that must be present within the IM&A integration team(s). The HR staff can address this need by assessing change management competencies when the integration team is being created and/or by providing training and change management services to the teams after they are formed.

Facing the threat of job loss and seeing others lose their jobs can be a traumatic and bitter experience. This is one reason why many excellent companies do everything possible to avoid layoffs, even after an acquisition. Despite the best intentions, even the most employee-friendly companies may conclude that some workforce reduction is necessary in order to eliminate redundant positions following an international merger or acquisition. In such situations, governmental policies and labor contracts may partially determine the layoff practices that are permitted. Nevertheless, the way a firm approaches reductions in the workforce can have long-ranging implications for employee loyalty and turnover.

Avoiding layoffs

Instead of cutting costs through layoffs, a company may choose to revise the timetable for achieving cost reductions, offer alternative employment arrangements to encourage the workforce to reduce the length of its workweek, and/or offer incentives to encourage employees to consider early retirement. Another approach to avoiding layoffs of redundant workers is to use internal transfers to other parts of the company. Other options that companies may use to avoid laying people off include:

- restricting overtime;
- not renewing contracts for temporary staff;
- temporary periods of leave;
- job sharing;
- retraining;
- providing seed funds and entrepreneurship training and encouraging employees to start their own businesses;
- transferring staff to other companies (e.g., suppliers, customers);
- reducing executive salaries and incentive pay;
- partnering with government agencies and professional societies to find jobs for displaced employees (*The Economist*, 2001; Hanoka, 1997).

By using such approaches, combines may be able to avoid some of the hidden costs associated with layoffs. These costs include:

- severance payments made to departing employees;
- fees paid to consultants who assist with the downsizing process;
- litigation from aggrieved workers;
- loss of trust in management;
- lack of staff who are needed when the new organization begins to grow;
- loss of reputation in the labor market, making future hiring more difficult;
- cynical and paranoid behaviors among layoff survivors; and
- declining customer satisfaction resulting from low employee morale (Colin, 2001).

Downsizing with respect

When employees must be let go, the process by which jobs are eliminated can make a difference. Loss of attachment, lack of information, and a perception of apparent managerial capriciousness as the basis for decisions about who will be terminated cause anxiety and an obsession with personal survival (Morrison, 1997). The negative cycle of reactions may not be inevitable, however. If survivors feel that the process used to decide whom to let go was fair, their productivity and the quality of their job performance may not suffer as much. It is not the terminations per se that create bitterness – it is the manner in which they are handled. Survivors often express feelings of disgust and anger when their friends and colleagues are fired. If they believe their own performance is no better than that of those who are let go, survivors may feel guilty that they have kept their jobs. Thus, in developing HR policies, procedures, and practices for effective downsizing and layoffs, even the needs of survivors require attention.

As with any major organizational change, the steps of diagnosing the current situation and developing a careful plan to implement change are essential. But the process of downsizing is not just about strategies and plans; it is also about relationships between the people in a company, and about personal character. The greatest challenges for companies and their managers are maintaining employee morale and regaining their trust while the actions of the company seem to say, "You are not valuable."

Retaining key talent

As we have already explained, Stage 1 of an IM&A process is the appropriate time to identify key talent. As the deal becomes more certain, specific plans for retaining that talent should be developed. Such planning may begin near the end of Stage 1 or early in Stage 2. Either way, it is during Stage 2 that the retention plans will ultimately succeed or fail. Watson Wyatt's research on IM&As found that retention of key talent was among the top three issues that needed to be addressed by an HRM integration plan, as illustrated in Table 5.1 (Yang, 2001).

Table 5.1 Percentage of respondents who believe that people activity is "critical" in international mergers

Specific people activity	*Percentage of respondents*
Retention of key talent	76
Communication	71
Retention of key managers	67
Integration of corporate cultures	51

Source: I.T. Kay and M. Shelton (2000) "The people problem in mergers," *The McKinsey Quarterly* (Number 4): 28

According to Kay and Shelton (2000: 29),

> People problems are a major cause of failed mergers, and you must ensure that most if not all of the people you want are still in place at the end of the integration period. This is best achieved by carrying out an employee selection process whose pace and substance match the kind of merger involved.

Given that everyone seems to understand the importance of retaining key employees, why do so many firms seem to stumble when it comes to meeting their objectives? One likely explanation is that the identification of key talent occurs too late – sometimes not until the person has already left the firm.

Guideline: Make talent retention a key performance objective of upper-level managers, give them the resources needed to achieve the objective, and monitor their performance against this objective.

Another cause of talent loss is that responsibility for talent retention is pushed down to lower-level managers, whereas a better approach would be to involve executives at the very top. Retention of key talent begins with communication. Employees whose talents are needed must understand that they are valued and that the firm wishes to retain them. This message is most effectively carried by managers positioned two or more levels above the employees of interest who themselves feel secure about their post-IM&A roles. These higher-level managers may also be more persuasive than the immediate supervisor of the person targeted for retention.

"It's really identifying your winners at all levels, in top sales, marketing, and technical leaders," says Jeff Christian, a Cleveland-based executive recruiter (Armour, 2000). Of course, in order for these managers to be effective, they must have the authority to negotiate meaningful retention agreements. Giving managers the authority to offer cash or other incentives to workers who stay through a merger or until a specific project is completed is one way to improve their ability to retain people. Another tactic is to alter the severance agreements of employees to provide an incentive for those employees who may worry about pending layoffs and depart prematurely. Because the best talent is also the most mobile, finding ways to forestall voluntary turnover should be a high priority during Stage 2.

Managing communications

Well-managed communications are valuable tools for retaining and motivating key employees, as well as for managing the many types of change that occur during combination and integration.

Guideline: It is impossible to communicate too much or in too many ways.

Effective communication is difficult under most circumstances, but the communication challenge is especially great during IM&As. Thus, it pays to use as many ways to communicate as possible. Thoughtful use of the Internet, internal company intranets, and e-mail is one way to dispel rumors and keep employees updated about pending changes, but remember that electronic communications should supplement, not replace, face-to-face discussions.

Managers in the acquiring firm have but one chance to extend a warm and convincing welcome to employees of a target firm, and that chance comes at the beginning of Stage 2. For this communication, personal contact with a lower-level manager is likely to be more effective than electronic contact with the top executive. Personal contact should also be used to convey complex information, so employees can ask questions and get clear answers immediately.

Guideline: The communication practices should be proactive and all information provided should be correct and accurate.

Effective communications anticipate employees' need for information; they do not merely provide answers to questions asked. Perhaps even more important than timely information is accurate information. For example, using the term *merger* to describe a deal that will be managed using the portfolio or assimilation approach to integration can cause unnecessary confusion and misunderstanding. Likewise, using the term *acquisition* to describe a deal that will be managed as a new creation or blended organization can send the wrong signal to employees and may create more resistance to change than is justified.

Knowledge sharing

A final HR task to attend to during Stage 2 is ensuring that lessons learned during the IM&A integration process are shared quickly throughout the organization. As J&J found, many of the same lessons were learned repeatedly across the business units, and these lessons were not always shared. Learning is a natural part of the integration process, and the need for some trial and error is unavoidable. Nevertheless, sharing problems as they are encountered and sharing solutions as they are found is one way to improve learning efficiencies. Large, decentralized firms seem more prone to inefficient learning related to routine processes and procedures because there is no natural central hub for information to flow through. For example, in a decentralized firm, staffing activities are typically conducted locally, with little or no central oversight. Consequently, each unit is likely to make the same mistakes as it gains experience in managing layoffs. In a centralized firm, the benefits of such learning accumulate more quickly. This is one of the reasons why an integration team should be established for every important process within the organization – including HR processes. In decentralized firms, such integration teams provide an efficient mechanism for the rapid transfer of learning.

Managing HR issues during Stage 3 (solidification and assessment) of IM&As

Once the international merger or acquisition has progressed through the stage of combination and integration, of whatever form, there remain several HR issues that need attention during solidification and assessment. Indeed, one danger at this stage is thinking that the IM&A process is finished and that issues addressed in Stage 2 no longer require attention. But this is seldom true.

Guideline: Disband integration teams slowly and only after the targets of their integration activity are completely stabilized.

Leadership

Leadership and staffing issues that may seem to have been resolved earlier may continue to unfold for quite some time. In the DaimlerChrysler example, during the two years after the combination was announced, Daimler made several leadership changes in the Chrysler Group, as the unit of DaimlerChrysler is now called (Tierney, 2000). At the beginning of 2001, Dieter Zetsche, a veteran Daimler executive, took over Chrysler's leadership, replacing a former Chrysler head, James Holden. Zetsche in turn created his own top management team composed of one Daimler veteran and five Chrysler veterans. All these changes were made because the earlier top management team of former Chrysler veterans failed in its efforts to stop the "breathtakingly fast decline of the bottom line" (Tierney and Green, 2000: 48). Thus the process of solidifying leadership may result in assessing and replacing the existing leadership. The need for new leadership may be due to inappropriate selection or changed conditions or both.

Strategy and structure

Just as the leadership at DaimlerChrysler had to be revised, the strategy and structure had to be assessed and revised. The new top management was given more control over the Chrysler Group largely because a senior Daimler executive was running it. He and his team developed a new strategy of cost cutting by reducing supplier costs and reducing product offerings. Instead of running the Chrysler Group as a cash-rich growth business, management began to manage it as a turnaround. Consequently, staff reductions were also needed. Thus HRM practices for evaluation and outplacement became critical.

Culture

Along with the changes in leadership and strategy, the culture changed. Zetsche and his team were much more egalitarian than their predecessors. According to one observer, "They [ate] in the employee cafeteria rather than the executive dining room at the headquarters in Auburn Hills, Michigan" (Muller *et al.*, 2001: 49). To support this new culture, strategy, and structure, changes were made in the performance appraisal and compensation systems, which clarified the new priorities of cost cutting, supplier management, flexibility, and improving employee morale.

DaimlerChrysler CEO Jürgen Schrempp, reflecting on these changes in the post-combination stage of the acquisition, estimated that recovery and solidification would take two to four years. Initially, back in 1998 upon purchasing Chrysler, Schrempp discussed immediate global synergies and probability. Perhaps the earlier success in its acquisition of Freightliner gave him the confidence that the Chrysler acquisition would be as successful. The contrasting experiences provided DaimlerChrysler with excellent opportunities for learning (Taylor, 2001; Vlasic and Stertz, 2000).

Responding to stakeholders

Institutional theory emphasizes the importance of involving and attending to the concerns of a firm's multiple stakeholders (Abrahamson, 1991). In IM&As, often the customers of the acquired firm suffer the most as products and services are changed or eliminated without warning. To avoid losing customers – especially those that the new firm may hope to serve in the future – it may be necessary to monitor how customers are responding to the new organization and make an extra effort to address their needs. For example, if a service is eliminated, the firm might help customers locate other providers of the service. Similarly, the concerns and considerations of the acquired firm's shareholders, employees, unions, community groups, and suppliers need to be evaluated and perhaps responded to. Ideally, the likely impact on these stakeholders of the IM&A was assessed earlier in Stage 1 or perhaps Stage 2, and by Stage 3 many actions should have been taken to address the concerns that were identified. As for the other activities that have already occurred, Stage 3 should now include an assessment of the effectiveness of actions taken, as well as the taking of any additional corrective actions that may seem appropriate.

Learning

For firms that will be engaging in future IM&As, capturing and consolidating the learning and knowledge that has been generated throughout the IM&A process is perhaps the most important activity during Stage 3.

Guideline: Regardless of whether the IM&A process has been declared a success or a failure, the knowledge created during the process should be captured and secured for future use.

As we have already suggested, retaining the integration manager is an objective that should be anticipated as early as Stage 1. The importance of retaining the integration manager is that if there is success, other executives will claim credit for that success. They will point to their skill in making the strategic decision, their cunning in negotiating the deal, and so on. Alternatively, if the deal seems to have failed, changes in business conditions or the partner's lack of candor during the due diligence process are likely to be blamed. Under either scenario, it is likely that the important role played by the integration manager will receive little attention. Similarly, it may be hard to believe that the lessons everyone has learned throughout the ordeal will ever fade from memory, become distorted with time, or simply walk out the door. Yet all of these are likely. Ensuring that the lessons learned will be retained requires intentional effort in Stage 3. In addition to retaining the integration manager and key players (such as integration team leaders and members), the organization should encourage all its staff to reflect on what they learned that could be useful for creating success in a future IM&A deal. These insights should be systematically surfaced, shared, and recorded for future reference.

Recognizing failure

Unfortunately, not all IM&As succeed, especially when they are the company's first experience. As described in CBA-in-Action 1, sometimes it is necessary to admit that an acquisition is not meeting the company's expectations and exit the arrangement. Because exits or CBA dissolutions are sometimes necessary, they are discussed in more detail in Chapter 7.

Lincoln Electric's international expansion falters

CBA-In-Action 1

Although the Lincoln Electric of Cleveland, Ohio, is today a very successful company, it went through some difficult times in the 1990s. The difficulties were partly due to the economic conditions around the world and partly due to the company's international strategy of expansion by acquisitions. It started back in 1986 when George Willis became CEO. He began to expand internationally in a big way. At this time, Lincoln Electric had operations in France, Australia, and Canada that had been in operation for many years. However, the company had not expanded internationally for many years.

Willis thought the economic times called for rapid international expansion. Thus rather than expand by building their own greenfield sites, which would require too much time, the company chose to make international acquisitions. Because Lincoln Electric had virtually no managers with international experience, it retained the managers in the newly acquired subsidiaries, several of which were in Europe. The companies were pretty much left to manage themselves. Most of the acquisitions were unionized and most did not have the piece-rate compensation system for which Lincoln Electric is famous.

By 1991, it was clear that the subsidiaries were losing money. The acquisitions were dragging down the entire company, forcing Lincoln to go into debt. Financial conditions got so bad that the company even had to borrow money to pay the traditional annual bonus to its U.S. workers in Cleveland.

In 1992, Don Hastings became CEO and acted quickly to take corrective actions. He began by bringing in several outside managers with international experience. He also closed several subsidiaries and reduced the product lines of others. Several modifications were made in the HR practices being used, and attempts were made to adapt Lincoln's individual incentive compensation system to the local conditions. In addition, a new

continued

management structure was created to oversee the company's international expansion efforts.

According to Don Hastings, harsh lessons were learned through these experiences, but now Lincoln Electric is better positioned than ever before to continue to move into the tumultuous realm of globalization.

Conclusion

As with international joint ventures, there are a significant number of HR issues in international mergers and acquisitions, as identified in Chapter 4. Although different HR issues take priority during the three stages of IM&As, a common objective in all stages is anticipating and managing change, and learning from experience. In addition, although it has not been a central theme in this chapter, managing cultural differences is a key HR issue for IM&As, as it is for any CBA. Because of the importance of culture and cultural differences in CBAs, we examine them in detail in Chapter 6.

Mergers and acquisitions of and by Deutsche Bank

Case Example

When an emissary of Sanford I. Weill, chief executive of Citigroup, approached executives at Deutsche Bank in February 2002 to gauge whether the German bank would be open to a takeover offer, the response was a categorical "no thanks," according to several sources close to the companies.

Scores of similar conversations have taken place in the past few years among executives at rival banks, in pursuit of the next big deal that will bring the economies of scale and the influence necessary to compete in the global financial services market. Most negotiations have become bogged down over issues of control, price, and culture. More recently, the depressed share prices of banks, pummeled by a lethal combination of rising bad loans and falling investment banking fees, have been a deterrent. But with share prices beginning to stabilize, executives are reexamining the potential for big cross-border acquisitions, analysts said. And this time, they added, there is more pressure to get deals done.

"Over the next three to four years, European banks will go through an accelerated wave of consolidation," predicted Davide Serra, an analyst with Morgan Stanley Dean Witter in London. "People are starting to look again at doing deals."

The list of would-be combinations is as long as it is varied. Some pairings, like a combination of Deutsche Bank and Citigroup, would make sense, analysts said. Deutsche Bank could offer Citigroup a stronger foothold in Germany, which is expected to be a hotbed for corporate advisory work over the next few years as companies take advantage of changes to the tax laws that will allow them to unwind cross-shareholdings without incurring huge liabilities. For Deutsche Bank, the combination would give it real influence on Wall Street, where its investment bank still lags. Josef Ackermann, however, chief executive of Deutsche Bank, is unwilling to give up control and is loath to consider a deal while his bank's share price is languishing.

Ackermann would love, however, to emulate Citigroup. He wants Deutsche to have the same broad array of businesses, and he wants the same power that Citigroup chairman Sanford I. Weill wields. On the second point, Ackermann will have his way. On January 31, 2002, Deutsche unveiled a plan to create a new executive committee, chaired by Ackermann, that will run day-to-day operations. That is a major departure. Under German law, companies are run by management boards called *Vorstände*, in which all decisions are made by consensus. Stretching the law to its limits, Ackermann demanded all the powers of an American CEO. Traditionalists were aghast, but Ackermann quickly quelled the dissent, ousting his most vocal critic, *Vorstand* member Thomas Fischer.

Ackermann's mission is to deploy the bank's capital more effectively. His plan is to sell most of the bank's money-losing or low-return businesses and sell its equity positions in firms such as Munich Re, and invest the proceeds in its strongest areas: investment banking, asset management, and investment advice for wealthy customers. He also wants to buy back up to 10 percent of outstanding shares. Some long-standing Deutsche businesses will come under the hammer. The bank's passive fund management business – the index-tracking money management unit, which has $153 billion on its books – will almost certainly go, as will its $3.37 trillion global securities custody business. He also expects to speed up the sale of Deutsche's investments in nonfinancial companies, which include stakes in DaimlerChrysler, tire manufacturer Continental, and cement producer Heidelberger Zemet. And as Citigroup, he may attempt to make more acquisitions within Germany.

Observers say the drivers for merger and acquisition activity in Germany are stronger than in other markets, which is good news for anyone with a strong position there. Hartmuth Jung, head of UBS Warburg's German business, says, "If the global M&A market goes down 50 percent, I do not know if it will grow, but it will not go down 50 percent because of reasons specific to Germany." Those reasons include the abolition of capital gains tax on companies' sales of stakes in other companies, the need for German corporations, more than any other in Europe, to restructure, and the deregulation of European industries, such as telecommunications and utilities, which will allow German companies, which were among the first to be deregulated, to buy into the markets, says Mr. Jung.

If Deutsche Bank does expand by making acquisitions within Germany, it may become as strong within Germany as it is outside Germany. But because Deutsche failed in its merger with Dresdner Bank, it will be keen on doing further deals as systematically as possible.

Because it was successful in integrating its acquisition of Bankers Trust in 1999, it knows that success in mergers and acquisitions is possible. Another result of that integration was a reorganization of the company and its HR department. Its 1,600 HR professionals also developed new competencies to better link their activities with the business (see the case

continued

example in Chapter 8). Thus the possibilities for success in future mergers and acquisitions look quite good.

Note: This case example was adapted from Kapner (2002a), Fairlamb (2002), "Deutsche Learns Well from UK, US models" (2001), "Mr. Ackermann Expects" (2002), Andrews (2002), Walker (2002), and "Deutsche Bank Is Shedding All Its Shares of Munich Re."

Managing cultural diversity in cross-border alliances

6

> In cross-border acquisitions or alliances, cultural differences can be viewed as either a handicap or a powerful seed for something new.
>
> Carlos Ghosn
> (Emerson, 2001: 3)

One of the single biggest variables in the success of cross-border alliances such as IJVs and IM&As is culture, and more specifically, cultural differences or distances between companies:

> Cultural distance is reflected and transmitted via human actors. In IJVs and IM&As, it is articulated in the composition of human resources, with employees and executives being the conduits for the cultural influences brought into the venture. These various employee groups bring in different inputs anchored in national, industrial and corporate cultures that make up the cultural mosaic of the IJV and the IM&A.
>
> (Shenkar, 2002: 1)

In this chapter, we use the term *culture* to refer to the unique pattern of shared assumptions, values, and norms that shape the socialization, symbols, language, narratives, and practices of a group of people. Thus culture provides a context (a mindset) for interpreting events and assigning meaning (Denison, 1996; Rafaeli and Worline, 2000; Trice & Beyer, 1993). Cultures develop in both large and small groups of people, so cultural differences occur at many levels. Some cultural differences become most evident when one is comparing large geographic regions, while others can be found at the level of countries, regions within countries, industries, organizations, occupational groups, demographic groups within a country, and so on (Jackson and Schuler, 2003). For any particular international joint venture, merger, or acquisition, cultural differences at many or all of these different levels are likely to be relevant. The distances between the cultures of organizations can have a significant impact on their relationships. In fact it may preclude their relationship (Ghemawat, 2001). It is, however, the specific nature and location of a CBA that determines which elements of culture become most salient and require the most attention.

National cultures

Depending on the cultural distance between the national cultures involved in a CBA, managing differences in country cultures or regional cultures may be of relatively great or of only minor significance. In some CBAs, such as those between U.S. and Canadian business, differences in country cultures are *relatively* small. In others, however, cultural differences in such key areas as leadership styles and decision-making procedures can be substantial (Brodbeck *et al.*, 2000). Even when an alliance occurs between companies within a single country, cultural differences may be significant, owing to regional differences. A study of more than 700 managers in large cities in each of China's six major regions suggests that there are at least three distinct subcultures in China: one in the southeast, another in the northeast, and a third covering much of the central and western parts of the country. The subculture of the southeast region is the most individualistic, whereas the subculture of the central and western areas is the most collectivistic. The culture of the northeast region falls between these two extremes. Thus, cultural diversity may create just as great a challenge for an alliance between companies from different regions in China as it would for other CBAs (Ralston *et al.*, 1996).

Variations (or similarities) in the institutional environments of the alliance partners may further complicate (or help to alleviate) the challenge of managing differences due to national cultures. For example, the European Union, the Asia-Pacific Economic Cooperation, and the North American Free Trade Agreement all represent institutional arrangements that seek to provide a common framework or perspective that can be used to guide some relationships between companies in the member countries (see Luo, 1999; Moran and Abbott, 1994). As these institutional arrangements become better established, it is likely that CBAs within an economic trade region will become easier even in the face of significant differences in national cultures. Nevertheless, even within economic trade zones, differences in institutional arrangements among countries result in differences in the functioning of corporate boards and top management teams as well as approaches to managing an organization's human resources (Brewster, 1995; Glunk *et al.*, 2001; Mayer and Whittington, 1999).

Industry culture

Similarly, differences in industry cultures may be important in some CBAs and nearly irrelevant in others. Industry cultures are likely to be relatively unimportant when an alliance is created between companies within an industry, but when organizations from distinct industries attempt to form an alliance, such differences may be as significant as differences in country culture. Industries boundaries are both fuzzy and unstable, so the question "What industry are we in?" is not always easy to answer. Furthermore, some companies compete by constantly pushing at the boundaries of the industry and, eventually, redefining the industries in which they compete (Hamel, 2001; Hamel and Prahalad, 1994). Nevertheless, at any point in time, the relevant industry for most

Box 6.1 Four dimensions in industry culture

Employee oriented: Concern focuses on the people sharing the work. ◄► *Job oriented:* Concern focuses on getting the job done.

Parochial: Employees identify with the organization in which they work. ◄► *Professional:* Employees identify with the type of work they do or their profession.

Open system: Many types of people can feel comfortable in the organization. ◄► *Closed system:* The type of person who fits is narrowly specified; it takes time for employees to feel at home.

Loose control: Codes of conduct allow for much variation among employees. ◄► *Tight control:* Written and unwritten rules exert tight control over behavior.

organizations is made up of a group of companies that offer similar products and services. Companies within an industry experience similar patterns of growth, and eventually a common industry culture may develop. Generally, companies within the same industry are a firm's most significant competitors, as well as their most likely partners in strategic alliances, including international mergers, acquisitions, and joint ventures.

Unfortunately, there is very little empirical research evidence available to use in understanding industry-based cultural differences. An exception is the work of Hofstede (1997), who suggested that industry cultures can be described using four dimensions as outlined in Box 6.1.

These dimensions build on Hofstede's earlier work on organizational cultures, described below. Although Hofstede's dimensions for describing industry differences have not been widely used in empirical research, his work supports the assumption that cultural clashes are more likely to be disruptive in alliances that are formed by firms from different industries.

Organizational cultures

As is true for industry cultures, describing differences in organizational cultures can be difficult because there has been little empirical work directed at understanding the nature of these differences and how they are manifested across different countries (Adler and Jelinek, 1986; Aguinis and Henle, 2002). One popular typology for describing organizational cultures uses two dimensions to create a typology of four cultures, with each culture characterized by different underlying values. In this typology, one dimension reflects the *formal control orientation*, ranging from stable to flexible. The other dimension reflects the *focus of attention*, ranging from internal functioning to external functioning. When these four dimensions are combined, they form a typology of four pure types of organizational cultures: *bureaucratic*, *clan*, *entrepreneurial*, and *market* (Hooijberg and Petrock, 1993; Quinn and Rohrbaugh, 1983).

On the basis of research in ten companies located in three European countries, Hofstede proposed using six dimensions to conceptualize organizational cultures (Hofstede, 1991; Hofstede *et al.*, 1990): *process versus results orientation*; *employee versus job orientation*; *parochial versus professional*; *open versus closed system*; *loose versus tight control*; and *normative versus pragmatic*. Rather than reflecting different values, these dimensions reflect differences in management practices (see also Peterson and Hofstede, 2000).

Using yet a third approach to conceptualizing organizational culture, the GLOBE project (Dickson *et al.*, 2000; House *et al.*, 1999) has made the assumption that differences in organizational cultures can be understood using the same dimensions that differentiate among national cultures.

Domestic cultural diversity

In any organization, differences in individual personality and behavioral styles contribute to domestic workforce diversity. Other forms of domestic diversity are associated with membership in various demographic groups. Regardless of which other forms of cultural diversity exist in CBAs, *domestic* cultural diversity is always an issue.

In the Davidson-Marley IJV, the Dutch workforce hired to staff the manufacturing plant shared a societal culture, but other forms of domestic diversity proved challenging nevertheless. Recruitment and selection practices intentionally sought to represent the demographic diversity (gender, age, and so on) of the Dutch labor market within the plant. Additional diversity was introduced unintentionally, however, because employees were hired in two distinct waves. All employees who were hired had to meet the same technical skill requirements, but different personalities were sought during these two hiring waves. In selecting the first 100 employees, the IJV sought people who were willing to contribute to building up the firm in its pioneering phase. Good problem-identification and problem-solving abilities were needed. In addition, the IJV looked for employees with an international orientation because these employees would be traveling to the United States or the United Kingdom to receive training.

Within the United States, research on domestic cultural diversity is based on the assumption that membership in some demographic groups results in socialization experiences that effectively create identifiable subcultures within a national population. Gender, ethnicity, and age are the characteristics most often associated with demographic cultural influences (Bloom, 2002). Certainly there is evidence of group-based differences in values and behavioral styles among members of different demographic groups. Within the context of North America, gender differences in verbal and nonverbal communication, influenceability, interpersonal styles, and leadership styles are well documented (Best and Williams, 2001; Carli, 1989; Eagly and Carli, 1981; Eagly and Johnson, 1990; Tannen, 1990, 1995). Also well documented are age and cohort differences in work attitudes and values (Elder, 1974; Rhodes, 1983; Thernstrom, 1973; "Work attitudes," 1986). Presumably, differences among ethnic groups and language groups within countries tend to mirror cultural differences between the host country and the original home country of an ethnic group. (However, with time, assimilation and adaptation may diminish the differences, and/or a new ethnic culture or language difference may develop.)

Of course, differences found among demographic groups within a country are shaped by and also contribute to the country's national culture. For example, gender differences appear to be more pronounced in some countries than others, as do the relationships between men and women (Best and Williams, 2001; Williams and Best, 1990). Furthermore, in other countries, it is likely that meaningful cultural variations are associated with other demographic subgroups; for example, cultural differences due to religion may be more salient while those due to race or ethnicity may be less salient.

Understanding how cultural diversity influences behavior

Scholars who study culture at different levels of analysis disagree about how to describe cultures, the social levels of analysis at which it is appropriate to apply the concept of culture, and many other issues that are beyond the scope of this chapter. (Interested readers can find an overview of these issues in Ashkanasy and Jackson (2001). For more detailed discussions, see Ashkanasy *et al.* (2000a).) Without attempting either to summarize or to resolve these debates, in this chapter we make some simplifying assumptions about the nature of "culture."

One assumption is that our understanding of the consequences of cultural diversity in CBAs can move ahead without our resolving the question about how best to assess the "content" of culture. We do not intend to suggest that empirical work of a comparative nature is unimportant. However, a complete understanding of the ways that the cultures of various subgroups are similar to or different from each other is not needed in order to begin to understand how the presence of cultural differences shapes behavior in organizations. That is, we assume that the structure of cultural diversity has some predictable consequences, and that these arise regardless of the content of the cultural diversity present in a specific CBA.

We also assume that the behavior of an individual is influenced by multiple cultures, which are associated with the person's multiple memberships in and identification with a variety of overlapping and intersecting social entities (societies, organizations, professions, ethnic populations, and so on). These multiple cultures provide the individual with a variety of value systems (which need not be consistent with each other) for interpreting and responding to events in the environment. Depending on the social setting, some of the value systems available to an individual become more salient and important in guiding behavior. This perspective of how cultures impact behavior is consistent with social identity theory, which views social identification processes as situationally determined (Salk and Shenkar, 2001).

A model for understanding cultural diversity and its consequences

Jackson *et al.* (1995) developed a model to illustrate how domestic diversity influences behavior in organizations. Here we have adapted their model to illustrate how many aspects of cultural diversity can combine to influence the behavior of employees in cross-border alliances. First, we describe the model shown in Figure 6.1, and briefly review some of the evidence used to develop it. Then we illustrate its implications for understanding the dynamics of managing cultural diversity in CBAs.

The many forms of cultural diversity

As shown in Figure 6.1, the model recognizes that the cultural context includes several layers or levels. To some extent, these layers of culture are nested, with the more inclusive levels of culture operating as constraints around the "lower" levels of culture. For example, the organizational cultures of single-business domestic firms tend to be constrained by and reflect their country and industry cultures. We do not intend to imply that the more inclusive levels of culture determine the cultures of more delimited social systems, however. Nor do we intend to suggest that a lower-level social system is fully nested within only one higher-level social system. Indeed, for CBAs, this is definitely not the case – instead, at least some individuals (e.g., the top management team) within any organization formed by a CBA are embedded in multiple organizational and country cultures, and perhaps also multiple industry cultures.

Recognizing that cultural diversity can be created in many ways, the model shown in Figure 6.1 organizes constructs into four general categories that are linked as follows: cultural diversity ➔ mediating states and processes ➔ short-term behavioral manifestations ➔ longer-term consequences. The model can be used to analyze the behavior of individuals, dyads, and larger social units, such as work teams or departments.

Beginning on the left, the content and structure of cultural diversity are viewed as (partial) determinants of the way people feel and think about themselves and each other. The *content* of cultural diversity simply refers to the specific values, norms, language, and other elements of a culture. As has already been noted multiple levels of cultural

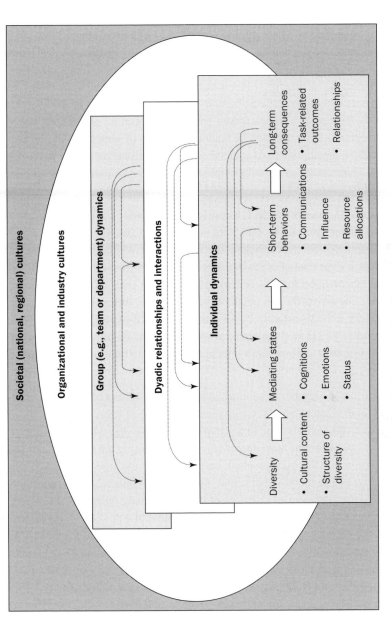

Figure 6.1 The dynamics of cultural diversity in cross-border alliances

© Susan E. Jackson and Randall S. Schuler

content will be relevant in most situations. For CBAs, societal, organizational, and industry cultures are likely to be particularly salient. However, demographic cultures also are likely to play a role in shaping the interactions between individuals and groups within the organization.

The *structure* of cultural diversity refers to how cultural differences are distributed within the team or organization. The specific circumstances of a particular CBA mean that both the structure and the content of cultural diversity may be unique to each alliance. For example, in the combination phase of IM&As, the structure of organizational-level diversity within the integration teams is likely to be balanced (or, some might describe it as polarized), especially if the partners try to merge the cultures of the two companies. If each of the partners is a domestic firm with little societal-level diversity represented, then the integration team also will be balanced in terms of societal cultural diversity. In this situation, the alignment of societal and organizational membership reinforces the cultural divide between the subgroups within the team, creating a cultural fault line (Lau and Murnighan, 1998).

Next, consider the example of an IJV that is located outside the countries of the two parents and staffed completely with local talent. In that case, there may be little societal diversity within the IJV. Nevertheless, if employees were hired from the local external labor market, a great deal of organizational and industry-based diversity may be present. If the local labor market for jobs is demographically diverse, and if employment practices encourage hiring across the full range of the labor force, then demographic diversity will also be present in the workforce. Under this scenario, the expectation might be that the structure of diversity should not create a strong fault line or polarization between any two groups. Nevertheless, cultural fault lines and polarization may arise even under this type of scenario.

In the Davidson-Marley IJV, a cultural fault line was inadvertently created among employees in the Dutch manufacturing plant. It developed because employees were hired in two distinct waves. The first group of 100 employees who were hired worked in a start-up operation and were deeply involved in working out the details of how the operation was run. After the new plant was established and growing, the IJV hired 200 more employees. For this wave of hiring, they sought people who were willing to accept and adjust to the management practices of the now thriving operation, and who could work well in teams. Thus differences in the job tenure of employees were aligned with differences in personality. Furthermore, as a result of the timing of the hires, these two waves of employees found themselves working under different employment contracts. And, owing to the seniority differences in the two groups, those who were hired first were always assigned to more advanced job categories and received higher pay. This divide within the workforce created unexpected conflicts, and in retrospect, the HR manager realized that it would have been better to hire on a continuous basis rather than in two distinct waves (van Sluijs and Schuler, 1994).

The *content* of cultural differences has received the most attention in past research. However, research on group dynamics clearly shows that the *structure* of cultural diversity has important consequences. For example, intergroup conflict is almost inevitable when cultural fault lines are present, regardless of the cultural values or norms that separate the groups. In contrast, when differences are more broadly distributed and diffuse, problems of coordination may be more problematic than overt conflict, especially in the early stages of a group's development. However, given enough time, very diverse multinational teams in which there is no opportunity for nationality-based cliques to form can overcome these problems and outperform more homogeneous teams in the long run (Earley and Mosakowski, 2000).

How cultural diversity influences employees' thoughts and feelings

The forms of diversity present in an organization can influence how people think and feel. Eventually, their thoughts and feelings are translated into observable behaviors. Attraction, discomfort, admiration, stereotyping, perceptions of status and power – all of these thoughts and feelings are influenced by cultural diversity.

Emotional reactions

Regardless of the basis for identifying people as similar or dissimilar (e.g., commonality of national, industry, organizational and/or demographic culture), people tend to feel more comfortable with and positive about others whom they perceive to be similar. Loyalty and favoritism characterize interactions with similar others while distrust and rivalry characterize interactions with those who are dissimilar. The tendency to be attracted to and biased in favor of similar others is so pervasive that it operates even when people judge their similarity on the basis of meaningless information (such as randomly determined group membership).

At the level of teams and larger organizational units, feelings of attraction or liking among members translate into group cohesiveness. Although there has been little research on the effects of shared societal, industry, or organizational cultures on group cohesiveness, there is a great deal of evidence showing this effect of similarity for other background characteristics, including age, gender, race, education, prestige, social class, attitudes, and beliefs (Jackson *et al.*, 1995). As will soon become apparent, this similarity–attraction–cohesiveness dynamic can have important consequences for the emotional landscape within which members of CBAs conduct their work.

Cognition

Cultural diversity also shapes the cognitive landscape of CBAs. In order to simplify and make manageable a world of infinite variety, people naturally rely on stereotypes to inform their evaluations of others, guide their behavior towards others, and predict the behavior of others. Mental models are another cognitive shortcut for making sense of a complex world and deciding how to act. In work organizations, the mental models of employees may include beliefs about the priority assigned to various performance objectives (e.g., speed versus friendliness in customer interactions) and well as beliefs about cause-and-effect relationships (e.g., what a group should do if it wants to increase speed). The content of stereotypes and mental models reflect past experiences, and are almost inextricably bound up with the content of a culture (e.g., see Beyer, 1981). This point is illustrated by cross-cultural research on negotiations and conflict resolution. Mental models of negotiation and conflict resolution appear to be somewhat culture bound. Although mental models in various cultures tend to share some common objectives, such as minimizing animosity, differences become apparent when one considers the beliefs people hold about how best to achieve this objective (Leung et al., 1992).

Another ubiquitous mental model that appears to vary across cultures is the model of personal and environmental influences that people use as explanations for their own and others' behaviors (e.g., see Kashima, 2001). Whereas North Americans explain behavior as due to a person's disposition, Hindu Indians tend to view forces in the environment as more important determinants of behavior (Miller, 1984, 1987). Other research suggests that North Americans tend to hold individuals accountable for their actions, whereas other cultures hold responsible the larger group to which the individual belongs (Chiu et al., 2001).

As these examples suggest, stereotypes and mental models do not simply reflect past experience; they influence what aspects of the environment people attend to and they guide the actions people take. Thus they can either contribute to or interfere with coordinated action. When cultural diversity results in greater diversity of stereotypes and mental models, misunderstandings among employees are more likely, so more time and effort will be needed to avoid or correct the harm that such misunderstandings may cause.

Status

Even in the flattest and most egalitarian social systems, some groups enjoy more status than others. In the United States, decades of national opinion polls and psychological research on prejudice and discrimination show that the status attributed to individuals corresponds to their sex, age, and ethnicity (Chronicle of Higher Education, 1992; Jaffe, 1987; Johnston and Packer, 1987; Katz and Taylor, 1988; Kraly and Hirschman, 1990). In CBAs, status hierarchies may reflect differences in the sizes and reputations of the organizations involved, as well as the specific circumstances of the alliance. Although we know of no research that has investigated status dynamics within joint ventures or M&As, anecdotal evidence suggests that employees of acquired firms such as Chrysler experience feelings of lost or lower status. Status relationships may also be shaped by an acquiring firm's use of the absorption approach to managing cultural diversity, which implies that the culture is to be subsumed or obliterated.

Status characteristics theory (SCT) specifies the processes through which evaluations of, and beliefs about, the characteristics of team members become the basis of observable inequalities in face-to-face social interactions (Berger *et al.*, 1966). Although cultures differ in the role that status plays in shaping interactions, status differences are recognized in all cultures.

The dysfunctional effects of status characteristics are likely to be greatest when low-status individuals have resources or expertise that the work group needs to perform their task, and high-status people do not. Compared to those with lower status, higher-status persons display more assertive nonverbal behaviors during communication; speak more often, criticize more, issue more commands, and interrupt others more often; have more opportunity to exert influence, attempt to exert influence more, and actually are more influential (Levine and Moreland, 1990). Consequently, lower-status members participate less. Because the expertise of lower-status members is not fully used (Silver *et al.*, 1994), status differences inhibit creativity, contribute to process losses, and interfere with effective decision making (Bottger and Yetton, 1988; Stasser and Titus, 1985; Steiner, 1972).

Status characteristics also create dissatisfaction and discomfort. Initially, group members behave more positively toward higher-status members (Ridgeway, 1982). Low-status team members often elicit negative responses from others, and because of their low status, they must absorb the negative reactions rather than respond and defend their positions (Ridgeway and Johnson, 1990).

In newly formed CBAs, observed conflicts often are attributed to disagreements that reflect an ongoing contest over the establishment of a status hierarchy among the members of the organization. In the case of acquisitions, the status hierarchy is perhaps most quickly established, with higher status going to members in the acquiring firm. In deals described as mergers, however, power-sharing structures may be set up to communicate the message that employees from the two firms are to be accorded equal status. Such structures seldom endure, however, and a clear status hierarchy eventually emerges. Similarly, joint ventures often are structured to communicate a message of equality among the partner firms. Inevitably, however, status hierarchies emerge and become established within the joint venture firm (e.g., see Yan and Luo, 2001).

Short-term behavioral reactions to cultural diversity

Short-term behavioral reactions to cultural diversity refer to observable interactions between people, including communications, resource sharing, and attempts to exert influence.

Communication

Cultures shape the way people communicate in a variety of ways, and because different cultures use different languages and communication styles, misunderstandings are common when people from different cultures attempt to communicate (e.g., see Gibson, 1999). Despite careful planning for the Davidson-Marley IJV, the U.S. engineers who designed the Dutch manufacturing plant sent measurements calculated in feet, inches, and U.S. gallons, which meant that local Dutch engineers had to convert all of the measurements before letting contracts and gaining approval from government officials. However, low-fidelity communication and misunderstandings are not the only short-term manifestations of cultural diversity – and they may not be the most important. Cultural diversity also shapes who speaks with whom, how often, and what they speak about. That is, cultural diversity shapes the structure of communication as well as the content.

In general, the structure of an organization's communication network is likely to reflect the structure of its cultural diversity because, just as people are attracted to similar others, they spend more time in communication with similar others (Brass, 1984; Lincoln and Miller, 1979). For example, work-related communications between men and women are less frequent in units that are more diverse with respect to sex (South et al., 1982). Formal and informal meetings among peers and with immediate subordinates are lower in racially diverse groups (Hoffman, 1985). And age and tenure similarities between co-workers were correlated with levels of communication among project teams of engineers (Zenger and Lawrence, 1989).

Although they are not well documented, these same dynamics are likely to shape communication networks in CBAs. Through their communications, employees manage information, tangible resources (e.g., equipment, tools, money), and human resources (e.g., skills, effort). To do so, they must exercise influence over each other. Influence attempts made for the purpose of changing the attitudes, values, beliefs, and behaviors of others are viewed as particularly potent short-term manifestations of cultural diversity. Ultimately, the meaning that organizational members assign to such influence attempts is likely to determine how effectively the organization uses its resources – including its human resources.

Resource allocation

Two categories of communication prevalent in organizations are task-related communication and relations-oriented communication, or instrumental and social exchanges (Elsass and Graves, 1999). Through task-related communication, members of an organization seek, offer, and negotiate for work-related information and resources. Each person's access to information and resources, in turn, has important consequences for the individual's performance as well as the group's performance. Access to resources also determines other important outcomes, such as whether a person can take advantage of personal and career-enhancing opportunities within the organization. Research conducted in laboratory settings shows that people who are similar share resources more readily (Brewer, 1979; Kramer and Brewer, 1984; Tajfel, 1978). Presumably, the same is true in organizational settings (Armstrong and Cole, 1996; Ilgen *et al.*, 1999).

Social influence

The basic dynamics of social influence include attempts aimed at changing the attitudes and behaviors of others as well as the responses made to such attempts. Social influence processes appear to be a universal aspect of group behavior that is found in most cultures (Mann, 1980). Nevertheless, the specific influence tactics used and the means through which conformity is expressed are somewhat culture bound. Comparative studies of social influence reveal a variety of differences among national cultures (Smith, 2001). For example, in collectivist cultures, people are relatively more responsive to influence attempts; that is, they conform more to social pressure from others (Bond and Smith, 1996). Comparative studies also show that managers from different cultural backgrounds use different influence tactics in their attempts to influence subordinates (Sun and Bond, 1999).

Unfortunately, there have been few investigations into how influence processes are affected by cultural diversity. However, findings such as these suggest that the contours of cultural diversity in an organization are likely to shape how, and how effectively, influence is wielded.

Long-term consequences of cultural diversity

So far, we have argued that the cultural diversity present in CBAs has important implications for employees' emotions, cognitions, and interpersonal behaviors. In this section, we describe the longer-term consequences that are the reasons why cultural diversity is important for organizations to understand and learn to manage. Several published reviews of the extensive literature addressing this topic suggest that cultural diversity can affect organizations and individuals in a variety of ways: some effects are potentially beneficial and others may be detrimental; some are directly relevant to the organization's performance and others are personally relevant to individual employees. (For more details, see Jackson, 1992a; Millikin and Martins, 1996; Williams and O'Reilly, 1998.)

Potential benefits of cultural diversity

In alliances that adopt either a blending approach or a new organization approach, it is likely that the executives who promoted the alliance believed that (a) the creation of an alliance would enable the partners to learn from their differences, and/or (b) the new organization would approach issues in new and innovative ways that were less likely to be found in either of the partner organizations.

As we noted above, CBAs are often viewed as learning opportunities – partners may hope to learn from each other regarding new technologies, new markets, new industries, and so on. The establishment of NUMMI by Toyota and General Motors is a well-known example of a U.S. auto maker's attempt to learn about the lean manufacturing methods that were being used so successfully in Japan. Conversely, Toyota was able to gain access that enabled it to learn about the competitive strategies of its partner and to more easily monitor developments within the U.S. auto industry (Doz and Hamel, 1998).

When learning is cited as an objective for alliances, the learning process often is depicted as one partner learning something that the other partner already knows. In other words, learning is viewed as knowledge transfer. For knowledge transfer opportunities to be valuable, the two partners must have different knowledge bases – for example, one partner may hope to acquire knowledge that the other partner has about a national market and its culture, a different industry, or a different technology or management system, etc. This view of learning may understate the value of diversity in alliances where learning is a key objective, however, because it ignores the potential value of diversity as a catalyst for creativity and innovation.

Creativity often arises when new problems are identified or new solutions are developed to address well-known problems. Generating *new* knowledge and new understanding are the heart of creativity. For teams working on tasks that require developing new and creative solutions to problems, diverse perspectives seem to be beneficial on several counts. During the environmental scanning that occurs in the earliest phase of problem solving, people with diverse perspectives can provide a more comprehensive view of the possible issues that might be placed on the group's agenda. Subsequently, discussion among members with diverse perspectives can improve the group's ability to consider alternative interpretations and generate creative solutions that integrate their diverse perspectives. As alternative courses of action and solutions are considered, diverse perspectives can increase the group's ability to foresee a wide range of possible costs, benefits, and side effects. Finally, diversity can enhance the group's credibility with external constituencies, which should improve their ability to implement their creative solutions (for a detailed review, see Jackson, 1992a).

It seems reasonable to assume that the presence of diversity creates opportunities for learning – including learning that occurs through knowledge transfer and learning that is associated with creativity and innovation. Unfortunately, however, there has been very little research on how individuals or larger organizations can take advantage of such learning opportunities. In fact, there are many reasons to believe that organizations often are not able to take advantage of the learning opportunities that diversity presents because cultural diversity also generates conflict and turnover.

Detrimental effects of cultural diversity

Cultural diversity seems to interfere with the development of cohesiveness among members of an organization. An important caveat to note here is that this conclusion is based almost exclusively on research investigating the cultural diversity associated with demographic differences. Nevertheless, the pattern of greater diversity resulting in lower levels of cohesiveness has been found for diversity in age, gender, race, education, prestige, social class, attitudes, and beliefs.

Low levels of cohesiveness can be detrimental to both organizations and individual employees. The positive feelings of attraction to coworkers that are present in a cohesive organization promote helping behavior and generosity, cooperation, and a problem-solving orientation during negotiations (for a review, see Isen and Baron, 1991). Cohesiveness may also translate into greater motivation to contribute fully and perform well as a means of gaining approval and recognition (Chattopadhyay, 1999; Festinger et al., 1950). If cultural diversity reduces these positive social behaviors, the performance of individuals as well as the organization as a whole is likely to suffer.

In addition to lowering feelings of attraction and cohesiveness among coworkers, dissimilarity often promotes conflict, which may influence one's decision to maintain membership in a group or organization. This was illustrated in a study of 199 top management teams in U.S. banks. During a four-year period, managers in more diverse teams were more likely to leave the team than were managers in homogeneous teams. This was true regardless of the characteristics of the individual managers, and regardless of how similar a manager was to other members of the team. Simply being a member of a diverse management team increased the likelihood that a manager would leave (Jackson et al. 1991). Presumably, more diverse teams experienced greater conflict and were less cohesive, creating feelings of dissatisfaction and perhaps increasing the perceived desirability of other job offers. Several other studies have examined the relationship between team diversity and team turnover rates, and most results support the assertion that demographic diversity is associated with higher turnover rates. Some evidence indicates that the relationship between diversity and turnover holds in cultures as different from each other as the United States, Japan (Wiersema and Bird, 1993), and Mexico (Pelled and Xin, 1997).

Guidelines for managing cultural diversity in cross-border alliances

Organizations that engage in CBAs do so for a variety of reasons. The Johnson & Johnson study found that companies need to pay more attention to culture up front because:

- Acquired company employees often identify cultural elements (e.g., flexibility in decision making) as integral to the company's success.

- Acquired companies often view their culture as faster-moving than that of their new, larger parent.
- It is possible that each side will perceive its culture as "better" and will not want to give up.
- Acquirees look at the credo and at J&J's action and expect to see credo-compatible behavior.
- Unmanaged cultural differences will lead to miscommunications and misunderstandings (Bobier, 2000).

Regardless of the specific reasons, however, companies must effectively manage cultural diversity of many forms in order to achieve their objectives. Ideally, the employees who participate in CBAs will be able to leverage their differences for the benefit of the organization while at the same time enriching their own experiences. But how can this ideal be achieved, given all of the interpersonal challenges that diversity creates?

Guideline: Before committing to a cross-border alliance, be vigorous in assessing the many types of cultural diversity that are likely to be present in the organization created by the cross-border alliance.

In IM&As, cultural audits conducted during the due diligence process are perhaps most widely used as tools for anticipating cultural differences in the new organization. If cultural differences between partners are judged to be too great, given the preferred approach for managing diversity (portfolio, blending, new creation, or absorption), a deal may be halted. More typically, the soft due diligence process is used to develop a plan for changing current HRM practices or instating new ones. Based on this, HRM practices can be selected to manage the existing distances in culture diversity. Although a similar approach could be used when planning IJVs, formal cultural audits are not usually conducted before an agreement is reached.

Even when cultural differences are accurately anticipated, they can be difficult to manage. Nevertheless, several principles have proved to be effective for reducing cultural prejudice and its consequences. The following principles were first offered by Allport (1954), and they have since been validated by hundreds of subsequent studies: (see Pettigrew, 1998). Specifically, managers should ensure that participants in the alliance:

- create a shared understanding of the objectives for the alliance;
- recognize that each partner contributes to the success of the alliance, and thus is deserving of equal esteem and respect;
- establish an organizational culture that rewards cooperation between members of different cultural groups, and penalizes behavior that appears to be biased or prejudicial;
- provide opportunities for members of different cultural groups to learn about and from each other;

- provide opportunities for members of different cultural groups to develop personal friendships; and
- support activities that encourage everyone to reflect on their own values and gain insights into how their values influences both their own behaviors and the ways that they interpret the behaviors of others.

To maximize the probabilities of success, participants in CBAs need to consider the implications of these six principles for managing each type of diversity present in the alliance and at each evolutionary stage of the alliance. Following these principles is likely to improve the chances of success of all types of CBAs, but the criticality of each principle at each evolutionary stage may depend on the integration management approach, portfolio, blending, new creation, absorption, as shown in Figure 4.1

As described next, a variety of human resource management practices may be helpful for organizations that wish to follow these principles. Although we describe the role of each area of human resource practice separately, we do not intend to imply that each practice works in isolation from the others. As is true for effectively managing human resources in any organization, a coherent and integrated system of practices is required to achieve the desired results. Together, the entire set of practices should communicate a single message to employees (e.g., see Jackson and Schuler, 2003). For example, an Italian automobile company, Fiat, undertook organization-wide programs that included the reevaluation of international positions as well as organizational culture change. Its approach moved beyond the use of a single HRM intervention – such as new staffing techniques or a training program – to include a systematic, large-scale effort to evaluate and adjust all aspects of how employees were treated (Schneider and Barsoux, 1997).

Work and organization design

Guideline: Whenever possible, rely on teams (not individuals) to conduct the activities involved in planning and implementing IJVs and IM&As.

Throughout all evolutionary stages of IJVs and IM&As, teams are a basic form of organization. During pre-combination and formation, teams typically serve to ensure that the perspectives of all alliance partners are represented when key decisions are made. During the early stages of evolution, teams may be used to assess cultural similarities and differences between the partners and plan for their integration. As an alliance evolves, teams may continue to be used to facilitate coordination on daily activities and ensure transfer of learning. In the DaimlerChrysler merger, for example, over 100 integration teams were used to handle coordination between the various functional areas and the different management levels in the organization (Charman, 1999). Most of the practices described below apply to the management of all the various teams and task forces likely to be present in IJVs and IM&As, as well as to the organization's workforce as a whole.

Staffing

Guideline: When making staffing decisions, gather reliable information about how employees respond to cultural differences. Competencies related to managing diversity should be given at least as much weight as technical competencies.

Throughout the lives of IJVs and IM&As, numerous staffing decisions must be made, including decisions regarding whom to hire, whom to promote, and perhaps whom to let go. In addition to ensuring that an alliance is staffed with people who have the technical proficiencies required, staffing practices can improve the organization's effectiveness by identifying individuals who are more likely to be effective working amid cultural diversity. Staffing practices also should be sensitive to the composition of teams (i.e., the content and structure of cultural diversity).

Staffing for cross-cultural competency

On the basis of their experiences and a review of the literature, Schneider and Barsoux (1997) proposed a set of behavioral competencies needed for effective intercultural performance. These included linguistic ability, interpersonal (relationship) skills, cultural curiosity, ability to tolerate uncertainty and ambiguity, flexibility, patience, cultural empathy, ego strength (a strong sense of self), and a sense of humor. When evaluating employees for staffing decisions, competency models such as this one provide useful guidance that can increase an organization's ability to staff its alliances with employees who easily adjust to and enjoy cultural diversity. However, it should be noted that competency models for cross-cultural adjustment often are developed on the basis of expatriates' experience (e.g., Mendenhall and Oddou, 1985; Tung, 1981). While expatriate assignments may share some similarities with IJV or IM&A assignments, there also are many differences. Much more research is needed to identify the personal characteristics most likely to contribute to success in these settings. When an organization's strategy requires that it participate in a large number of IJVs and IM&As, it has the opportunity to conduct such research. Doing so can help it further refine its understanding of how various personal characteristics relate to the performance of employees in culturally diverse organizations.

Guideline: When staffing teams and larger work units, avoid creating situations in which strong cultural fault lines are likely to create unmanageable conflicts.

Staffing for composition

As we have noted, cross-cultural alliance partners often establish teams to ensure the airing of multiple perspectives prior to decision making (Apfelthaler *et al.*, 2002). Especially during the early stages of the alliance's evolution, these teams often are staffed with equal numbers of representatives from each partner involved in the alliance. For example, following a merger, this tactic might be used ensure that the two companies have equal representation in the new top management team (Schweiger *et al.*, 1992). This tactic also is likely to be used when forming the board that oversees an IJV, when staffing IM&A integration and transition teams, and so on.

While representational staffing has many benefits, it may inadvertently lead to unnecessary conflict, divisiveness, and turnover if it creates teams characterized by strong fault lines. Fault lines can be avoided if staffing decisions take into consideration the structure and content of diversity created by a combination of people selected to staff a team. In other words, selecting the "best" people for a team assignment involves more than evaluating the performance potential of individuals: it requires evaluating the performance potential of the team as a whole.

In addition to avoiding the creation of teams or departments with clear fault lines, staffing decisions also need to consider the status dynamics that are likely to arise within a team or organizational unit. When members of a group perceive a clear status hierarchy, lower participation and involvement can be expected from those on the lower rungs of the hierarchy, regardless of their actual expertise and knowledge.

Training and development

Guideline: Offer training designed to improve employees' skills in managing their diversity, but don't ignore training in technical and business skills.

Training and development activities can address a number of challenges created by the cultural diversity present in IJVs and IM&As. Training to improve cultural awareness and competencies may seem the most relevant form of training for improving intercultural relations, but appropriate business training should also be helpful.

Cultural awareness and competency training

Perhaps most obviously, cultural awareness and competency training can quickly teach employees about cultural similarities and differences, and perhaps diminish their reliance on inaccurate stereotypes. Although stereotypes can be resistant to change, they can be modified if sufficient disconfirming evidence becomes available (Triandis *et al.*, 1994).

As was implied by our earlier discussion of the many types of cultural diversity present in some IJVs and IM&As, awareness training should not be limited to learning about national cultures; employees may also benefit from information about differences (and similarities) due to regional locations, industries, organizations, and membership in various demographic groups. Besides imparting knowledge, effective training provides employees with opportunities to practice and hone their interpersonal skills. Nor should awareness training be viewed as a one-time event. Educational briefings may be helpful initially, but as the alliance evolves, more intensive team-building workshops and joint problem-solving sessions will likely be needed as employees experience the many implications that cultural diversity has for their daily interactions.

Business training

The potential benefits of cultural awareness training seem obvious, but business training also can improve the alliance's ability to manage its cultural diversity. Business training can help to establish two of the conditions that enable diverse groups to reap the benefits of their diversity: an understanding of shared goals, and mutual respect. Unless participants in an alliance believe they share the same interests, they may assume that a competitive relationship exists between the alliance partners. Furthermore, unless they understand why the capabilities and resources of each partner are needed to succeed in achieving their shared goal, they may perceive that the contributions of one partner are more important, more valuable, and thus more deserving of respect. Through business training, employees in an alliance can develop an appreciation for how the capabilities and resources of each partner can contribute to success. For example, if IJV partners enter a relationship that is not based on a fifty-fifty equity relationship, employees in the venture may assume that the higher-equity partner will ultimately have more influence and control, placing the lower-equity partner in a position of lower status. Yet in such a venture, it is likely that the intangible resources of the lower-equity partner are essential to the venture's success (Yan and Gray, 1994). Thus, teaching employees about the complementary value of capital and intangible resources provides employees with a solid foundation for developing mutual respect.

Performance management

For any organization, performance management is an important and very complex aspect of human resource management. For IM&As, creating a unified performance management system is perhaps the greatest challenge faced by organizations that seek to blend two disparate cultures (Fealy et al., 2001). For IJVs, a major challenge is creating a performance management system that aligns the interests of managers in the venture with those of the parents (Evans et al., 2002). In addition to contributing to employees' performance in the technical aspects of their jobs, performance management systems can improve cross-cultural relations by ensuring that employees' efforts are directed toward shared goals, providing them with feedback that provides insights about how people from other cultures interpret their behaviors, and rewarding them for developing the competencies required to be effective in a culturally diverse organization.

Guideline: Use the performance management system as a communication tool that provides guidance and direction for achieving shared goals and objectives.

Training programs can inform employees about the shared goals of alliance partners, but performance management systems must convince employees that the rhetoric is also the reality. Ideally, at each evolutionary stage, all employees involved will understand how their performance is assessed and how performance assessments relate to the goals for the alliance. Rewards and recognition for performance that contributes to achieving the alliance's goals serve to reinforce the message.

Guideline: Use feedback procedures that are sensitive to the cultural norms of the person receiving the feedback.

The norms that govern giving and receiving feedback in various cultures differ greatly, yet in any culture, giving and attending to feedback is necessary for maintaining effective relationships. Cultural differences mean that feedback communications are particularly prone to misunderstandings and misinterpretations. One response to such problems is to avoid giving feedback to people from other cultures. Well-designed performance management practices can ensure that employees receive the feedback they need in a culturally appropriate way.

Guideline: Use rewards and recognition to encourage employees to develop their cultural competencies.

Often organizations provide training but do not mandate full participation, nor do they reward employees who apply the training lessons in their work. According to a study involving several hundred U.S. organizations, the success of domestic diversity interventions was enhanced when supporting sanctions were in place. Requiring everyone to attend cultural awareness and competency training communicates their importance, as does providing rewards to employees who provide evidence of improvement (Rynes and Rosen, 1995).

Organizational development and change

Guideline: When developing management practices for the formal organization, consider their consequences for the informal organization, and then monitor these consequences systematically.

Organizational development (OD) and change activities can serve many purposes during the formation and subsequent management of CBAs. Here we focus on OD aimed at developing the informal organization. Research and anecdotal evidence alike point to the important role of personal friendships in the success of cross-cultural alliances. For example, in explaining the factors that resulted in a successful joint venture between an Italian and a U.S. firm, managers pointed to the strong friendship between the two chairmen of the parent companies. Conversely, the lack of personal friendships between employees at FESA – a joint venture between Japanese Fujitsu and Spanish Banesto – made it difficult for them to develop the level of trust that was required in order for learning and knowledge transfer to occur (Yan and Luo, 2001).

Owing to the many forms of cultural diversity that often are present in CBAs, employees may find it more difficult than usual to develop close personal relationships with their colleagues from other cultural backgrounds. Yet the positive feelings associated with one close friendship with someone from an "outgroup" culture (e.g., the joint venture partner) are likely to generalize to the entire group (Pettigrew, 1997). Thus, OD activities that help employees develop even a few friendships may be quite beneficial to an alliance. As is true for all HRM practices, however, a major challenge is designing activities that have the intended effects across all segments of the organization. As we have described, OD interventions are most effective when the assumptions that guide the OD activities fit the assumptions of the culture (Aguinis and Henle, 2002; Hui and Luk, 1997; Jaeger, 1986). Within culturally diverse organizations, meeting this condition is particularly challenging. The assumptions underlying an OD effort may be congruent with the cultural background of some employees, but unless there is little cultural diversity, the same assumptions will not be shared by all employees.

Conclusion

As businesses globalize, they will continue to use cross-border alliances as a means to expand and grow both their operations and knowledge base. To succeed, such businesses must effectively manage the many forms of cultural diversity inherent in such organizations. Although international joint ventures and international mergers and acquisitions represent only two types of cross-border alliances, our discussion here illustrates how cultural diversity can affect alliances of other types. We hope that by now, it is obvious that the challenge of managing cultural diversity is distinctly different from the challenging of managing expatriates. Yet researchers and practitioners alike have devoted much more time and resources to the task of expatriate management than they have devoted to the task of understanding and learning to manage cultural diversity effectively. The challenge of managing cultural diversity involves much more than assessing the degree of cultural fit between alliance partners and creating plans to close (or otherwise manage) the cultural gap, for example, by designing a new human resources management system. Creating alignment among the formal systems is a necessary first step, but additional efforts are needed to ensure that organizational structures do not create additional barriers to cross-cultural collaboration and to develop a workforce with the competencies needed to work effectively amid cultural diversity.

Terra-Lycos

All parties involved had high hopes in May 2000 when Madrid-based Terra Networks SA, Europe's second-largest Internet service provider, agreed to pay $14.4 billion in stock for Lycos Inc., the U.S. Web search service. Terra executives said they were optimistic that Lycos would provide their company with access to some 30 million U.S. Hispanics and help it compete better in Asia and Europe.

Analysts and investors gushed. The deal, they said, would succeed because Terra would also provide Lycos with the ability to offer standard Internet access along with wireless Internet services over laptop computers and cell phones. "These things put together will make for a powerful company," Brian Grove, portfolio manager at Vaughan, Nelson, Scarborough & McCullough, said after the deal was announced.

As in so many other cross-border transactions, the cheering soon stopped. On February 1, 2001, four months after the deal was closed, Terra Lycos SA CEO Bob Davis quit, ending tension between him and his European bosses over who was calling the shots. Several key executives followed him out the door. Terra's share price has dropped 80 percent since the deal was announced, closing at $11.84 on March 9, 2001. "The merger's at risk," says Jordan Rohan, analyst at Wit Sound-View, who rates Terra's stock as "sell." "We're seeing that it's hard to blend these companies together."

So are principals in many cross-border mergers. Nonetheless, reasons for the upturn in cross-border deals are varied. Regulations barring such mergers have been scrapped in many countries. Trade barriers have fallen as well, providing an incentive for companies to compete globally. The euro's arrival has spurred European companies to shop globally by providing deeper capital pools for financing the deals. Also contributing to the cross-border boom is goading from consultants and investment bankers who stand to make huge fees on cross-border transactions. In 1999, for example, Morgan Stanley Dean Witter & Co. earned $71 million for its work on the sale of AirTouch Communications, Inc. to Vodafone Group PLC.

Cross-border deals go awry for varied reasons as well: key executives depart, power-sharing plans prove unrealistic, disparate cultures fail to mend. "Domestic mergers are hard enough. Companies overpay or have unrealistic expectations," says John Katzenbach, a

Case Example

continued

former McKinsey & Co. consultant who now runs his own firm advising companies on handling mergers. "When you add in the physical and psychological space between two international companies, problems escalate."

Language also matters. In its January 2001 study, KPMG found that the success rate of cross-border deals rises when the companies share the same tongue. Mergers between U.S. and U.K. companies were 45 percent more successful than the average, while deals between U.S. companies and those from elsewhere in Europe were 11 percent less successful than the average rate of return of all cross-border deals.

Clashes between executives sharing power can cause some mergers to unravel. These arrangements rarely work in domestic deals. At Citigroup Inc., for example, Sanford Weill and John Reed planned to run the financial services company jointly. In February, Reed retired early as co-chairman and co-CEO and Weill cemented his control.

Executives who share power collide more often in overseas mergers, consultants say, because the combined company's two top leaders are often based far from each other and are not compatible. In May 2000, for example, when Terra Networks announced its Lycos bid, Terra chairman Juan Villalonga tapped Bob Davis as CEO and told analysts and investors that Davis had a free hand to shape the company. "Terra acquired more than a collection of Internet properties; it bought a team to develop Web sites and add value to Terra's Spanish/Latin American access business," says Andrea Rice, an analyst at Deutsche Banc Alex Brown.

Davis was not an obvious fit with Terra's culture. For starters, he did not speak Spanish. Also, say analysts familiar with the company, Davis was really most comfortable at home in Massachusetts. Most of his life he had never strayed far from his roots in Dorchester, a middle-class Boston neighborhood. He went to Northeastern University in Boston and got an MBA from Babson College in Wellesley, Massachusetts, 14 miles west of Boston. Before moving to Lycos, based in Waltham, Massachusetts, he had spent fourteen years at other Massachusetts-based firms.

By the time the merger was sealed in October, the ties between Davis and Terra were already frayed. Villalonga had quit amid allegations of insider trading. Davis went left dealing with Villalonga's successor, Cesar Alierta, who named Joaquim Agut, a top European executive at General Electric Co., as Terra Lycos's chairman

Agut said that he was not interested in sharing control with anyone. "I am the executive chairman of the company – the one and only," he said in an interview published in *Actualidad Económica*, a Spanish business magazine.

That spelled trouble. Within four months, Davis was gone; he joined Boston venture capital firm Highland Capital Partners. "We found ourselves in an environment with two leaders, and that's a difficult thing to do," Davis said in a conference call with investors and analysts after his resignation. Other executives soon bolted, including Ron Sege, president of U.S. operations, and Abel Linares, COO.

Note: This case example is adapted from A. Levy, Bloomberg/Newsroom, and used by permission.

Managing cooperation, control, structure, and exit
7 in cross-border alliances

> HR buys (deals where the employees are seen as more valuable than the company's products) are becoming more prominent. If a company can buy another firm cheap enough and pick up 50 or 100 networking engineers who have skills in key technologies, it's not a bad idea.
>
> Mark Shafir
> Investment Banking, Thomas Weisel Partner

While the dynamics of the global economy make for ups and downs in the nature and strategies of business, it appears that CBAs will continue. Thus it remains important to try to make them successful. In this regard, it helps to understand the major issues in their management and structure.

> It is frequently observed that the ownership structure for a proposed joint venture stands out as a central issue on which potential partners bargain really hard and even fall into deadlocks during the venture's founding negotiations. In many cases of joint venture negotiations, ownership structure may serve as a threshold: If an agreement is reached, negotiation will continue; if no, nothing is going to happen.
>
> (Yan and Gray, 1994)

As with the understanding and management of cross-cultural diversity described in Chapter 6, cooperation, trust, control, and structure require more detailed discussion. Thus, while these issues were introduced in earlier chapters, they are developed more fully here. The chapter concludes with a description of alliance exits.

Cooperation

The success of cross-border alliances, mergers, and acquisitions largely depends on inter-partner cooperation during subsequent operations and management. Interfirm cooperation and trust correlate positively with alliance longevity, effectiveness, and performance (Yan, 1998). Cooperation, however, does not emerge automatically.

All the parties involved in an alliance, merger, or acquisition have an inalienable *de facto* right to pursue their own interests at the expense of others. Consequently, cross-border partnerships are often characterized by instability arising from uncertainty regarding the partner's future behavior.

The problem of cooperation arises in situations of conflict and interdependence. Conflict stems from the fact that individuals and organizations may have goals that are mutually exclusive. Interdependence requires mutual accommodation if all parties are to meet otherwise incompatible goals. The need for cooperation arises where both interdependence and conflict are simultaneously present. Cross-border partnerships combine several types of resources not belonging to any one firm. Each company lacks some of the other's resources; each would be unable to gain the benefits of the cross-border cooperation independently. Each firm depends on its partner to achieve its goals for the alliance. Thus, each firm needs to take into account how its partner may respond to its behavior, and how this response will affect the outcome of the cross-border partnerships.

Conflicts may occur at almost any stage of CBAs. In the early stages, differences in the partners' goals, low trust, resource homogeneity, and ambiguous contracts are among the internal factors that drive conflict. During the later stages, conflicts between partners may arise owing to opportunistic behavior, disagreement about operational policies, the emergence of unanticipated local contingencies, and changes in the partners' strategic plans. Such conflict may impair the creation of expected synergies. Increasing formalization and monitoring of the partners may also cause conflict as the partners struggle to maintain their autonomy in the face of growing interdependence. The increase in resource transactions among partners over time implies that their domains will shift from being complementary to being similar, which increases the likelihood of territorial disputes, conflict, and competition. Thus, even a long-surviving alliance with strong norms of equity and trust can experience some inter-partner conflict.

In IJVs, alliance success depends not only on cooperation between the parents, but also on collaborations between the IJV management and the parent firms. Managers in the IJV direct their staff to accomplish goals that may or may not correlate with the objectives of either parent company. IJV managers may even be offered incentives to behave opportunistically in dealing with the parent firms. A minority parent may dominate the venture if it can convince the IJV managers to be more cooperative and supportive than they are with its partner. When partners' objectives diverge, a parent's relationship with IJV managers becomes even more important.

Figure 7.1 schematically describes approaches for improving trust and cooperation, each of which is discussed in detail in what follows.

Accentuating Cooperation and Trust

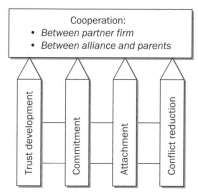

Figure 7.1 Approaches for improving trust and cooperation in cross-border alliances

Trust

Inter-partner cooperation requires trust in order to succeed. Trust and cooperation have at times been treated as synonymous. However, they are two different but correlated concepts. *Trust* refers to the willingness of a party to be vulnerable to the actions of another party based on the expectation that the other will perform a particular action important to the trusting party, irrespective of the ability to monitor or control that other party. Trust frequently leads to cooperative behavior. Nevertheless, in theoretical terms, trust is not a necessary condition for cooperation to occur, because cooperation does not necessarily put a party at risk. In the short term, a firm can cooperate with a company it does not really trust as long as the expected benefits from cooperation outweigh corresponding costs.

Trustworthiness is determined by several factors, particularly a party's ability, benevolence, and integrity. Ability is a party's skills, competencies, and characteristics that enable it to have influence within some specific domain. If such abilities are complementary to those of the partner firm, their contribution to trustworthiness will be higher. Benevolence is the extent to which a firm is believed to want to do good to the trusting party, setting aside any profit motive. Benevolence suggests that the trusted party has some specific attachment to the trusting party. The relationship between integrity and trust involves the trusting party's perception that the other party adheres to a set of principles that the former finds acceptable. Acceptability precludes a party committed solely to the principle of profit seeking from being judged high in integrity. Such issues as the consistency of the party's past actions, credible communications about that party from other sources, belief that the party has a strong sense of justice, the degree to which the party is concerned with the other party's needs, and the extent to which the party's actions are congruent with its commitment all affect the degree to which the party is judged to have integrity.

Commitment

The degree of commitment to a CBA is likely to be conditional upon certain characteristics of the alliance. The commitment of the partners is likely to be higher, for example, the more socially meritorious or strategically important the output is deemed to be. Commitment will also tend to be higher if the distribution of rewards from the venture, when it is successfully completed, is deemed equitable to all parties. Envy of the share of gains appropriated by another partner not only diminishes motivation but also encourages cheating. The psychology of commitment, if understood correctly, can be used by one party to manipulate another. Securing commitment through manipulation is a dangerous strategy for a party, however, because it will lead to some form of reprisal from the other party.

Personal and structural attachments

Governance mechanisms such as contractual stipulations and managerial control systems are insufficient for controlling opportunism and elevating cooperation. Ongoing business relationships often become overlaid with social content that generates strong expectations of trust. Personal and structural attachments between exchange partners then become critical dynamic forces for improving cooperation (Luo, 2001).

Inter-party attachment is a time-dependent binding force between exchange partners that can promote maintenance of an existing relationship. It is manifested in personal relationships (personal attachment) or ties between exchange partners at an organizational level (structural attachment) (Inkpen and Beamish, 1997). *Individual attachment* reflects socialization by *boundary spanners* (i.e., senior CBA managers representing each party) during their involvement in exchange activities (including those occurring before CBA formation) between the same interacting organizations.

Structural attachment reflects the history of the partners working together as one after the CBA is formed. Personal attachment is heightened with the tenure of boundary spanners, and structural attachment increases along with the duration of the alliance relationship. Both attachments counter the pressure for dissolution stemming from resource misfit and prevent exploration of alternative partnerships. Instead, they encourage taking advantage of relationship-specific opportunities that will escalate joint payoffs. They further positively affect levels of trust, commitment, and forbearance, as well as organizational duration, stability, and evolution.

Individual attachment

Attachment is the result of an evolving history of partner interaction. Individual attachment accrues over the period of time during which particular organizational representatives are involved in exchange activities. It is mainly represented by personal relationships based on personal knowledge and trust established in previous interactions (e.g., prior cooperation or negotiation) and accumulated after a CBA is formed. Determinants of personal attachment include (a) *interpersonal relationships*; (b) *tenure of boundary spanners*; and (c) *interpersonal learning of individual skills and knowledge*. Personal attachment increases when each of these three determinants is enhanced.

Although the two are related, personal attachment differs from personal relationship in that attachment concerns the degree to which boundary spanners are bound together, while a personal relationship is only one binding force between senior CBA managers. The turnover rate of individual boundary-spanning managers has a direct influence on personal attachment, since its development is time dependent. Because personal relationships are normally not transferable, a high turnover of managers can lead to a loss of relationship continuity and reduction of individual attachment. Individual organizational members thus constitute a repository of assets created from relationship-specific capital. Lastly, boundary spanners bind more when they are personally "attracted" to each other. Inter-party complementarity in terms of the resources, capabilities, and competencies contributed to a CBA generates financial and operational synergies. Since some of these resources are embedded in specific individuals, organizational routines, or in specialized assets that only specific individuals can apply or manage, synergetic effects are strengthened when knowledge complementarity between boundary spanners is high. Personal attachment is an increasing function of interpersonal learning, which is then a positive function of such complementarity.

Structural attachment

Structural attachment develops through experience in a collaborative relationship and through investments the partners make in the relationship over time. Structural attachment concerns the extent to which two parties are organizationally and structurally bound within a CBA through jointly formalized and routinized procedures or policies for managing interorganizational exchanges and nurturing the accomplishment of joint goals. *Formalization* is the degree to which formal roles and procedures govern interorganizational activities. It may include specific plans, detailed rules and procedures, clear division of labor, formal job descriptions, predetermined forms of communication and control, a clear decision-making hierarchy, a system of inter-partner coordination, and information flow, among others. As an indicator of a firm's ability to institutionalize effective procedures and efficient practices, *routinization* is the extent to which a series of coordinated activities are undertaken semiautomatically; that is, without significant bureaucratic direction or verbal communication. CBA-in-Action 1 illustrates how Unilever tried to formalize human resource policies and practices after acquiring Brazil's Kibon in 1997.

Inter-party familiarity is a prerequisite for formalization and routinization of joint procedures. When firms have worked together in the past, they tend to have a basic

Unilever's human resource experience in Latin America

Unilever's (U.K./Netherlands) recent acquisition in Brazil – of Kibon in 1997 – marked another expansion of the company's already strong presence in Latin America's largest market. The company's cautious, yet methodical, approach to acquisitions has allowed it to retain Kibon's local flavor while simultaneously integrating it into Unilever's global network. Its management of human resources illustrates the firm's ability to mix internationally savvy executives with the best local talent and practices.

The global firm's approach is a mix of taking the best of the local culture and combining it with the firm's global intentions. Its success with Kibon stems from a deliberate but gradual integration process, particularly with regard to personnel changes. Rather than immediately impose control from the top, Unilever strategy centers on two important initial stages. Unilever implemented its business strategies only after a careful analysis of Kibon's corporate culture and specific characteristics. This included its positioning in the market, key corporate values, and the practices and behavior of its leadership. The company has assimilated some elements of Kibon's culture and turned them to its own advantage.

Unilever promoted dialogue with staff during the initial period after the acquisition, then defined its priorities and assumed leadership. Management zeroed in on two priority areas: the ice cream manufacturing process and R&D. Its preliminary studies of Kibon's best operations helped management make appropriate decisions about future layoffs and restructuring. Once the groundwork was laid, Unilever did not hesitate to make changes. After carefully studying the acquired company, it quickly set out to forge a new identity and strategy and to rationalize production. This involved taking certain tough measures.

While removing Kibon's entire board of directors, Unilever made a special effort to hold on to key personnel in priority areas, namely production and R&D. It sent positive signals to the relevant staff regarding career opportunities and financial prospects (including higher compensation and bonuses) within the new business group. As far as noncore processes were concerned, staffers willing to integrate remained with the company, while personnel and executives who did not agree with the integration process as it was being conducted left.

Unilever prides itself on its decentralized approach. This decision-making style helps to alleviate tensions when a large multinational such as Unilever takes over a smaller company. Kibon went from being an independent entity to becoming part of the Unilever global family. Management had a better chance of retaining talented employees if it kept parental control and bureaucratic procedures to a minimum. A small corporate center manages Cessy Lever. This team was charged with incorporating Kibon into the overall local structure but allowed the ice cream business to operate as a separate unit.

understanding of each other's strengths and weaknesses. The partners may have developed commitment because of a connection that existed before forming a CBA. The older a relationship, the greater the likelihood that it has passed through a critical shakeout period of conflict. Therefore, firms often form CBAs with firms with which they have had transactions in the past, through either trade or investment. Major sources of structural attachment include the formalization and routinization of exchange arrangements, such as the establishment of policies and procedures for managing JV operations. Previous cooperation, duration of a current CBA, and partner commitment or investment in inter-party ties are not direct sources of structural attachment, but are important factors that affect formalization and routinization.

Attachment development

The development of structural attachment depends on interorganizational cooperation, commitment, and trust, the issues being discussed above. Here we focus on how personal attachment can be improved. There are several practices that facilitate the development of personal attachment involved in cooperation.

Guideline: Establish and maintain friendly personal contacts among the leaders in the alliance, especially among leaders representing the interests of different partners.

It is important that friendly personal contact is regularly maintained between the leaders of the cooperating organizations, and this contact should be visible to all those working under them. This means planning for personal visits between partner chief executives at least once a year, and giving these full publicity. Apart from the intrinsic merit such visits have in ironing out any differences of view between the partners and laying down broad plans for the future, they very importantly set an example and establish a climate of cooperation for the people working at deeper levels in the CBA.

Guideline: For IJVs, the length of temporary assignments from the parent to the venture should be as long as possible. For IM&As, the length of assignments to temporary integration task forces and committees should be as long as possible.

Cooperative and trusting relationships require time to develop. When the length of assignment to an alliance is short, say three years or under, the chances of achieving mutual bonding are reduced. Not only is there personal unfamiliarity to overcome, but, if a language has to be learned or improved, this clearly takes time as well. Personnel on longer-term appointments are also more likely to invest in establishing relationships within the alliance, for they see it as a more significant part of their overall career path. Western, and especially U.S., companies tend to attach people to alliances on contracts of four years maximum, whereas Japanese companies tend to attach their people for up to twice as long. Partners in countries where relationship is a requirement for business cooperation commonly complain that personnel assignments to their alliances are too short for any bonding to occur.

Guideline: The recruitment and selection of people to work in a CBA should be conducted as systematically as they would be for any other key position.

Because the development of strong personal relationships is key, people who are to work in an alliance should not be selected merely on the basis of technical competence, important though this is, but also on an assessment of their ability to form good relationships with people from other organizational and national cultures. Track records can tell a lot in this respect. Some global companies have, for this reason, now created opportunities for successful alliance and expatriate managers to be able to remain in interorganizational and international assignments without detriment to their long-term advancement within the home corporation. People with open-minded and prejudice-free personalities are likely to be more successful at personal bonding within alliances. These characteristics can be assessed through careful observation and, if appropriate, through systematic personality tests.

Guideline: Create as many ways as possible for employees from the partnering organizations to socialize informally with each other and also with members of the external community.

Activities such as sports and social events as well as charitable and sponsorship activities in the local community can do a lot to break down social barriers. They help to bring about an acceptance of the alliance within its local community, and a strengthening of its external identity. At the same time, they are collective events that help to build up an internal identity within the alliance itself.

Reducing conflicts

Most experienced managers accept that conflict in CBAs is inevitable, given the rich diversity of capabilities, cultures, and constraints of each partner. There is likely to be a mixture of disputes over "hard" financial or technological issues and frictions of a "softer" cultural and interpersonal nature. In each case, it is important to have mechanisms for resolving such conflicts in place from the very outset of the alliance's existence.

Guideline: When analyzing situations and choices, assume that the perspectives of the partners will be different and make an extra effort to understand and analyze the actions and/or positions of the partner firm from its perspective.

In addition to providing new insights into the partner's issues and options, making sincere attempts to understand the perspective of an alliance partner demonstrates respect for the partner. This approach, for instance, helped Fuji and Xerox overcome the common dividend dilemmas between the U.S. and Japanese firms. U.S. MNEs generally prefer high dividend payout, owing to pressure from Wall Street and institutional investors, whereas Japanese shareholders accept low payout in return for profits reinvested for growth. So, by understanding the constraints of both sides, each partner was more willing to opt for the middle ground: Fuji Xerox dividends generally hovered around 30 percent of earnings.

Guideline: Set key milestones and management principles jointly.

Jointly setting a specific goal for an alliance encourages partners to be flexible when resolving problems. Many conflicts stem from unclear or misread signals between partners in an alliance. It is therefore important jointly to develop a basic set of operating principles for the alliance. Improved communication between managers from each party also nurtures problem solving and conflict reduction. For example, the communications system in Fuji Xerox comprises a co-destiny task force, presidential summit meetings, functional meetings, resident directors meetings, and personnel exchanges. Such communications channels significantly bridge the differences between Fuji and Xerox. Having regular meetings is an important step to jointly setting principles for alliance operations. These meetings should establish the facts of any matters at issue and record the discussion and any solutions proposed. The records of such meetings provide a basis on which problems can be addressed at a higher level between the partners. An important aim of meetings and other formal conflict resolution mechanisms is to ensure that the disputes do not get turned into, or mixed in with, interpersonal conflicts.

Guideline: IJVs should steer clear of the goals and strategies of the parents.

Many executives view conflicts and overlap between an alliance and its parent organizations as a potential minefield of problems. A CBA should steer clear of parent operations strategies, geographic expansion, and product lines. For example, many of the difficulties and tensions in the Rolls-Royce–Pratt venture of forming International Aero Engines to manufacture V2500 engines stemmed from competitive conflicts with the parents. The V2500, a competitor of CFM International's own products, also competes directly with two Pratt engines, the JTAT 200 series and the Pratt 2037, as well as Rolls-Royce's RB211 engine.

Guideline: Develop formal rules and guidelines that make matters such as correct financial procedures and the protection of technology clear to all alliance partners.

Developing formal specifications will probably require a significant investment of time by senior partner managers at a very early stage of the alliance, even before it comes into operation. While formal measures cannot guarantee the amount and quality of information sharing, procedures such as password access to computer networks, the circulation of well-documented material before meetings, and the regular dissemination of data on the alliance's performance can be of considerable assistance in information sharing.

Guideline: Encourage everyone to develop a willingness and ability to remain flexible.

Maintaining flexibility is a virtue for avoiding conflicts. Given the fact that market and environment conditions change, partners must be adaptable. Although a contract may legally bind partners together, an adherence to a rigid agreement may hamper adaptations regardless of how well conceived the original contract or agreement may have been. Box 7.1 provides additional detailed guidelines for handling inter-partner conflicts within CBAs (The Economist Intelligence Unit, 1999).

Box 7.1 Practical suggestions for conflict management in cross-border alliances

- Do not expect to finesse fatal flaws. Deals with the wrong partner or with a faulty structure cannot be managed, only renegotiated, abandoned or sold.
- Promote win–win partnerships, not win–lose pacts.
- Encourage flexible responses – alliances, acquisitions, and mergers are fast moving. Cultivate a corporate culture that embraces change.
- Maintain ongoing senior management commitment. Alliances and acquisitions with true potential will not run themselves. They need the involvement of upper management as well as an outgoing management approach at the operational level.
- Enter as equally strong partners and remain strong in your respective core competencies. Alliances are hard enough without having to prop up your ally.
- Be open to new alliance and acquisition options – they may be staring you in the face.
- Allow the venture the chance to go on its own. Grant it the independence and power that accompany success.
- Listen to partners and profit from disagreements. Staff working with allies or acquired entities must be capable of inverting the traditional "alien is erroneous"

assumption while maintaining a healthy skepticism – a case of expect the best and prepare for the worst.

- Focus on the desired end result. The primary goal of alliance management is to guarantee not that the relationship be a smooth one, but that it achieve its business target. There are many examples of successful ventures with chaotic management.

Control

It is important to distinguish between *de jure* control, achieved from majority share of ownership, and *de facto* control, which is the control a partner actually exercises. The latter is not necessarily tied to equity position. In general, companies may be able to exercise *de facto* control even with minority equity positions. For example, the dependence of alliances on parent firms for strategic resources such as capital, technology, management skills, and market access provides parent firms with means of exerting effective control. Firms will be powerful relative to others to the extent that they can control resources needed by others, and also reduce their dependence on others for resources. In addition, managerial control can be either positive or negative. Positive control is exercised when a parent firm is in a position to influence activities or decisions in a way consistent with its own interests and expectations. Negative control may be used to prevent the implementation of decisions or activities it does not agree with.

The exercise of management control in CBAs is far more complex than in controlling stand-alone companies. The partners in CBAs often are engaged in mixed-motive games in which cooperative and competitive dynamics occur simultaneously (Yan and Luo, 2001). The desire and competition for management control over the alliance originate in the partners' general fear of uncertainty with respect to whether their expectations will be fulfilled. Particularly when alliances operate in a cross-country and cross-cultural environment, one can imagine that the level of uncertainty and unpredictability to be experienced by the partners is significantly higher than in a domestic environment. CBA-in-Action 2 illustrates an example of managerial control in an Iveco–Ford alliance.

In IJVs, gaining control over the IJV's management can serve as a proactive strategy intended to ensure that the way an alliance is managed conforms to the parent's own interest. This is particularly true when the partners have differing agendas for forming the alliance and their strategic objectives are not perfectly compatible. In this case, the alliance's efforts and outcomes valued by one partner are not necessarily appreciated by the other. Therefore, for each partner, achieving hands-on management control over the alliance's operation can enable itself to gain the right of participation in the alliance's decision making, through which it ensures that its strategic goals will be vigorously

Managerial control in Iveco-Ford

Although Iveco-Ford is an equally owned strategic alliance, it was agreed that Iveco should take the lead in operating control. Consequently, Iveco-Ford is managed on a daily basis as if it were a division of Iveco. With meetings only three times a year, the board does not review day-to-day operations in great detail, though major decisions, such as new capital increases, market withdrawal, or changes in products, require unanimous board approval. The board was composed of people whose competencies and skills were suitable to the running of the alliance. It serves an important purpose in motivating strategic goal setting and budgeting. The Iveco-Ford board members must hammer out their differences in order to reach unanimity on a number of strategic items, while Iveco listens to Ford's concerns on items that Iveco can approve alone. Most of all, the process requires the sharing of information to avoid negative surprises that might break down confidence between the partners.

pursued by the alliance management. The strategic direction in which the alliance moves and the ways in which the pooled resources are allocated and utilized will have direct and critical impact on the alliance's outcomes (Geringer and Hebert, 1989).

Means of managerial control

As Figure 7.2 shows, several mechanisms of managerial control are available to firms. These are described in more detail next.

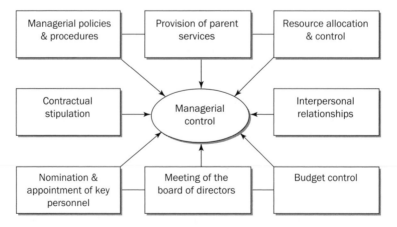

Figure 7.2 How to maintain control in cross-border alliances

Nomination and appointment of key personnel

Control requires knowledge of events and circumstances. Such knowledge is most readily available to partners when their own personnel run or monitor key operations and critical functions such as marketing, R&D, or corporate finance. The appointment of key personnel as a control mechanism is especially important when the alliance organization (e.g., the IJV or an acquired subsidiary) is geographically remote.

Meetings of the board of directors

Although a majority equity holder is in an advantageous position in terms of composition and representation on the board, a minority partner has room to manipulate the frequency of meetings and agenda coverage. In addition, a dominant partner cannot consistently overrule or refuse to compromise with its weaker partner without building significant ill will. Minority parents can prevent their majority partner from implementing unilateral decisions by negotiating a veto right over decisions important to their interests. Of course, control at the board level is not simply a matter of votes. Control also results from the ability to influence other board members on important issues. This is to a large extent a matter of competency, bargaining power, and negotiation skills. As a result, minority partners have an opportunity to influence the management of a CBA if they are able to fill the board with people who have a strong grasp of the CBA's operational and strategic issues, good bargaining skills, and empathy with the partner's culture.

Managerial policies and procedures

The behavior of executives in a CBA is influenced by various managerial policies and procedures devised by the owners. Since an alliance contract usually does not stipulate or specify these policies and procedures, a minority partner can be more proactive by playing a bigger part in formulating and adjusting such policies and procedures. Reward and report systems are particularly effective for the purpose of control. The former determines the incentive structure and performance evaluation, and the latter determines the flow, dissemination, and accuracy of information.

Budget control

Five aspects of budget control can be implemented: (a) emphasis on the budget during performance evaluations – that is, using quantitative criteria in evaluating manager performance; (b) participation in the budget setting – that is, the degree of involvement a partner has during budget development; (c) budget incentives – that is, linking pay and promotion prospects to meeting budget goals; (d) budget standard-setting difficulty – that is, the difficulty with which budget goals are set; and (e) budget controllability filters – that is, extenuating factors that are brought into the performance evaluation process. In general, minority partners can use all five budget control mechanisms to increase their overall or specific control over a CBA's operations and management.

Provision of parent services

In order to increase the likelihood that specific tasks in an IJV are performed in conformity with their expectations, parent firms may offer staff services and training, sometimes at no cost to the IJV. Such services can be provided irrespective of equity ownership level. Increased control thereby accrues to parent firms in the following ways: (a) greater awareness of the parent to conditions within the CBA because of enhanced dialogue with the alliance employees; (b) increased loyalty from alliance employees who identify more with the parent and have assimilated its ethos; and (c) increased predictability of behavior in the CBA because its managers are more likely to use the guidelines within which they have been trained. Similarly, within IM&As the acquired firm, or the less dominant partner in a merger, can be proactive in offering to take responsibility for staff services and training, and thereby gain some additional control.

Interpersonal relationships

A CBA partner can increase its control if it builds and maintains trustworthy, enduring personal relationship with upper-level managers representing the other partner firm. In fact, this approach has helped many global companies, as minority parties, successfully control their CBAs in developing countries. By arranging for managers from local firms to work at foreign headquarters, helping solve personal difficulties they face, or offering favors as needed, foreign companies are able effectively and efficiently to cultivate and solidify relationships with local executives, who will, in turn, remain loyal to the foreign company. This will eventually promote the foreign company's managerial effectiveness.

Structure

A critical aspect of alliance development concerns *changes* in the control structure over time. *Structural reconfiguration* concerns the extent to which the alliance changes its structure of governance over time. An alliance is structurally unstable if control over its strategic and operational management shifts frequently. However, it is structurally stable if its control structure remains unchanged for extended periods of time. There are both *driving* and *restraining forces* underlying structural changes in and reconfiguration of CBAs.

Driving forces

Structural instability is prompted by (a) *unexpected contingencies*; (b) *undesirable alliance performance*; and, for IJVs, (c) *inter-partner competitive learning*. Unexpected contingencies include both internal factors, such as changes in strategies, and external factors, such as changes of government policies regarding foreign investment. Undesirable performance also triggers instability. Poor performance implies that the alliance has failed to achieve at least one key objective. Restructuring or reallocation of control may be viewed as a possible remedy. IJVs (especially in high-tech industries) also provide an arena in which the partners are engaged in a "race to learn." This competitive motive complicates the partnership. The potential for misunderstanding and mistrust increases when IJVs involve learning-oriented versus output-oriented goals. Learning can change partner interdependency, thereby creating pressure for recontracting or reorganizing of the IJV. Asymmetries in learning can shift the relative bargaining power between the partners, and thus make the original bargain obsolete, because the faster learner is likely to raise its "price" for further cooperation. Consequently, reallocation of control becomes necessary, or jockeying for power will follow.

Restraining forces

Meanwhile, there are structural inertial forces in organizations, which counter change and help retain certain organizational characteristics. Once these characteristics are acquired at the organization's founding, they are held unchanged over a long period of time. This phenomenon is known as *organizational imprinting*. Major sources of structural inertia include (a) *partner initial resource contributions*; (b) *the original (im)balance of bargaining power*; and (c) *pre-alliance relationships between the partners and between the managers* (i.e., personal attachment as mentioned above). CBAs will generally retain their initial configuration of resources for an extended period of time. The balance of relative bargaining power between the partners reached at the alliance's inception may be resistant to change, as it provides a reference point against which the relative power positions of the partners are monitored. Another organizational source of imprinting that may exist is the prior relationship between the partners. The preliminary sense of mutual commitment and trust puts the alliance in a fast lane toward the further development of trust. To this extent, trusting partners tend to behave in a trustworthy manner in dealing with each other, and expect to generate a trustworthy response in return. This spiral process enhances and further develops trust in the relationship. Alternatively, if the initial level of trust is low, a downward spiral may operate.

Flexibility and reorganizations

As all partnerships are subject to unforeseeable change, whether external or internal, success in the management of CBAs requires flexibility. Relationships and operations need to be monitored and revisited periodically. Success often depends on the partners' ability to make adjustments in their relationship as necessary, overcoming operating misfit with structural and procedural changes in the boundary-spanning process, and renegotiating and repositioning the partnerships to reestablish strategic fit.

Effective alliance leaders prepare for operational crises and contingencies by identifying critical incidents that may affect the alliance and by looking for early warnings: Is one party constantly dragging its foot on deadlines, information or participation? Is there frequent conflict or confusion over roles and responsibilities? Are goals being met and are costs in line? Is information flowing easily – upward, downward and laterally? Is one partner nursing grudges about an unequal distribution of resources, time, cooperation, or commitment? Such concerns need to be brought to the surface, discussed, and dealt with jointly and constructively. If the relationship has become contentious, it may be important to let a disenchanted partner "win" on some issues in order to reestablish trust and goodwill. Even if partners do their best to maintain the relationship and carry out a win–win interaction at the operational level, major changes in the business environment may call into question the "strategic" value of the alliance. Sometimes changes require that the relationship be renegotiated or transformed into another agreement. At other times, the only choice may be to dissolve the relationship. In either case, the foundation of trust and positive interaction on an operational level makes it easier to take the steps necessary to deal with a fluid business environment.

Political and economic conditions may doom even the healthiest CBAs. For instance, the large majority of U.S.–Russian joint ventures have failed because political evolution in Russia and economic conditions faced by these ventures have discouraged the growth of CBAs there. Thus many multinational companies have been using an incremental evolutionary approach to developing alliances in Russia. Positive news could also require adjustments. By mid-1994, for example, Display Technologies, Inc., the IBM–Toshiba joint venture, made a decision to double its capacity in response to market demand. In conclusion, unexpected changes will occur in any relationship. Success depends, to a great extent, on the partners' flexibility to adapt to these changes and refocus and reposition the alliance when necessary.

Thinking ahead: exit as a natural outcome of IJVs

Unlike mergers and acquisitions, all IJVs will sooner or later be terminated. IJV divorce does not necessarily signal failure; it often means that the business logic for the alliance no longer applies. The transitory character of IJVs often stems from the nature of parent firms' strategic intent when forming them. As IJVs evolve over time or face various hazards, whether internal or external, partners need to have mechanisms in place to guide the exit process (Serapio and Cascio, 1996).

It is indeed important for international managers to spend a great deal of time on the formative decisions, such as partner selection, equity arrangement, and responsibility allocation. There is no reason at all, however, to overlook the termination considerations. Yet we have witnessed numerous cases where, when it becomes time to end the venture, there are no mechanisms in place to guide the process. Even though termination is a natural event in the JV life cycle, parent companies often fail to plan for it when they are setting up their ventures. Many executives realize that reaching clear agreement at the outset of an IJV on how the endgame will be handled is an important organizational mechanism to ensure success.

Reasons for terminating CBAs

The reasons behind commercial divorces vary. First, differences in strategic or operational objectives often lead to such divorce. Many practitioners and academics alike attribute many of the problems in U.S.–Japanese alliances in auto parts to this incompatibility in strategic goals. U.S. suppliers often have a narrow focus: to gain access to the Japanese auto transplants in the United States. Their counterparts, however, have broader goals: to secure a foothold in the U.S. market. Such incompatibility can be operational as well. Partners may also disagree over whether they should exploit their original investment or continue to invest capital and/or technology in the venture instead. For example, a former alliance between Corning and Ciba-Geigy of Switzerland derailed because of growing differences in the two partners' ambitions and commitment.

Second, differences in managerial styles can be the reason behind the termination. In the case of the Corning–Vitro alliance, the two partners had different ideas on how to define and provide "service" to customers. Corning was concerned about prompt service to retailers, such as Wal-Mart and K-Mart. Vitro had different ideas, however. Having operated for years in a closed Mexican economy with little competition, Vitro was concerned only about product reliability.

Third, exit may be attributable to differences in conflict resolution. In many alliances in China between Chinese and foreign companies, for instance, the Chinese partners prefer not to pre-specify explicit conflict resolution terms, especially judiciary or arbitration resolutions, in an alliance contract. From their perspective, leaving these terms ambiguous may nourish inter-partner cooperation in the long term. When they form partnerships with Western firms, however, this ambiguity can lead to the exit of alliances. For example, Lehman Brothers sued Sinochem and Sinopec, the two giant state-owned Chinese firms, in 1994, for failing to honor their obligations in swap transactions. This accusation, however, was rejected by the Chinese partners, which argued that there was no explicit stipulation on these transactions in the agreement. As a result of this open confrontation, the partnership between Lehman Brothers and the two Chinese giants was ended.

Other reasons underlying the end of IJVs include inability to meet shifting targets (e.g., Du Pont and Philips terminated their alliance in optical media for this reason), inability to meet financial requirements (e.g., financial strains prompted Chrysler to sell its stake in Diamond Star Motors to Mitsubishi), inability to predict partner competencies (e.g., AT&T ended its partnership with Philips as it found that Philips NV's clout did not go far beyond the Dutch market), and inability to predict regulatory policies (e.g., Rohm & Hass terminated its electronic chemical alliance with Tokyo Okha Kogyo to accommodate European regulatory concerns about possible overlaps with its pending acquisition of Morton International).

Of course, the best scenario for IJV dissolution is that the venture has already met its strategic goals, as set by both parties. In particular, when each party aims to acquire knowledge from the other, this alliance does not have to maintain its longevity. For instance, Hercules and Montedison, two former competitors in polypropylene products, established an alliance and pooled together $900 million in assets to create Himont in November 1983. Each side enjoyed a competitive advantage in the industry that the other lacked and wanted. Through research and technological breakthroughs, Himont added new properties and applications for polypropylene and grew worldwide to include over 3,000 employees, thirty-eight manufacturing plants, and distribution capabilities in 100 countries. As a leader in the chemical industry with a return on equity of 38 percent, Himont earned at least $150 million per annum from new products. After successfully fulfilling its objectives (i.e., having learned new technologies), Hercules sold its equity stake in Himont to its partner. Box 7.2 summarizes the above reasons for terminating IJVs and other CBAs.

Box 7.2 Reasons for terminating cross-border alliances

- Differences in strategic or operational objectives
- Differences in dynamic commitment
- Differences in organizational adaptation
- Differences in decision-making authority
- Differences in managerial styles
- Differences in conflict resolution
- Inability to meet shifting targets
- Inability to meet financial requirements
- Inability to predict partner competencies
- Inability to predict regulatory policies and decisions
- Inability to satisfy one or two partners' goals or strategies
- Alliance goals met

Scenarios surrounding CBA dissolution

The scenarios surrounding CBA dissolutions or exits can vary greatly. Some endings are planned while others occur with little warning. Some are friendly, others unfriendly. Finally, sometimes the partners are in agreement about the need to dissolve the CBA, while other times there is disagreement over this point.

Planned or unplanned

Some dissolutions are planned while others are not. Exits planned by both parties are more likely to imply the end of the alliance's mission than are unplanned ones. As a result of the twelve-year limit imposed by the U.S. Federal Trade Commission, both General Motors and Toyota Motors knew from the beginning that their alliance, NUMMI, would have to plan for divorce. The dissolution of the collaborative partnerships between General Motors and Daewoo Motors, Meiji and Borden, and AT&T and Olivetti are examples of unplanned divorces.

Friendly or unfriendly

Alliance dissolutions can be friendly or unfriendly. The divorce between Vitro and Corning, mentioned earlier, is an example of an alliance that ended on friendly terms. Both companies amicably agreed to terminate their equity ventures, and Corning paid Vitro its original investment in the alliance. In contrast, unfriendly divorces are often contested in courts or end up in arbitration.

Agreement

The last scenario concerns whether or not all parties have agreed to the termination. Hercules (U.S.) and New Japan Chemical, for instance, agreed in 1999 to disband their equally owned alliance, Rika Hercules, after determining that managing the businesses separately would allow them to better preserve and expand the advantageous positions of both businesses.

Having a partner that refuses to terminate presents more difficulties in dissolution. To illustrate, a major U.S. computer company attempted to terminate its alliance with a Japanese partner because of a major shift in its strategic focus. The Japanese partner, however, refused to accept the proposition of termination because ending the alliance meant a loss of face.

Methods of terminating a CBA

As presented in Figure 7.3, there are also three different methods of termination, namely, *termination by acquisition* (equity transfer), *termination by redefinition* of the alliance, and *termination by dissolution*.

Figure 7.3 Exiting from cross-border alliances

Acquisition of the alliance

In the first case, the IJV is terminated with one of the partners acquiring the stake of the other partner. Termination by acquisition could also take the form of one partner selling its equity stake in the alliance to another company (e.g., British Aerospace selling its equity stake in Rover to BMW), or both partners selling their shares to a third company. In general, most companies prefer reallocation of ownership between existing parent firms. These changes in ownership and resource commitments are a function of both firms' evolving relationships to the venture. Termination by acquisition is most common in international equity alliances. For instance, as already mentioned, New Japan Chemical recently agreed to buy out the share of its partner, Hercules, in their alliance, Rika Hercules. After this acquisition, the two partners intend to maintain a friendly relationship, including technological exchanges.

Redefinition

Termination may also occur by the redefinition of the alliance agreement. In lieu of termination, partners to an IJV may agree to redefine or restructure their original agreement. For example, Matsushita Electric Industries Co. of Japan (MEI) and Solbourne Computer, Inc. of Colorado entered into an ambitious partnership in 1987 to compete with Sun Microsystems' SPARC computers. When the venture failed, MEI and Solbourne agreed in 1992 to redraft their initial agreement into a more limited partnership arrangement. In this case, redefinition or restructuring resulted in the creation of a new alliance. In other words, the life cycle of the old alliance has ended while the life cycle of the new alliance has just begun.

Dissolution

Finally, the IJV can be dissolved as a jointly controlled entity. One option here is to sell off the assets and dissolve the organization completely. Alternatively, the alliance may be allowed to operate as an autonomous organization, free from the control of the original parents.

Procedures for terminating CBAs

Regardless of which condition has provoked termination or which type of termination is occurring, the process should be managed in accordance with procedures stipulated in the initial alliance contract or its supplements. These procedures generally include statements that specify the *conditions for termination*, *timing*, *disposition of assets*, *disposition of liabilities*, and *dispute resolution mechanisms*.

Conditions of termination

In many countries, both developed and developing, the regulations governing the termination and dissolution of alliances are contained in the alliance law and its implementing regulations. According to Chinese Equity Alliance Law, for instance, an alliance may be dissolved when it incurs "heavy losses" or when one party fails to execute its obligations. If a loss is incurred owing to a breach of contract, the violating party has to bear financial liability for the loss. Other conditions in most countries' corporate or alliance laws concerning alliance dissolution include expiration of duration, inability to continue operations owing to losses caused by *force majeure*, inability to obtain the desired objectives of the operation while simultaneously seeing no future for development, and occurrence of other reasons for dissolution as prescribed by the contract or articles of association.

Timing of termination

The timing of a possible termination establishes up front the amount of commitment or flexibility each party has with respect to the alliance. If two companies have mutually agreed not to retract their participation in the joint activity, then they have sent a strong signal to each other indicating their level of dedication to the project. A benchmark event may be set, such as allowing termination of the venture only when it has reached a stage of self-sufficiency that does not leave either partner vulnerable.

Disposition of assets

The partners should specify the methods to be used in valuing assets. Partners should negotiate how the alliance will liquidate its assets and how the partners will share in the assets. Asset valuation or pricing is a major source of disagreement during a divorce. The contract should stipulate whether one partner will be given the opportunity to bid for the equity share of the other. The basis for asset valuation should also be clarified. It may be based on the actual amounts invested by the partners, the findings of an independent appraiser, or an offer from one of the partners or an external buyer.

Disposition of liabilities

There needs to be a clause that stipulates the disposition of liabilities. How partners deal with the liabilities of the alliance and how the venture deals with contingent liabilities should be clarified. For example, terminating a venture in host countries such as Italy, Spain, or Belgium can be very expensive because of the significant severance benefits that the governments of these countries require employers to pay terminated employees. To illustrate, terminating a 45-year-old manager with twenty years of service who is earning $50,000 (U.S.) per year costs about U.S.$130,000 in Italy, $125,000 in Spain, and $94,000 in Belgium, compared to an average $19,000 in the United States. Partners to an alliance must be prepared to address these and other types of liabilities related to termination.

Dispute resolution mechanisms

Finally, the contract should regulate the methods of resolving disputes. Disputes may be resolved judicially or through arbitration. Partners to an alliance should be aware of the advantages and disadvantages of each alternative before selecting a particular mode of dispute resolution. If the partners agree to resolve disputes judicially, they are usually free to specify which country's laws will govern any dispute. An additional step in this process is to reach an agreement on what must be accomplished in order to allow one of the partners to continue operating the venture. This is an operational definition of what the alliance requires to survive, if not to prosper. It may include specifying a target market penetration or a milestone in the transfer or development of a given technology.

Conclusion

In order to help increase the likelihood of success for CBAs, companies attempt to work in collaboration with companies that can be trusted and with which cooperation is more likely than conflict. Although cooperation and trust can be developed between CBA partners over time, finding partners with which trust and cooperation already exists may ensure that the alliance develops as quickly as possible. Frequent and open communications appear to be vital to the development and continuation of trust, collaboration, and commitment in the alliance. Once cooperation and trust exist between alliance partners, issues of conflict, power sharing, control, and structure of the relationship become easier to manage and resolve.

Of course, the probability of failure for any alliance is relatively high. Even under the most favorable conditions of trust and cooperation between partners, an alliance may outlive its usefulness. Thus, establishing an agreed-upon plan for exit or termination of such an arrangement seems reasonable.

Because of the importance of trust and cooperation in CBAs, it is important that they be systematically considered, both in the selection of partners and in the evolving relationship between alliance partners. In both cases, the HRM professionals can have an important role to play in CBAs. This role and others are described in greater detail in the next and concluding chapter.

Dynamic collaborations between Westinghouse and Mitsubishi

Case Example

The collaboration between Westinghouse and Mitsubishi dates back to licensing agreements forged in the 1920s. Over the years, the partners have built up an army of cooperative links in R&D, product development, manufacturing and marketing. However, changing global market conditions and pressures on the partners for new strategies necessitate a dynamic cooperative relationship between the alliance partners.

Westinghouse and Mitsubishi Heavy Industries (MHI) have long enjoyed a classic licensing arrangement in steam turbine and gas turbine technology. As is often the case in such a licensing relationship, however, the student eventually accumulates as much knowledge as the teacher, jeopardizing the deal. During the mid-1980s, MHI's lower-level engineers in particular became disillusioned with a relationship in which the Japanese firm paid royalties for Westinghouse technology that MHI had greatly advanced. Westinghouse equally acknowledged that the licensing partnership was outdated, because of the new product and technology innovations achieved by MHI.

Yet senior management at both companies still wanted to preserve the relationship, for several reasons. For one thing, global market conditions were tough, and both sides believed they would be more effective competing as partners rather than alone. Also, technically MHI could not use the technology once the licensing agreement had expired, since licensing is a rental and not a transfer of ownership. In addition, MI-11 and Westinghouse wanted to build on many years of a good relationship. Both managements felt they could achieve new product, market, and technological breakthroughs by working as strategic partners.

continued

Consequently, as the agreements came up for renewal, MHI and Westinghouse worked out a new direction and vision for the alliance. When the agreement covering steam turbines came up for renewal in February 1989, the partners replaced the old licensing agreement with three new contracts that are completely without royalties. The key features of the new agreement include the following:

Business cooperation. MHI and Westinghouse agreed to jointly develop and advance technology. The agreement also covers cooperation in product development. The partners further identified plans to create partnership strategies to build a global presence and cooperate in marketing on a case-by-case basis where such cooperation would enhance competitiveness.

Technology cooperation. The partners will collaborate in R&D, either in the same research labs or at their own separate locations. However, all R&D patents will be jointly owned by MHI and Westinghouse. The contract also granted MHI rights to use the Westinghouse technology in perpetuity.

When MHI and Westinghouse designed their new arrangements, both sides realized that alliances need constant attention and maintenance, so they created a series of committees to accompany the new partnership and foster close contacts. The three committees include, among others:

1   A steering committee – top management at MHI and Westinghouse meet semiannually to discuss the alliances and evaluate the direction and strategy of the partnership. The partners aim to have a frank discussion on key issues: what each firm expects from the alliance; how the partnership can improve competitiveness; how rival firms react to the new liaison; and an outline for one-, two-, and ten-years agendas for the different activities and operations.
2   A technology committee – this committee brings together engineers and managers from MHI and Westinghouse to discuss product, technology, and new strategies. There is no formal schedule for meetings, but the engineers are encouraged to meet frequently.
3   A marketing committee – the marketing team pools executives from both partners to brainstorm on how to build market share and prize open new markets. As with the technology committee, the marketing group is encouraged to meet regularly.

Following the success of the new MHI–Westinghouse relationship in steam turbines, the partners decided to adopt the same strategy for gas turbines. Even though that licensing agreement did not technically expire until 1992, senior management signed a similar set of agreements for gas turbines in July 1991. The decision to move quickly has paid off. The new MHI–Westinghouse global strategic partnership recently won the Yu-Yu twin cities project in Korea to build two new power plants. Westinghouse will act as the lead vendor, with MHI as its partner.

Westinghouse also cooperates with Mitsubishi Electric (Melco). Riding on the tide of successful changes in the Westinghouse–MHI relationship, the two firms set out on the same road in mid-1991. Initially, a corporate umbrella agreement between the senior management of Westinghouse and that of Melco constituted the keystone of the alliance. The umbrella accord included a cluster of Westinghouse technologies licensed to

Mitsubishi. Royalty and other fees from the technologies were paid directly to Westinghouse senior management and later disbursed internally to the different divisions. This agreement functioned smoothly for years. Mitsubishi obtained the necessary technology to build a big business in the power-generation industry. For its part, Westinghouse received a steady stream of revenue and also expanded the geographic scope of its technology. Yet turbulent global market conditions and changing corporate objectives and strategies threatened to unbundle the closely knit relationship.

Several developments placed the umbrella agreement in jeopardy. First, Westinghouse's markets for power generation in the United States were shrinking, while the Asian markets were expanding. It did not make sense for Westinghouse to push on while its markets floundered. As one Mitsubishi executive said, "It was never a case of one partner being dumb while the other was savvy. The world changes, markets change. And companies must react."

Consequently, Westinghouse refocused its energies from working with mature, low-growth industries such as certain areas of power generation toward higher-growth segments. Key businesses, particularly the transmission and distribution section, were sold to competitor Asea Brown Boveri. Westinghouse also withdrew its participation in a fifty-fifty joint venture with Melco in high-voltage power circuit breakers. Other sectors were restructured and downsized. The amount of business connected to the umbrella agreement fell from a high of fifty projects to only a handful. Yet the royalties had already been paid by Melco and disbursed by senior management, leading to tension at lower levels when projects ran aground.

A second factor jeopardizing the umbrella agreement is that the licensee–licensor relationship became obsolete. Elmendorf points out that Mitsubishi had clearly advanced the technology. The Japanese firm had developed many improvement patents as well as introducing new technologies and products to the market. Much of the resentment among Mitsubishi engineers stemmed from their desire to operate on a level playing ground with Westinghouse. And other executives concurred, saying that there comes a time in any prosperous licensing relationship when the two sides must operate as equals, to keep problems and tension from suffocating the relationship.

Subsequently, both partners worked to transform the alliance from a licensee–licensor relationship to a global strategic partnership. Westinghouse and Melco allowed the umbrella agreement to expire when it came up for renewal in April 1991. Instead, they replaced it with a series of agreements covering products, sourcing, and relationships:

1 *Products.* The partners listed several product areas in which they agreed to collaborate in R&D, new technology and product development, manufacturing, and marketing. Their products cover the field for large rotating electric generators that are either hydrogen- or air-cooled. To strengthen the new relationship, Melco recently established an office in Orlando, Florida, the operating center for Westinghouse's power-generation businesses. The two partners also exchanged engineers, with one Melco engineer working in a Westinghouse plant in Orlando and two Westinghouse engineers transferred to Melco facilities in Japan.

continued

2 *Sourcing.* After Westinghouse shed several low-profit businesses in power generation in the late 1980s, the U.S. MNE faced serious gaps in its product line for the construction and maintenance of power plants. Therefore, Westinghouse and Melco signed a series of supplier agreements in which the latter acts as principal supplier for equipment such as transformers, switch gear, and so on.

3 *Relationship.* In a relationship mirroring the MHI–Westinghouse deal, both partners were committed to working together worldwide. Management also wanted to encourage as much cooperation and communication as possible between all levels of management and engineers to help reconcile previous differences and problems. Hence, Melco and Westinghouse also adopted the three-committee strategy of steering, technology, and market committees to nurture cooperation and compete as partners in the global marketplace.

Cross-border alliances and the HRM profession

We were debating between establishing the center in Australia or Singapore. We had to evaluate local employment laws, the cost and availability of housing, and what it would cost to recruit and relocate the multilingual employees needed to staff the center. We also researched tax issues, the competitive salary structure, medical facilities, and the healthcare system. There's a myriad of decisions in which HR must participate to go back to the business unit and say: "This is what you should do, this is what it will cost, and this is how long it will take to get the new business or division up and running."

Tim Harris
Former HR Head, Novell

When it comes to operating in a global context, most organizations and most HR professionals are at an early stage of learning. Globalization is forcing managers to grapple with complex issues as they seek to gain or sustain a competitive advantage. Faced with unprecedented levels of foreign competition at home and abroad, operating an international business is high on the list of priorities for top management. So are finding and nurturing the human resources required to implement an international or global strategy.

As CBAs become more common, the role of HR professionals increasingly requires the competency to blend domestic and international HR activities. In the case of IM&As, for example, successful acquirers conduct a thorough due diligence process to ensure that they understand the HR issues and risks associated with the deal. When they screen potential partners or target firms, they assess both the obvious strategic and financial opportunities and the human and cultural elements that can undermine an otherwise sound deal. Is the management talent pool sufficiently deep to sustain some unwanted turnover? What labor relations issues will confront the new organization? How similar are the cultures of the two firms? (Mirvis and Marks, 1992). Such assessments require the active involvement of HR professionals.

Cisco has pursued the acquisition strategy as well as any company as a means of expanding its product lines. John Chambers, CEO of Cisco, says very clearly that integrating the newly acquired company into the Cisco culture is very important, and Cisco carefully evaluates the culture of the companies it is thinking about acquiring. For Cisco, "culture" refers to the values of the company and the way it treats people. Cisco looks for companies that manage people in ways that fit Cisco's own culture, which means that people are rewarded for their performance, and encouraged to be creative and team oriented. During the due diligence process, the senior vice president of HR works in partnership with the head of corporate acquisitions to assess these cultural elements. Certainly, there is a clear role for the human resource professionals, and the company respects the value they add to the due diligence process (Jackson and Schuler, 2003).

Human resource professionals can play a similar role in companies engaged in IJV activity, but they are not always given the opportunity to do so. According to one study (Frayne and Geringer, 1990), on average only about 4 percent of the time spent in creating an IJV is time spent resolving HR issues. By contrast, at Davidson-Marley, addressing HR issues was high on top management's agenda from the earliest planning discussions.

Roles for HR professionals

Human resource professionals play a critical role in the globalization process by helping companies evaluate the HR prospects and possibilities involved in moving to different regions of the world.

As we have seen in prior chapters, there are numerous HR issues to be addressed when planning and implementing CBAs. Some HR issues are best handled by the senior HR leader in partnership with other senior executives. Many others, however, require the involvement of various experts in the HR department. In addition, the roles of HR professionals may be slightly different depending on whether they are located in the parent firms developing an IJV, in the IJV itself, or in companies engaged in an international merger or acquisition. Despite the many differences in the HR activities required in these various situations, there are many commonalities also. In this chapter, we focus on those commonalities and offer several guidelines for HR professionals involved in CBAs.

Human resources roles in CBAs

Table 8.1 provides a summary of the HR roles required for successful CBA activity. Like any HR professional whose work crosses national borders, HR professionals working in CBAs must deal with issues such as international taxation, relations with the host government, and language translation. A host government can, for example, dictate hiring procedures or insist that a company provide training to local workers. Local cultural and religious practices may make it necessary to modify the company's local approach to managing HR practices. Human resource professionals in all global companies also face the problem of designing and administering programs for more than one national group of employees, and they must therefore take a more global view. In comparison with HR professionals working in domestic environments, HR professionals in global companies often realize that the human and financial consequences of failure are more severe in the international arena. For example, expatriate failures and terrorism are persistent, high-cost problems for international companies.

Table 8.1 The key roles and their meaning for the HR leader in cross-border alliances

Key roles	Meaning for the HR leader
Partnership	Shows concern for multiple sets of stakeholders
	Understands how money gets made, lost and spent in a global context
	Knows the market and how CBAs can fit the business
	Works effectively with other HR leaders
Change facilitator	Can execute change in strategy
	Can get others to work with partners
	Can think conceptually and articulate thoughts
	Is able to get others to change from competitor to partner
	Knows how to differentiate for competitive advantage
Strategy implementor	Has the ability to build commitment and trust
	Responds to needs of several organizations
	Recognizes the importance of teamwork across organizations
	Is sensitive to needs for integration and differentiation
Strategic	Is capable of educating line managers about trust and learning
	Knows the plan of top executives and can influence partner selection
	Is involved in the formulation of CBA strategies
	Can create structures and cultures for learning
Innovator	Sees the talent needed for executing CBA strategies
	Can adapt to changes in the stages of the CBA development
	Manages the tensions and conflicts resulting from different perspectives
Collaborator	Knows how to work with partners to create a win–win situation
	Sees the wisdom of sharing over competing
	Works with new organization to insure its success
Builder	Knows best HRM practices
	Appreciates HRM system considerations
	Can convey HRM practices to others

Cross-border alliances increase role complexity

Compared to HR professionals working within an autonomous organization without significant alliances, HR professionals engaged in CBA activity often deal with greater complexity. Thus, their jobs can be quite challenging. A major source of added complexity is the need to manage relationships between the partner companies in addition to managing relationships within one's own company. Because power must be shared among the partners, HR policies and practices cannot simply be imposed; they must be jointly designed, negotiated, and implemented in an atmosphere that maintains trust and collaboration.

Competencies needed by HR professionals

Box 8.1 describes the competencies needed by HR professionals today. These competencies are organized into three broad categories: business competencies, leadership competencies, and change and knowledge management competencies.

Box 8.1 Business competencies, leadership competencies, and change and knowledge management competencies

Business competencies

- Industry knowledge
- Competitor understanding
- Financial understanding
- Global perspective/knowledge
- Strategic visioning
- Partner orientation
- Multiple stakeholder sensitivity

Leadership competencies

- Strategic analysis
- Managing cultural diversity
- Creator of learning culture
- Planning skills
- Adaptability
- Learning facilitator
- Value shaper
- Manager of uncertainty

Change and knowledge management competencies

- Consulting and communicating
- Group process facilitation
- Designing and working in flexible structures
- Partnering and parenting
- Negotiating
- Network building
- Creating HR alignment
- Managing learning transfer

In addition, of course, HR professionals need the full array of technical HR competencies. All HR professionals should strive to develop this full set of competencies, including those who expect to be involved in CBAs. Armed with these competencies, HR professionals will be well positioned to meet the challenges of managing CBA activity.

Guidelines for HR professionals involved in cross-border alliances

For HR professionals, CBAs provide excellent opportunities to apply their expertise to HR issues that are critically important to the success of the business. Regardless of the specific type of CBA, they can increase the value of their efforts by following a few simple guidelines (for more detailed discussions, see Child and Faulkner, 1998; Child et al., 2001; Pucik, 1988).

Guideline: Get involved early.

The HR leader and staff should be involved in the formation of the CBA from the earliest planning stages. Before the decision to proceed has been made, the HR department should evaluate alternatives to an alliance and assess the objectives to be achieved by an alliance. With their expertise in measuring attitudes and opinions, the HR staff can assist by ensuring that all stakeholder concerns have been identified, and that all of the social costs and benefits are considered. Early involvement of the HR staff ensures that they can be proactive rather than reactive in addressing HR issues as they arise. It also facilitates subsequent communications and negotiations between the HR staff and other experts involved in the deal, because everyone is better informed of others' perspectives and concerns.

Guideline: Stress the importance of being clear about how the new organization will be designed.

Whether a CBA involves forming an IJV or entering into an international merger or acquisition, a new organization will almost certainly be created. If the form that this new organization is to take is not clearly understood early in the process, it will not be possible to make a smooth transition to the desired new future. Clearly envisioning the future organization is the first step to creating that future. As HR professionals understand, the success of the new organization will depend on how well the strategic intent fits with the objectives and structure of the new organization, the relationship of this organization to the other CBA partners, and the quality of the people working in the new organization. HR policies and practices such as staffing, performance measurement, training, and remuneration are central to establishing a new organization that is capable of realizing the strategic intent. Unless everyone involved in the alliance is clear and in agreement about the vision for the future, it will be nearly impossible to create an effective HR system for the new organization.

Guideline: Communicate the strategic intent.

Executives and managers sometimes believe that most employees are not interested in understanding the larger strategic picture of the firm, and perhaps could not understand strategic issues even if they were explained. Human resource professionals, on the other hand, know that employees who understand the organization and its strategic objectives are more likely to be highly motivated and productive. Thus, to fulfill its responsibility for corporate communications, the HR department should cooperate with operational managers to make certain that the strategic intent of a CBA is adequately communicated to all employees. Offering training programs for managers is one way to prepare them to deal effectively with the ambiguity and complexity of CBAs. In addition, the HR staff can assist by preparing stories and news announcements for company newsletters and electronic bulletin boards on the company intranet. Whenever news about the company's CBA activity is reported, HR staff can assist by making sure that the news stories provide information that will help employees answer the question, "What does this mean for me, my job, and my career?"

Guideline: Adopt a cooperative relationship with the HR professionals in alliance organizations.

Regardless of the specific type of CBA, cooperation among the HR professionals in the partner organizations will be essential to the long-term success of the alliance – just as cooperation among other professional staff is needed. Because the HR staff become involved in so many issues that directly affect employees throughout the partner firms, employees have many opportunities to "see" how the HR staff from the partner firms relate to each other. If they are supportive and respectful of each other, employees learn that cooperation is both possible and valued, and are likely to follow this example. If the HR staff show disrespect and make comments that undermine each other's efforts, employees may imitate these destructive behaviors also.

Guideline: Develop learning mechanisms for the HR department as well as for others throughout the organization.

The importance of learning from CBA experiences has been repeatedly mentioned throughout this book. It seems apparent that the HR staff should be deeply involved in developing mechanisms to ensure that learning occurs throughout the organization and between organizations. Like everyone else, the HR staff also need to learn. Among the key opportunities that HR staff have to promote organizational learning are these:

- *Staffing to learn*. The accumulation of invisible assets should be the key principle guiding the staffing strategy – for each organization and each unit within the partner organizations. Staffing and development plans should be established to allocate talent where it is most needed, and procedures should be developed to facilitate the flow of talent among the partners.
- *Using training to stimulate the learning process*. Several types of training activities can be used to create a positive climate for learning. For CBAs, building skills in cross-cultural communication is perhaps most important. For managers who will be involved in IJVs, training should be used to build the skills needed for alliances that involve the mixed motives of collaboration and competition. Managers must be able to establish open communication and trust in order to promote the smooth transfer of know-how. Finally, interorganizational learning can be promoted by ensuring that all training programs are offered to all partners in the alliance, to maintain balance. Whenever possible, employees from the partner organizations should be trained together. This helps expose the different perspectives of employees from the partner firms and also builds personal bridges between the partner organizations.
- *Rewarding learning activities*. Management behavior that encourages organizational learning, such as sharing and diffusion of critical information, should be explicitly recognized and rewarded. HR staff can help achieve this objective by ensuring that learning objectives are included in job descriptions and performance measures, and they also can develop specific recognition and reward programs.

Conclusion

As all the chapters have suggested, there are many human resource issues to be managed in successful cross-border alliances, particularly international joint ventures and international mergers and acquisitions. In this chapter and others, we have described many of these issues and offered a few guidelines for how to address these issues effectively. The guidelines suggested are grounded in the experiences of managers and the relevant scholarly literature – including both theories of strategic human resource management and empirical studies of various types of alliances. Nevertheless, because cross-border alliances are a relatively new phenomenon in the history of organizational research, there are many lessons that are still to be learned. Much more systematic research is still needed before the many issues that arise in managing cross-border alliances are fully understood. As the research on managing cross-border alliances effectively continues to unfold, we hope the guidelines offered in this book prove useful to both managers and scholars who are concerned with understanding and succeeding in the world of alliance management. With the likelihood of increasing cross-border alliance activity around the world, the future seems to provide many opportunities for HR professionals, working in partnership with line managers and other employees, to improve the effectiveness of global business organizations while also improving the satisfaction of the many stakeholders whose lives are affected by CBAs.

The new HR roles at Deutsche Bank

Deutsche Bank (DB) has more than 90,000 employees organized into five globally operating business divisions and a corporate center. While successful by traditional standards, in 1999, after having just successful acquired and integrated Bankers Trust, it was faced with the new reality for most companies that if it did not change rather dramatically, it would soon lose its position in the industry. The new reality was being created by events such as disintermediation, deconstruction, deregulation, and e-business. All of these events were making traditional business models obsolete.

In order to help DB deal with the changes needed for it to be successful in the new business environment, the HR department and its professionals recognized that they had to become a strategic partner, linked to the business and to the line managers who had to execute new business models and strategies. To become a better strategic partner, the HR department identified the major aspects of the environment facing DB, and it started a global transformation program for 1,600 HR professionals. Essentially the program was designed to create an HR department that could respond more strategically and more capably to the rest of the bank's management and employees.

The global transformation had four parts: strategy, structure, management, and competency. These parts recognized that for the bank to succeed, it needed to have great human resources. So the HR department had to link its activities with the needs of the business. To do so effectively, it had to change its structure and it had to manage itself like a business unit. Critical to these changes in the HR department itself were the changes in the roles and competencies of the HR professionals. In essence, the 1,600 HR professionals realized they had to play all the new roles shown in Table 8.1, not just the strategic management role, and have the competencies necessary to play them as well as possible. Together with HR consultants, the senior HR leaders developed a learning program, using Deutsche Bank University, to help the HR professionals obtain the competencies necessary to play the new roles that were a part of the new reality for the Bank. As of 2002, the program is having success, even though the business environment remains very challenging.

The international joint venture
of Davidson-Marley BV

Formation of an international joint venture:
Davidson Instrument Panel*

Randall S. Schuler, Susan E. Jackson, Rutgers University, U.S.A.,
Peter J. Dowling, University of Canberra, Australia, Denice E. Welch and
Helen De Cieri, Monash University, Australia

Executive summary

Going international no longer is a matter of choice for many U.S. firms. Yet the risks and costs associated with "going global" are enormous. Many things can impede success when setting up an international joint venture (IJV). With systematic planning and foresight, however, these barriers can be reduced to mere road bumps. This article identifies and discusses these barriers, including several human resource management (HRM) issues. How these barriers can be addressed systematically is illustrated through a case study of Davidson Instrument Panel and its joint venture with a partner in England

Introduction

OK, so you're thinking about manufacturing and selling your company's wares abroad, but you're more than a little daunted by the risks. Why not join forces with a foreign partner? That way, you can split the start-up costs and divide up any losses, not to mention gaining quicker international credibility, smoother distribution, and a better flow of information. Then again, maybe you'd rather not share your potential profits – or the secrets of your company's success – with anyone. That's fine. But don't be surprised if, after trying to crack a foreign market on your own, you develop a new enthusiasm for joint ventures (Hyatt, 1988: 145).

Even if you haven't attempted to crack a foreign market on your own, you may be ready for an international joint venture (IJV). Such is the case with many U.S. firms today, especially since the advent of Europe 1992 and recent events in Eastern Europe. In fact, there may be little real choice for firms that desire to expand globally. According to Nicholas Azonian (Vice President of

* Funded by a grant from the Human Resource Planning Society. The authors thank Joseph E Paul and Jonathan T. Hopkins at Davidson Instrument Panel. Citations for articles in Appendix A are listed in the Bibliography.

Finance at Nypro, an $85 million plastic injection-molding and industrial components manufacturer in Clinton, Massachusetts, with a presence in six countries and four IJV factories in the United States): "Without these foreign ventures, we'd be very limited in terms of our knowledge, our technology, our people, and our markets. We'd be a smaller company in every sense of the word" (Hyatt, 1988).

Of course, the benefits of IJVs are not limited to small companies. Sales of companies in which Corning Glass has a joint partnership are nearly 50 percent higher than the sales of its wholly owned businesses. According to James Houghton, Corning's CEO, speaking of international opportunities and joint venture alliances:

> Alliances are the way to capture that window. By marrying one party's product to the other's distribution, or one party's manufacturing skill to the other's R&D, alliances are often quicker than expanding your business overseas – and cheaper than buying one.
>
> (Stewart, 1990)

With high failure rates and increasing competitiveness, launching an IJV offers little guarantee of success. Some of the most significant barriers to success involve people issues – issues relating to international human resource management (HRM). This article describes many of the issues associated with forming and managing IJVs and illustrates how one IJV is addressing many of them. Because this venture is in the early stages of formation, this article addresses only critical start-up barriers. A subsequent article is scheduled to describe more extensively issues related to establishing the HRM practices to be used in the facility. Another article is scheduled to describe how everything is working and what adjustments have been made. The current article addresses the IJV from the viewpoint of its U.S. partner, Davidson Instrument Panel. Subsequent articles will reflect viewpoints of the British partner and the joint venture itself.

Davidson Instrument Panel

Davidson Instrument Panel is one of thirty-three divisions of Textron, an $8 billion conglomerate headquartered in Providence, Rhode Island. Davidson and its two sister divisions (Interior Trim and Exterior Trim) make up Davidson-Textron. All three divisions are component suppliers to automotive original-equipment manufacturers. Davidson-Textron is the largest independent supplier of instrument panels for the U.S. automobile industry.

Originally begun as a maker of rubber products for drug sundries in Boston in the early 1850s, Davidson moved its operations to Dover, New Hampshire, in the 1950s. Its headquarters now are in Portsmouth, New Hampshire, where staff of fewer than fifty oversee the operation of two manufacturing plants: one in Port Hope, Ontario, and another in Farmington, New Hampshire. The 1,000-person operation in Port Hope is unionized; the 900-person operation in Farmington is not.

The nature of the U.S. automobile industry has changed dramatically during the past twenty years, and the effects have been felt by all the "Big Three" auto makers. As the automobile industry has become globalized, success has turned on quality products that fit right and perform smoothly and reliably. But while quality has become a major concern to the auto industry, so have cost and innovation. New products and new technology are vital to the success of the Big Three, but without cost reduction, new products cannot be offered at competitive prices.

The characteristics of the auto industry are reflected in the companies supplying it. Davidson Instrument Panel is no exception. To succeed, the company must adapt to the demands of the new environment. Doing so will bring rewards such as market share and, perhaps even more important, an extensive cooperative relationship with the Big Three. Essentially, the days of multiple bidding – where winning meant delivering at the lowest cost with no assurance that the next year's bid would be the same – are gone. Today, automobile companies use sole sourcing for many of their supply needs. Accompanying this is a greater sense of shared destiny and mutual cooperation:

> The component suppliers are having to change with the times. The multinational car manufacturers increasingly want to deal with multinational suppliers, giving them responsibility for the design and development of subassemblies in return for single supplier status.
> (*Financial Times*, March 1, 1990: 8)

Thus it is not unusual for design engineers from suppliers to provide full engineering design of the components they will supply their customer

An important aspect of this new cooperative, sole-sourcing arrangement adopted by the Big Three automotive makers is the willingness to conceptualize and form longer-term relationships. For Davidson Instrument Panel, this has meant the opportunity to establish an IJV.

In the summer of 1989, Davidson agreed to establish an IJV to supply instrumental panels to a Ford Motor Company plant in Belgium beginning in 1992. It chose as its partner for this venture a British firm named Marley.

What seemed like a good opportunity is not always a success, of course. U.S. studies estimate the failure rate of IJVs to be between 50 and 70 percent (Harrigan, 1986; Levine and Byrne, 1986). Because this new IJV is in its early stages, evaluation of its success would be premature. Probabilities of success can be estimated by comparing the actions of Davidson Instrument Panel to the recommendations of others and against mistakes made by others in their early stages. These comparisons may offer guidance to firms seeking to "go global" through such alliances.

Although there is no single agreed-on definition of an IJV, one definition is: "a separate legal organizational entity representing the partial holdings of two or more parent firms, in which the headquarters of at least one is located outside the country of operation of the joint venture. This entity is subject to the joint control of its parent firms, each of which is economically and legally independent of the other" (Shenkar and Zeira, 1987a).

Using an IJV as a mode of international business operation is not new (Ohmae, 1989a, b, c). But economic growth in the past decade of global competition, coupled with shifts in trade dominance and the emergence of new markets, has contributed to a recent increase in the use of IJVs. According to Peter Drucker, IJVs are likely to grow in importance in the 1990s:

> You will see a good deal of joint ventures, of strategic alliances, of cross-holdings across borders. Not because of cost, but because of information. Economists don't accept it, but it is one of the oldest experiences that you cannot maintain market standing in a developed market unless you are in it as a producer. As an exporter, you will be out sooner or later, because you have to be in the market to have the information.
> (Drucker, 1989)

Reasons for forming an IJV

Harrigan (1987a) argued that since a joint venture draws on the strengths of its owners, it should possess superior competitive abilities that allow its sponsors to enjoy synergies. If the venture's owners cannot cope with the demands of managing the joint venture successfully, Harrigan advised the owners to use nonequity forms of cooperation such as cross-marketing and/or cross-production, licensing, and research and development consortia. Some companies shun joint ventures, preferring 100 percent ownership to the drawbacks of loss of control and profits that can accompany shared ownership (Gomes-Casseres, 1989). However, many firms, regardless of previous international experience, do enter into IJV arrangements. The most common reasons cited in the literature are.

- host government insistence (Datta, 1988; Gomes-Casseres, 1989; Shenkar and Zeira, 1987b);
- to gain rapid market entry (Berlew, 1984; Morris and Hergert, 1987; Shenkar and Zeira, 1987b; Tichy, 1988);
- increased economics of scale (Datta, 1988, Morris and Hergert, 1987; Roehl and Trui, 1987);
- to gain local knowledge (Datta, 1988; Lasserre, 1983; O'Reilly, 1988) and local market image (Gomes-Casseres, 1989);
- to obtain vital raw materials (Shenkar and Zeira, 1987b) or technology (Gomes-Casseres, 1989);
- to spread the risks (Morris and Hergert, 1987; Shenkar and Zeira, 1987b);
- to improve competitive advantage in the face of increasing global competition;
- cost-effective and efficient responses forced by globalization of markets (Datta, 1988; Harrigan 1987a, b; Shenkar and Zeira, 1987b).

For many firms, several of these reasons apply. Some of the outcomes above may be unanticipated but later recognized and welcomed. For example, Nypro entered into a joint venture with Mitsui to operate a factory in Atlanta that could serve as a U.S. source of videocassette parts for Enplas, a Japanese concern. Enplas taught Nypro some lessons in both cost-saving management skills and quality control, according to Gordon Lankton, Nypro President and CEO:

> "Why did you reject this shipment?" Lankton would ask. "The label on the boy," they would answer, "was crooked."
> "We eventually learned," says Lankton. Now, Nypro's Atlanta plant is its most productive, with sales per employee averaging $2,000. By comparison, most of Nypro's other nine plants hover around $1,250
> (Hyatt, 1988).

For Davidson Instrument Panel, gaining local knowledge, spreading risks, improving competitive advantage, and becoming more global were important reasons for their IJV. In addition, it wanted to extend its relationship with Ford Motor Company as much as possible – and being a sole-source supplier would mean working with the customer as much as possible.

Failures of IJVs

IJV failure rates (50–70 percent) reflect the difficulty of establishing a successful IJV. Reasons for failure include:

- The partners cannot get along.
- Managers from different partners within the venture cannot work together.
- Managers within the venture cannot work with the owners' managers.
- Partners simply renege on their promises.
- Markets disappear.
- The technology involved does not prove as good as expected.

Failure rates are difficult to measure. The criteria for defining success or failure depend on the parent companies' expectations and motives for establishing the joint venture. "Joint ventures can be deemed successful in spite of poor financial performance, and conversely, they can be considered unsuccessful in spite of good financial performance" (Schaan, 1988). For example, financial performance may take second place to profits from management fees or royalties from technology transfer.

It's a marriage

Many writers compare IJVs to a marriage (Tichy, 1988). The analogy seems to spring from those factors necessary for success, and problems inherent in UVs owing to their contractual nature. To manage an IJV for success, it is important to understand the joint venture process, which includes these five parts:

1   finding an appropriate partner;
2   courting (the prenuptial process);
3   arranging the marriage deal;
4   launching the venture (the honeymoon period); and
5   building a successful ongoing relationship.

Observers (Gomes-Casserres, 1987; Harrigan, 1986; Lyles, 1987) have suggested that effective use of joint ventures requires managers to develop special liaison skills to cope with the mixed loyalties and conflicting goals that characterize shared ownership and shared decision making. Joint venture managers also need to have – and to instill – team-building values and receptivity to ideas generated outside the organization.

Increasingly it is recognized that good joint venture marriages are not created with a handshake and a stroke of the pen. Instead of rushing headlong into a flurry of strategic partnering, savvy managers now are moving slowly into long-term relationships with their cross-national counterparts. They are trying to avoid many of the mistakes created by the "knee-jerk" venturing behaviors of the early 1980s. One way to help make an lJV work is to. establish equal partnerships. According to James Houghton of Corning Glass, "To work, alliances must be true marriages, not dates. A fifty-fifty deal usually works best because it commits both parties to success" (Stewart, 1990). In addition – according to Gordon Lankton of Nypro – "Just finding a knowledgeable partner for a joint venture isn't enough, though. You have to make sure that partner's long-term goals are in sync with your own" (Hyatt, 1988).

Critical issues in managing IJVs

Consensus has it that the very nature of joint ventures contributes to their failure: they are a difficult and complex form of enterprise (Shenkar and Zeira, 1987b, p. 30) and many companies initiate IJVs without recognizing and addressing the major issues they are likely to confront (Morris and Hergert,

1987). Success requires adept handling of three key issues. Below, we describe each of these key issues. We then discuss how Davidson is preparing to deal with them.

Issue 1: Control

Who actually controls the operation can depend on who is responsible for the day-to-day management of the IJV. Ownership distribution may matter less than how operating control and participation in decision making actually are apportioned (Harrigan, 1986). For a parent with minority ownership, for example, the right to appoint key personnel can be used as a control mechanism (Schaan, 1988). Control can be achieved by appointing managers loyal to the parent company and its organizational ethos. Of course, loyalty to the parent cannot be guaranteed. "The ability to appoint the joint venture general manager increases the chances that the parents' interests will be observed, but it is no guarantee that the joint venture general manager will always accommodate that parent's preferences" (Schaan, 1988: 14).

Top managers will be expected to make decisions that deal with the simultaneous demands of the parents and their employees in the enterprise. At times, such decisions will by necessity meet the demands of some parties better than those of other parties. If the partners do not anticipate such decisions, they may fail to build in control mechanisms to protect their interests. Weak control also can result if parent-company managers spend too little time on the IJV, responding to problems only on an ad hoc basis. Finally, control-related failures are likely to occur if control practices are not reevaluated and modified in response to changing circumstances.

Issue 2: Conflict

Business and cultural differences between UV partners often create conflict. Working relationships must be based on trust.

Because joint ventures are inherently unstable relationships, they require a delicate set of organizational and management processes to create trust and the ongoing capacity to collaborate. This means that senior executives must be involved in designing management processes that (1) provide effective ways to handle joint strategy formulation; (2) create structural linkages; (3) provide adequate day-to-day coordination and communication; and (4) establish a win/win climate (Tichy, 1988).

Many misunderstandings and problems in IJVs are rooted in cultural differences (Datta, 1988). Differing approaches to managerial style are one area that can create problems. For example, one party may favor a participative, managerial style while the other may believe in a more autocratic style of management. Another area that can be problematic is acceptance of risk taking when one parent is prepared to take more risks than the other. Such differences often make the process of decision making slow and frustrating. The resulting conflict can be dysfunctional, if not destructive. The big challenge is to work through top management disagreements and avoid deadlocks (Thomas, 1987).

Issue 3: Goals

The partners in an IJV often have differing goals. This is especially likely when an IJV is formed as a solution for reconciling incongruent national interests. For example, a parent may be obliged to share ownership with a host government despite its preference for complete ownership and control. In such a case, the two partners are likely to be concerned with different constituencies; business strategies may differ as a result. For example, the local partner may evaluate strategic choices on the basis of how effective they are likely to be in the local market while the multinational parent would favor strategies that maintain image and reputation in the global market (Gomes-Casseres, 1989). Cultural

differences also may affect strategy. For example, Americans are alleged to have a shorter-term focus than the Japanese (Webster, 1989).

Differing levels of commitment from the parents provide yet another source of difficulty (Datta, 1988). The commitment of each partner reflects the project's importance to the partner. When an imbalance exists, the more committed partner may be frustrated by the other partner's apparent lack of concern; or the less committed partner may feel frustrated by demands and time pressures exerted by the other, more committed partner. The level of commitment by parties to the IJV can contribute to success or failure (Bere, 1987).

Davidson's preparation for these critical issues

Management at Davidson Instrument Panel recognized the importance of these three issues to their IJV. They were careful in selecting a partner, based on more than twenty-five years of licensing experience in Western Europe with four different licensees. From these potential partners they chose the one (Marley in England) with which they had the most in common. This commonality included the following:

- Both use consensus-style management.
- Both are part of a larger organization that is relatively decentralized.
- Both desire to move to the Continent with a manufacturing presence.
- Both have similar views on how to grow the business.
- Both have similar philosophies on how to run a business and how to manage human resources.
- Both desire a fair and open relationship.

These several dimensions of commonality should help minimize the difficulties that can arise due to differing goals and objectives.

Thus far, the parents have made several strategic decisions in establishing the IJV, including where to locate the new plant and who will be responsible for what functions. Davidson's preferences for how these decisions would be made were important influences in its selection of Marley as a partner. Located in Europe, Marley gave Davidson knowledge of the market. Far more than this, it gave it functional fit and personal contacts. While Marley understood the marketplace, Davidson had expertise in manufacturing the administrative systems. Thus, while Davidson supplied the technology and the systems, Marley supplied knowledge of the markets and the contacts needed to get the plant built

Locating the facility

Where to locate the plant was an important decision – and an early test of the parents' compatibility. Together, the parents gathered extensive information and visited many sites. Of value here was Davidson's position as a division of a large conglomerate that could provide tax and legal guidance. (Textron had an office in Brussels that provided this service.) During the initial site-selection process, Davidson collected information related to possible locations from the U.S. consulates of the relevant countries. According to Joe Paul, Vice President of Administration at Davidson, the consulates provided extensive information about business conditions; they also provided names and telephone numbers of employment agencies, training centers, union officers, and local business organizations. Davidson also acquired information from Deutsche Bank, the international banker for Textron.

The decision was made to locate in Born, the Netherlands. This decision was made after considering and eliminating France, West Germany, and Belgium. These four nations were possibilities because of their proximity to the Ford plant in Genk, Belgium, and because all four governments offer cash grants to firms locating in the coal region these nations share. With relatively high unemployment, the governments of the four nations offer incentives to firms regardless of parent-company nationality. The particular site in the Netherlands was selected because it is within thirty minutes of the Ford plant, a location that would facilitate compliance with Ford's just-in-time requirement.

According to Jonathan T. Hopkins, Vice President of Worldwide Business Development at Davidson, the location also was selected in part because labor unions in the area indicated a willingness to consider accepting job flexibility and a relatively small number of job classifications. These features were important to both parents because they operate using principles of employee involvement and egalitarianism. Both parents want these principles reflected in the management style of the new plant in Born. Davidson's experience in running a unionized plant in Canada proved valuable to foreseeing some of these labor-related issues.

Another important consideration was the availability of job applicants. The area now has a 15 percent unemployment rate. In addition, two government-controlled firms are expected to privatize and downsize, thus increasing the pool of applicants with work experience. These considerations were deemed by the parent companies to be more favorable in the Netherlands than in the other three nations.

HRM issues

As the establishment of the IJV between Davidson Instrument Panel and Marley continues over the next twelve months, six HRM issues are likely to unfold (Shenkar and Zeira, 1990). In light of the shared goals and objectives of the two partners, the extent to which these issues become problem areas may be minimal. Nevertheless, the substance of these issues needs to be addressed explicitly (Lorange, 1986).

Assignment of managers

Each partner may place differing priorities on the joint venture; therefore, a partner may assign relatively weak management resources to the venture. To be successful, not only should the assigned managerial resources have relevant capabilities and be of adequate quality, but the overall blend of these human resources must have a cultural dimension. Recognizing the importance of key personnel appointments, the parents have agreed to collaborate in the selection of a general manager. They already have agreed on the search firm that will help them identify candidates, and they now are in the process of jointly deciding the final criteria to be used in the selection process. Although the selection criteria are not yet finalized, Davidson has expressed some desire to have a person with manufacturing experience in plastics who is from the Netherlands. Once this individual is selected (scheduled for early 1991), he or she will come to Davidson's headquarters in New Hampshire for several months. During this time, the individual will become familiar with Davidson's technology, manufacturing systems, and HRM practices and philosophies.

Specific selection, performance appraisal, and compensation practices will be left to the discretion of the new general manager, but it is expected that this individual will adopt the Davidson-Marley philosophy of employee involvement participation, job flexibility, egalitarianism, and teamwork. These are practices both parents adopted in their own operations to facilitate high quality. Davidson and Marley feel that local labor councils are flexible and open to these practices, but the task of actually negotiating specifics will be done by the IJV's management staff. At that point, control issues are likely to become salient.

Transferability of human resources

Are the parents willing to transfer critical human resources to the new business

venture? Given the long time frame of most joint ventures, strategic human resources sometimes have to be transferred from the parent on a net basis during the initial phase. In this case, because of the skills of the two partners, Davidson Instrumental Panel is supplying the human resources relevant to the manufacturing systems and the administrative systems. Marley is responsible for actually building the plant but Davidson is designing the interior of the facility to fit its technology. In addition, Davidson already has assigned three design engineers from its facility in Walled Lake, Michigan, to be expatriates in Europe. These engineers work with fourteen contract designers recruited in Europe to design the component that will be manufactured in the plant. Marley has located a sales manager in the Netherlands, and will supply sales and marketing support to the company.

Davidson also will be supplying the new controller, who will install the administrative systems. Textron's accounting firm, which has offices in the United States and Europe, is ready to provide assistance to the financial officer who will eventually be selected for the IJV. (Textron's accounting firm also serves Davidson.) Davidson's accounting procedures will have to be adapted to the European environment, which will be done through the accounting office in Europe assisting the new financial officer. Over time, remaining HRM decisions will become the responsibility of the IJV as it begins to operate like an independent business organization.

Manager's time-spending patterns

The IJV has to carry out a set of operating duties simultaneously with its development of new strategies. This raises the issue of the appropriate emphasis to give operating and strategic tasks; sufficient human resources must be allocated for both. The situation is similar to that of an independent business organization: the IJV must be able to draw sufficient human resources from the operating mode to further develop its strategy. If the parent organizations place strong demands for short-term results on the IJV, this may leave it with insufficient resources to staff for strategic self-renewal. In this particular case, the need for strategic planning and new business development is somewhat less, owing to the expected availability of a major customer, namely Ford Motor Company. In addition, Marley's marketing expertise and knowledge of the Continent should serve as a support mechanism that minimizes the time the new IJV initially needs to spend on longer-term issues. Over time, the balance between focus on operations versus strategic planning will shift as the IJV becomes more independent and the short-term operating tasks become more manageable.

Human resource competency

Deciding how to evaluate IJV managers will be another major challenge. It has been claimed that several joint ventures have failed because of inappropriate staffing (Lorange, 1986). Myopic, biased parent organizations may make poor selection decisions, or they may be tempted to use the IJV to off-load surplus incompetent managers. Performance evaluation therefore is important. The long-term relationship and shared objectives of Davidson and Marley make inappropriate staffing decisions less likely in this case. Also, early decisions to limit reliance on expatriates to the controller and three design engineers are likely to minimize problems arising from off-loading surplus managers.

Management loyalty issues

Management of loyalty conflicts must be considered an integral part of the HRM of IJVs. Assigned executives (expatriates) usually are loyal to the IJV and are expected to stay with the IJV for a long period of time. If a conflict arises between parents and the IJV, management can be expected to side with the IJV. For Davidson and Marley, the assignments of design engineers and the controller are primarily for start-up purposes. These employees' loyalty may remain with Davidson because of the explicitly temporary nature of their assignments.

Career and benefits planning

A recent survey of expatriates found that 56 percent felt their overseas assignments were either immaterial or detrimental to their careers – a finding that indicates potential motivational problems any IJV may encounter. The motivation of executives assigned to an IJV can be enhanced by the creation of a clear linkage between the assignment and an assignee's future career. Some assurance of job security may be needed to offset perceived risks. As with any overseas assignment, assignment to a joint venture may make the manager's future career appear uncertain. If the parent company has not thought through this issue, this uncertainty may be justified. Thus, parent organizations should offer career planning to counter the ambiguity and risks associated with an IJV assignment and to limit the potential for unsatisfying repatriation experiences.

Apart from career-path disturbances, the assignment to an expatriate post usually requires relocation to a foreign country – with all the disruption to family and social life that such a posting entails. Benefits packages must be designed to maintain the economic and social lifestyle of the manager so that the individual does not lose through the IJV assignment. In the present case, the number of expatriate employees involved is so small that these issues have not been considered major. They will become more significant with the assignment of the controller. At that time, Davidson's own experience with R&D expatriates and the experience of Textron will be helpful.

Lorange (1986) argued that IJVs must have their own, strong, fully fledged HRM function. The individual in charge must establish ways to work closely with each parent company, particularly during the early years. The two major roles of the IJVs HRM function are (a) to assign and motivate people via job skills, compatibility of styles, and communication compatibility; and (b) to manage human resources strategically, so that the IJV is seen as a vehicle to produce not only financial rewards, but also managerial capabilities that can be used later in other strategic settings. To the extent that an IJV is staffed with temporary managerial assignees, transferring people to an IJV every few years would not result in strategic continuity of management.

In addition to the two major HRM roles noted by Lorange (1986), the new IJV will have to establish its own set of human resource practices, policies, and procedures. It will immediately use these to staff the new operation. We look forward to tracking this process with the new general manager, before and after production has begun.

Summary

In this article, we discussed several sources of potential risk for IJVs. A comparison of the research literature with the experience of one IJV (that of Davidson Instrument Panel in the United States and Marley in England) provided suggestions for U.S. firms contemplating an IJV in the near future. We also discussed several international HRM issues associated with IJVs, focusing on the initial human resource planning and selection decisions that two partners face in forming an IJV. Finally, we identified several unfolding international HRM issues that the two partners – Davidson and Marley – are likely to face over the next twenty-four months. These issues will be followed and will become subjects of subsequent articles [reproduced in the rest of this Appendix].

The formation of an international joint venture: Marley Automotive Components

Randall S. Schuler, Rutgers University, USA, Peter Dowling,
University of Canberra, Australia and Helen De Cieri,
Monash University, Australia

Executive summary

In Maidstone and Lenham in Kent, and Bitton near Bristol, England, is the operation of Marley Automotive Components Ltd. In the late 1980s it entered into an international joint venture (IJV) with the U.S. company Davidson Instrument Panel Textron of Portland, New Hampshire. An earlier article by the authors examined Davidson's perception of the IJV, including their reasons for the joint venture, the critical human resource issues they were facing and how they were planning to ideal with several unfolding human resource issues. This article now portrays Marley's perceptions of the same issues. The purpose in using this case study to describe IJV issues is to offer information on human resource issues to readers considering an IJV as the route to globalization. Hopefully, this information will help companies to increase the chances of a successful IJV experience.

Introduction

Because of increasing globalization and its attendant costs and risks, many firms are entering into international joint ventures (IJVs). Although joint venture formation is proving to be an integral part of business

strategy for multinational firms such as
Glaxo, Grandmet, IDV, and Thorn-EMI,
entering and operating them successfully
is by no means a sure thing (Main, 1990).
Research indicates that the failure rate
of IJVs is between 50 and 70 percent
(Harrigan, 1986; Levine and Byrne, 1986).
Some of the most significant barriers to
success involve people issues – issues
relating to international human resource
(HR) management. Consequently, these
issues are the focus of this article.

Specifically, this article describes many
of the international human resource issues
associated with forming and managing IJVs.
It does this through an intensive case study
of an IJV in its early stages of formation and
development. It addresses critical start-up
issues from the view of the British partner,
Marley Automotive Components Ltd.
These are the same issues addressed from
the view of the U.S. partner, Davidson
Instrument Panel, reported in an earlier
article (Schuler *et al.*, 1991). Given that
the IJV has developed since our first article,
this article also addressed several other
unfolding HR issues identified in that first
article [reproduced as the first part of this
Appendix].

The parents: Marley PLC and Davidson-Textron

Marley PLC

Marley is one of the leading manufacturers
of building materials in the United Kingdom
and has similar operations in many countries
throughout the world. Marley's products
extend from roof tiles, roofing felt, bricks,
aerated concrete blocks, and concrete paving
to PVC flooring, plastic plumbing, and
drainage goods. Marley also derives part of
its profit stream from property transactions
by exploiting the value of sites surplus
to operational requirements. In addition,
Marley is recognized and well established
as a major supplier of quality components to
the European motor industry. The particular

division that deals with the motor industry is
called Marley Automotive Components Ltd.
This division employs approximately 1,400
workers out of a total Marley workforce
of 11,000.

The nature of the automobile industry has
changed drastically during the past twenty
years, and the effects have been felt by all
auto makers. As the automobile industry has
become globalized, success has turned on
quality products that fit right and perform
smoothly and reliably. But while quality
has become a major concern to the auto
industry, so have cost and innovation.
New products and new technology are vital
to success, but without cost reduction, new
products cannot be offered at competitive
prices.

The characteristics of the auto industry
are, of course, reflected in all companies
supplying it. Marley Automotive
Components Ltd. is no exception. To
succeed, it must adapt to the demands of
the new environment. Doing so will bring
rewards such as market share and, even
more important perhaps, an extensive
cooperative relationship with major
automobile manufacturers.

Essentially gone are the days of the
multiple bidding system, where winning
meant delivering at the lowest cost, with
no assurance that the next year will be the
same. Today, the automobile companies
use sole sourcing for many of their supply
needs. Accompanying this is a greater sense
of shared destiny and mutual cooperation:
"The component suppliers are having, to
change with the times. The multinational
car manufacturers increasingly want to
deal with multinational suppliers, giving
them responsibility for the design and
development of sub-assemblies in return
for single supplier status" (*Financial Times*,
March 1, 1990: 8). Thus, it is not unusual to
have design engineers from suppliers doing
full engineering design of the components
they will supply to their customers.

An important aspect of the new cooperative,
sole sourcing arrangement adopted by
automotive makers is the willingness

to conceptualize and form longer-term relationships. For Marley Automotive this meant the opportunity to establish an international joint venture. In the summer of 1989, Marley agreed to establish an IJV to supply instrumentation panels to a Ford Motor Company plant in Belgium starting in 1993. It chose as its partner for this venture the U.S. firm Davidson Instrument Panel.

Davidson Instrument Panel

Davidson Instrument Panel is one of thirty-three divisions of Textron, an $8 billion conglomerate with its headquarters in Providence, Rhode Island. Davidson Instrument Panel and its two sister divisions, Interior Trim and Exterior Trim, make up Davidson-Textron. All three divisions are component suppliers to the automotive OEMs (original equipment manufacturers). Davidson-Textron is the largest independent supplier of instrument panels for the U.S. automobile industry.

Originally begun as a maker of rubber products for drug sundries in Boston in the early 1850s, Davidson moved its operations to Dover, New Hampshire, in the 1950s. Its headquarters now are located in Portsmouth. A staff in Portsmouth of fewer than fifty oversees the operations of two manufacturing plants: one in Port Hope, Ontario, and the second in Farmington, New Hampshire. The 1,000-person operation in Port Hope is unionized, and the 900-person operation in Farmington is not.

The IJV: Davidson-Marley BV

By way of review and update, Davidson Marley BV, the name of the IJV, is a fifty-fifty partnership between a U.S. firm and a British firm. It is located in Born, the Netherlands. Situated near Maastricht Airport, the location was selected because it is near Davidson Marley's primary customer, Ford. Proximity to Ford was important, because the company required

its sole source suppliers to meet its just-in-time inventory requirements. The location was also selected because of favorable accommodation by the local authorities and the fact that it is close to the Netherlands Car BV production plant (a potential customer). The facility is being constructed so that expansion can be easily incorporated and approved by the local council. The plot of land is sufficient for expanding by a factor of at least four.

There were several reasons for the IJV between Marley and Davidson. First, Ford Europe asked Marley (which had been supplying its needs for the Sierra line in the United Kingdom) to supply its needs for its world car to be produced at the Genk plant. Consistent with the world car concept, however, Ford Europe wanted worldwide sourcing. A joint arrangement with Davidson Instrument Panel made a great deal of sense. It filled the worldwide sourcing requirement and it was a company Marley knew and trusted. Marley had been a licensee of the Davidson technology for instrument panel skins and the foam injected to give it shape and substance.

This long-term arrangement had given each other time to get acquainted and learn about the other's management style and philosophy. The compatibility in their styles provided confidence that an IJV might be successful. They were also compatible in what they could contribute to an IJV. Marley had marketing skills, knowledge of the European market, and the ability to oversee construction of the new facility and provide administrative support. Davidson had the technological expertise and complementary administrative skills.

Another reason for the IJV was to share the risk of a new venture. While Davidson wanted to get into Europe and Marley wanted to expand its automotive business, there was no guarantee that Ford would be successful in Genk. Marley's primary businesses are construction related. To reduce its dependence on the construction cycle, it had decided to expand its automotive business. However, Marley did not want to do this without minimizing the risks. The sharing of rewards was worth the sharing of the risk with a long-term business associate.

A joint venture with Davidson at a greenfield site in Born also offered Marley the opportunity to introduce a new management style and structure. During the 1980s, more than 100 Japanese firms have established operations in the United Kingdom. In doing so, they have implemented their human resource practices of workforce flexibility, minimal job classifications, and use of teams with a total quality strategy. Though practically unknown in British industry, including Marley's other operations, these practices seemed to be working well. They are described in extensive detail by Peter Wickens, the personnel director of Nissan Motor Manufacturing UK (1988). The opening of the greenfield site in the Netherlands, and also the creation of another joint venture in the United Kingdom with a Japanese company, offered Marley the opportunity to learn more about the Japanese policies and practices and possibly extend them to other operations. This desire was certainly consistent with Davidson's methods of operations, since it has implemented many similar practices in its plants in New Hampshire and Ontario, Canada.

In deciding upon the IJV arrangement, Marley and Davidson had a choice here: they could either build on a greenfield site or take over a brownfield site. While the brownfield option is faster and avoids all the aspects of construction, the two partners thought it was more important to build to their own specifications. It was critical to both that everything be designed to be compatible with a teamwork, flexible job assignment orientation.

A final reason for the IJV location was the potential it offered for competitive flexibility. Locating the plant in Born places it near Audi, Volkswagen, Mercedes, and Volvo operations. While these companies often supply their own instrument panel needs, Davidson-Marley BV could potentially offer a better product at a lower price. To help develop this potential, Marley established a small marketing company.

While the list is not meant to be exhaustive, these were the major reasons for the IJV from Marley's perspective. They are certainly consistent with Davidson's motives and with those suggested in the literature (Datta, 1989; O'Reilly, 1988; Gomes-Casseres, 1989; Harrigan, 1987a; 1987b; Main, 1990; Shenkar and Zeira, 1987a). Nonetheless, this does not ensure success or diminish the risk of failure.

Reducing the risk of IJV failure

Managing IJVs can be very difficult. The difficulties, and thus the reasons for failure, include;

- The partners cannot get along.
- Managers from different partners within the venture cannot work together.
- Managers within the venture cannot work with the owners' managers.
- Partners simply renege on their promises.
- Markets disappear.
- The technology involved does not prove as good as expected.

Both Marley and Davidson think that they can overcome the odds of failure in their IJV. Much of their confidence rests on the fact that they know what it takes for a good partnership to survive and flourish:

1 shared objectives (a joint mission);
2 cooperation as equals (based on parity, no domination or paternalism);
3 openness, mutual trust and respect of others as persons and their values, capabilities, and objective understanding of their intentions;
4 building on each other's strengths;
5 reducing each other's limitations;
6 each has something the other needs (resources, access, etc.);
7 pooled capabilities and resources permit taking on tasks neither could do alone;
8 two-way flow of communication

(breakthrough of communication blocks);

9 mutually perceived benefits;

10 commitment of leadership and middle management to find some shared values, without ignoring the fact that they are not identical;

11 co-learning flexibility;

12 a win–win orientation.

Despite the many positive features of the Davidson-Marley BV IJV, there is a consensus that the very nature of joint ventures contributes to their failure – they are a difficult and complex form of enterprise (see Brown, 1990; Main, 1990; Shenkar and Zeira, 1987b). As described in our earlier article (Schuler *et al.*, 1991), the critical issues which IJVs face revolve around *control, conflict, goals, management styles*, and *degrees of commitment*.

Who controls the IJV – from its inception through to the early critical staffing appointments – can lead to failure. The Davidson-Marley BV IJV has a board of directors with two members from each parent. All major decisions are to be decided by this board. Whenever local Dutch management or their staff encounter key issues, the board decides. To ensure that IJV development and production deadlines are not compromised, Ford requested that Marley retains one less share in voting on major issues until production starts in January 1993. This arrangement would help address any critical issues of control and conflict if such were to arise during the start-up period.

Other positive factors included joint selection of the general manager and human resource manager, and an arrangement whereby Marley supplies the local marketing knowledge and makes the arrangements with the local suppliers, while Davidson supplies the technology and the financial systems (including the financial controller for the operation). These arrangements thus remove many potential disagreements and conflict, and form part of the IJV agreement. Thus, errors of omission are avoided by extensive discussion of issues and formal recording of all agreements.

In terms of goals, management styles, and degrees of commitment, Marley believes that it has compatibility with Davidson on these three issues. It is important that firms interested in IJVs give serious consideration to the degree of cultural homogeneity. This is particularly the case with regard to North American and Western European countries, which share a similar Western cultural heritage. These cultural similarities tend to obscure difficulties. Such obfuscation is all the more likely when the differences are subtle, and not obvious during initial negotiations. For example, when dealing with Asian firms, because Western managers *expect* differences, they will be more sensitive to cultural diversity. When dealing with firms that are perceived to be culturally similar, managers will be less sensitive to differences which while being subtle are still important (Brown, 1990).

As a case in point, there are important differences in language usage between English-speaking countries: Americans tend to use the term "plant" to refer to the building in which operations take place and machinery is located, while the British use the term "plant" to include machinery. "Natural wastage" means voluntary resignations and retirements in the United Kingdom but something rather different in the United States, where it means leaving through natural attrition! It is important that both parties to a joint venture clearly define key terms early on in discussions to minimize the problems attendant with miscommunication. This suggests that firms entering into a joint venture establish a glossary of terms regardless of whether they think they have a common language. Where differences in definition exist or in broader matters such as what selection methods to use, it seems advisable to go with local custom.

Thus while it appears as if Marley and Davidson are on top of the critical issues that can give rise to IJV failure, they still face many human resource issues that are beginning to unfold in the evolution of their partnership. These issues include the assignment of managers, transferability of human resource, managers' time-spending patterns, human resource competency, management loyalty issues, and career benefits and planning (Shenkar and Zeira, 1990). The following sections show Marley's views on these issues.

The assignment of managers

The general manager for the IJV has been selected. He was selected by both parent firms from three Dutch short-listed candidates identified by the search firm Spencer Stuart. The process was done in a way consistent with European practices. Marley recognized the importance of adjusting to the employment practices of the host country rather than just imposing parent-country practices on the otherwise local (i.e., European) operations. While there is considerable divergence with regard to the development of relatively high minimum standards of employment conditions as a consequence of European integration, there is divergence in terms of both specific human resource practices and implementation of HR policies. For example, in comparing the UK and France on the use of reference checking, "UK firms are still using references as proof of someone's fitness to do the job. More than 70 per cent of UK firms use them compared with just over 11 per cent in France" (*Personnel Today*, February 5, 1991: 5).

In selecting the general manager for the IJV, Marley gave significant weight to experience in manufacturing. Interviews were used to evaluate the degree of fit with the operating style and management philosophy of the parents. Employment tests such as tests measuring aptitude and personality were not used.

Once appointed, the general manager participated in selection of the IJV's human resource manager in February 1991, which was done using a similar process. These managerial appointments coincided with the final property purchase and ground breaking for the new plant.

While both of these individuals could have been brought in even earlier to achieve greater feelings of ownership and involvement, this was not done owing to cost considerations and the need to carry out these initial recruitment assignments jointly. However, this group has now been given the freedom to select, appraise, train, and compensate the 250–300 employees who will be hired by August 1992. The current, relatively high unemployment rate in this region (around 8–9 percent) should ensure a sufficiently large applicant pool. Although Marley had nominal lead responsibility for initial recruitment, the strategy for recruitment, training, and compensation was developed jointly by senior human resource executives at Davidson and Marley agreed upon by the Davidson-Marley board.

Transferability of human resources

Both parent firms are committed to the success of the IJV and are transferring experienced employees to it. Even with the most systematic planning process, unforeseen events will occur. For example, the engineers assigned to design the plant were supplied by Davidson. While highly qualified, they calculated measurements in feet, inches, and U.S. gallons. The local Dutch engineers had to convert these non-metric measures when letting contracts to Dutch firms and gaining approval from local authorities. Since Davidson will supply the financial controller, U.S. accounting procedures will be used and a corresponding set of accounts will need to be established to meet Dutch auditing requirements.

Allocation of start-up responsibilities

Initially, IJV staff will need to focus on immediate, short-term issues in establishing the joint venture. The IJV staff are not under pressure to produce an immediate profit since the business plan allows for a reasonable time horizon to achieve profitability. Marley has established a sales and marketing group in the Netherlands for the IJV to look for new contracts. Both parent firms will offer training programs and support, including technical training for key employees who will in turn train the other employees. Start-up costs will be shared by both parent companies.

Conflicts of loyalty

For both parent companies, the work of the planning teams is essentially completed. The financial controller (a U.S. expatriate) is scheduled for a three-year term, after which a local will take over. The staff will then be entirely Davidson-Marley BV, and conflicts of loyalty to either parent company should be minimal – particularly as the venture grows and achieves success, according to Mr. Chris Ellis, Business Development Director of Marley.

The general manager and his key staff members are employed by Davidson-Marley BV and as such have career paths anchored within the joint venture rather than the parent companies.

Progress to date

To date, the two parent companies of Davidson-Marley BV appear to be benefiting from a careful planning process and a longer-term perspective with regard to profitability. Although trial production runs are just beginning at the time of writing, there have been no obvious signs of partnership dissolution or disaster. Nonetheless, both parents are monitoring their relationship, checking for danger signals of a deteriorating relationship, including the existence of statements such as the following:

1 "They have long term objectives, we don't."
2 "They get more than they give."
3 "Their strengths (market access) were overestimated."

4 "We don't communicate any more; we just let them do their thing."
5 "They compete with us more than they cooperate."
6 "They (or we) haven't assigned the best people."
7 "Our combined decision making is too slow, compared to the competition."
8 "We are not organized to learn from them (or our people don't feel they can learn much from them), but they absorb everything we give them."
9 "We have agreed that the best way to work is not to work together."
10 "They are developing organizational capabilities that will make us unnecessary in the future."
11 "Whoever cooked up this deal was pretty naive."
12 "Our commitment to the success of this partnership is *declining* rapidly: mutual trust and respect are minimal."

Conclusion

For an increasing number of firms in many countries, "going international" is no longer a choice – regardless of firm size or product. The world has become far too interconnected for many products and services to be offered within a domestic market context only. Faced with this reality, many firms in the advanced Western economies are seeking to establish their presence in the world market. For example, many large British firms such as BP, ICI, and Marks & Spencer have already developed a global presence. These firms entered the global arena relatively early via the direct establishment of their own subsidiaries. This mode of internationalization is less of an option for many firms today because the establishment of subsidiaries requires substantial commitment of time and resources.

Thus many firms are considering entry into global markets via various forms of cooperative venture and strategic partnerships. One form of partnership currently receiving considerable attention is the international joint venture (IJV). The IJV is popular because both parties are able to share risk exposure (i.e., political and financial risk) and to optimize the strengths of each partner (e.g., cash, experience, or technology). There are, however, many potential problems involved with the establishment of an IJV. These problems are often related to the quality of the relationship between the two partners, and the human resource decisions that flow from the relationship. We believe the Davidson-Marley BV case is a good example of an IJV where both partners have worked hard to develop the initial relationship and have taken human resource issues into consideration throughout the planning process. While this does not guarantee that Davidson-Marley BV will be successful, we believe the behaviors of the parent firms to date are good predictors for the future success of the IJV.

Note

The authors express their appreciation for the support provided by a research grant from the Human Resource Planning Society, New York, and for generous time and assistance from Chris Ellis, Business Development Director, and Norman Taylor, Personnel Manager, both of Marley Automotive Components Ltd.

Davidson-Marley BV: establishing and operating an international joint venture

Randall S. Schuler, Rutgers University, U.S.A., and Ed van Sluijs, GTIP, The Netherlands

Executive summary

The company of Davidson-Marley BV, the international joint venture (IJV) of Davidson Instrument Panel (U.S.) and Marley PLC (U.K.), is situated in Born in the Netherlands. Two previous articles [reproduced as the first two parts of this Appendix] described this IJV from the viewpoints of the two parents. This article is primarily dedicated to describing it from the viewpoint of the IJV itself. In particular, the views of the general manager and the human resources manager are presented in order to describe their perceptions of how well the IJV was established and how well it is poised for the future. These views describe the relationships not only with the parents themselves but also with the local community, with particular emphasis on the human resource practices that are both feasible and effective in the Netherlands. Together with the two previous articles, the intent of this investigation is to provide readers interested in international joint ventures with as much useful information about the human resource management (HRM) issues as possible. The major goal has been to advance our understanding of how IJVs can be more effectively established and managed.

Introduction

For an increasing number of firms in many countries, "going international" is no longer a choice but a necessity – regardless of firm size or product. The world has become far too interconnected for many products and services to be offered within a domestic market context only. Faced with this reality, many firms in the advanced Western economies are seeking to establish their presence in the world market. For example, many large British firms such as BP, ICI, and Marks & Spencer have already developed a global presence. These firms entered the global arena relatively early via the direct establishment of their own subsidiaries. This mode of internationalization is less of an option for many firms today because the establishment of subsidiaries requires substantial commitment of time and resources.

Thus, many firms are considering entry into global markets via various forms of cooperative venture and strategic partnerships. One form of partnership currently receiving considerable attention is the international joint venture (IJV). The IJV is popular because both parties are able to share risk exposure (i.e., political and financial risk) and to optimize the strengths of each partner (e.g., cash, experience, or technology). There are, however, many potential problems involved with the establishment of an IJV. These problems are often related to the quality of the relationship between the two partners, and the human resource decisions that flow from the relationship. These problems, however, may be minimized by having an understanding of them before entering into an IJV. Accordingly, a study was designed whereby a base of understanding could be provided to those interested in IJVs. This is the third and final part in the study that has as its primary focus the HRM issues in international joint ventures.

The first part of the study described the U.S. parent of the IJV, Davidson Instrument Panel (Schuler *et al.*, 1991). In the second part the British parent is described (Schuler *et al.*, 1992). In this, the third part, we are describing the IJV itself, Davidson-Marley BV.

Background

By way of review and update, Davidson-Marley BV is a fifty-fifty partnership. It is located in Born, the Netherlands. Situated near Maastricht Airport, the location was selected because it is near Davidson-Marley's primary customer, Ford. Ford is located in Genk, Belgium, less than 45 minutes by truck. Proximity to Ford is important, because the company require its sole source suppliers to meet its just-in-time delivery and sequential delivery requirements. The location was also selected because of favorable accommodation by the local authorities and the fact that it is close to the Netherlands Car (NedCar) BV production plant (a potential customer) and other car manufacturers. The facility has been constructed so that expansion can be easily incorporated and approved by the local council of Born. The plot of land is sufficient for expanding by a factor of at least four. To provide a perspective for this description of Davidson-Marley BV, here is a review of the two parents and the reasons for their decision to enter into an international joint venture.

Marley PLC

Marley is one of the leading manufacturers of building materials in the United Kingdom and has similar operations in many countries throughout the world, Marley's products extend from roof tiles, roofing felt, bricks, aerated concrete blocks, and concrete paving to PVC flooring, plastic plumbing, and drainage goods.

Marley also derives part of its profit stream from property transactions by exploiting the value of sites surplus to operational requirements. In addition, Marley is recognized and well established as a major supplier of quality components to the European motor industry. The particular division that deals with the motor industry is called Marley Automotive Components Ltd. This division employs approximately 1,400 workers out of a total Marley workforce of 11,000.

The nature of the automobile industry has changed drastically during the past twenty years, and the effects have been felt by all auto makers. As the automobile industry has become globalized, success has turned on quality products that fit right and perform smoothly and reliably. But while quality has become a major concern to the auto industry, so have cost and innovation. New products and new technology are vital to success, but without cost reduction, new products cannot be offered at competitive prices.

The characteristics of the auto industry are, of course, reflected in all companies supplying it. Marley Automotive Components Ltd. is no exception. To succeed, it must adapt to the demands of the new environment. Doing so will bring rewards, such as market share, and even more important perhaps, an extensive cooperative relationship with major automobile manufacturers. Essentially gone are the days of the multiple bidding system, where winning meant delivering at the lowest cost, with no assurance that the next year will be the same. Today, the automobile companies use sole sourcing for many of their supply needs. Accompanying this is a greater sense of shared destiny and mutual cooperation: "The component suppliers are having to change with the times. The multinational car manufacturers increasingly want to deal with multinational suppliers, giving them responsibility for the design and development of sub-assemblies in return for single supplier status" (*Financial Times*, March 1, 1990: 8). Thus it is not unusual to have design engineers from suppliers doing full engineering design of the components they will supply to their customers.

An important aspect of the new cooperative, sole sourcing arrangement adopted by the automotive makers is the willingness to conceptualize and form longer-term relationships. For Marley Automotive this meant the opportunity to establish an international joint venture. In the summer of 1989, Marley agreed to establish an IJV to supply instrument panels to a Ford Motor Company plant in Belgium starting in 1993. It chose as its partner for this venture the U.S. firm Davidson Instrument Panel.

Davidson Instrument Panel

Davidson Instrument Panel is one of thirty-three divisions of Textron, an $8 billion conglomerate with its headquarters Providence, Rhode Island. Davidson Instrument Panel and its two sister divisions, Interior Trim and Exterior Trim, make up Davidson-Textron. All three divisions are component suppliers to the automotive OEMs (original equipment manufacturers). Davidson-Textron is the largest independent supplier of instrument panels for the US automobile industry.

Originally begun as a maker of rubber products for drug sundries in Boston in the early 1850s, Davidson moved its operations to Dover, New Hampshire, in the 1950s. Its headquarters now are located in Portsmouth, New Hampshire. A staff in Portsmouth of fewer than fifty oversees the operations of two manufacturing plants, one in Port Hope, Ontario, and the second in Farmington, New Hampshire. The 1,000-person operation in Port Hope is unionized, and the 900-person operation in Farmington is not.

Reasons for the IJV

There are many reasons for IJVs; none of them guarantees success.

There are several reasons why Marley PLC and Davidson decided on this international joint venture. First, Ford Europe asked Marley (which had been supplying its needs for the Sierra line in the United Kingdom) to supply its needs for its world car to be produced at the Genk plant. Consistent with the world car concept, however, Ford Europe wanted worldwide sourcing. A joint arrangement with Davidson Instrument Panel made a great deal of sense. It filled the worldwide sourcing requirement and it was a company Marley knew and trusted. Marley had been a licensee of the Davidson technology for instrument panel skins and the foam injected to give it shape and substance.

Another reason for the IJV was to share the risk of a new venture. While Davidson wanted to get into Europe and Marley wanted to expand its automotive business, there was no guarantee that Ford would be successful in Genk. Marley's primary businesses are construction related. To reduce its dependence on the construction cycle, it had decided to expand its automotive business. However, Marley did not want to do this without minimizing the risks. The sharing of rewards was worth the sharing of the risks with a long-time business associate.

A joint venture with Davidson at a greenfield site in Born also offered Marley the opportunity to learn more about modern manufacturing management style and structure. In the IJV itself, they are implementing human resource practices of workforce flexibility, minimal job classifications, and use of teams with a total quality strategy. These modern manufacturing practices are described in extensive detail by Peter Wickens, the personnel director of Nissan Motor Manufacturing UK (1988). The opening of the greenfield site in the Netherlands offered Marley the opportunity to learn more about these new management practices and possibly extend them to other operations. This desire was certainly consistent with Davidson's methods of operation, since it has implemented many similar practices in its plants in New Hampshire and Ontario, Canada.

A final reason for the IJV location was the potential it offered for competitive flexibility. Locating the plant in Born places it near Audi, Volkswagen, Mercedes and NedCar operations. While these companies often supply their own instrument panel needs, Davidson-Marley BV could potentially offer a better product at a lower price. To help develop this potential, Marley established a small marketing company.

While not meant to be exhaustive, these were the major reasons for the IJV. They are certainly consistent with those suggested in the literature (Datta, 1988; Gomes-Casseres,

1989; Harrigan, 1987a, b; Main, 1990; O'Reilly, 1988; Shenkar and Zeira, 1987a). Nonetheless, this does not ensure success nor diminish the risk of failure.

Davidson-Marley BV

As described in the two previous articles, both parents thought that their relationship with each other would minimize the risks of their IJV. Despite the many positive features of the Davidson-Marley BV IJV, there is a consensus that the very nature of joint ventures contributes to their failure – they are a difficult and complex form of enterprise (see Brown, 1990; Main, 1990; Shenkar and Zeira, 1987b). As described in our earlier articles (Schuler *et al.*, 1991, 1992, reprinted as the earlier parts of this Appendix), the critical issues that IJVs face revolve around *control, conflict, goals, management styles*, and *degrees of commitment*.

While it appears as if Marley and Davidson were on top of the critical issues that could give rise to IJV failure, there are many other important human resource issues that are specifically related to the evolution of their partnership. These issues include the selection of managers, transferability of human resources, and conflicts of loyalty issues (Shenkar and Zeira, 1990). Whereas the two previous articles had the parents' views on these earlier issues and some of the evolving issues, the following section has those of Davidson-Marley BV.

Selection of managers

The general manager

The general manager for the IJV, Mr. Huub Cilissen, has been selected. He was selected by both parent firms from three Dutch short-listed candidates identified by the search firm Spencer Stuart. In selecting the general manager for the IJV, the parents gave significant weight to experience in manufacturing. Interviews were used to evaluate the degree of fit with the operating style and management philosophy of the parents. Employment tests measuring aptitude and personality were not used.

An important consideration in the final selection of Mr. Cilissen appears to have been the fact that he was from the region. Born is located in the southern province of Limburg, an area that has distinctive social customs and dialect. While the selection of a Dutch person from outside this region might not have proven detrimental to the IJV's operation, having a local person offers many advantages in a small facility with a participative, egalitarian management style.

As indicated in our earlier articles, the final decision to hire the general manager was delayed about a year for several reasons including salary costs. According to Mr. Cilissen, however, all agree that this delay has proven to be more costly than any possible savings. Thus instead of being hired in October 1990 (only five months before ground breaking), he should have been hired in October 1989. Local contracts, contracts, agreements, and discussions had to begin in 1989, so the parents had to hire consulting firms. His earlier involvement would have eliminated this and provided him with more opportunities to get involved. It is important for IJV parents to remember that they are hiring a local general manager to be responsible for their operation. Without providing significant autonomy and responsibility from the earliest possible point, the potential to select the best candidate may be diminished.

The human resource manager

Once appointed, the general manager participated in the selection of the IJV's human resource manager in February 1991. The actual selection process, however, was begun in parallel with the selection of the general manager.

The human resource manager, Mr. Jean Theuns, was also brought in through a search firm. His upbringing in Limburg and previous successful work as human resource manager in a Japanese subsidiary in the Netherlands were two very positive qualities for his selection.

The facility manager

Concurrent with the appointment of the general manager and the human resource manager was the selection of the facility manager, Mr. Herman Vaassen, also Dutch. He was also identified by a search firm and hired on the basis of the same criteria as the human resource and general managers. Together, these three operated very much like a trio in working their way into the operation that the two parents had already begun to establish for them.

During their hiring process these three had been informed that the operation of the plant was "up to them." Reality set in quickly once they were hired. With fairly detailed plans already written by the two parents, the actual degree of freedom these three had over their respective areas was rather minimal. These three suggested that for the purpose of creating greater feelings of involvement and ownership, the parents of the IJV could have at least been more subtle in introducing their plans, budgets, and ways of operating. For example, they could have just introduced rather broad guidelines and policies and then left it up to the IJV managers to develop the specific applications. Perhaps because the two parents were operating in a foreign country, they felt a greater need to structure policies and practices in order to minimize risk and uncertainty.

The degree of freedom given to newly recruited IJV senior managers is a sensitive matter. While these three individuals could have been brought in even earlier to achieve greater feelings of ownership and involvement, they were nevertheless given the freedom to select, appraise, train, and compensate the 150–200 employees who were hired in the autumn of 1992. Although Marley had nominal lead responsibility for initial recruitment, the strategy for recruitment, training, and compensation was developed jointly by senior human resource executives at Davidson and Marley and agreed upon by the Davidson-Marley board (two members from Marley and two from Davidson). It is now, however, clearly in the hands of Mr. Theuns to operate the human resource activities. Because these activities represent an important, and perhaps unique, way of successfully operating in the Netherlands, they are described in specific detail in a later section of the article.

Transferability of human resources and allocation of start-up responsibilities

Both parent firms are committed to the success of the IJV and have transferred experienced employees to the IJV. For example, Davidson transferred in the first engineering manager and first facility manager. Again, to maximize the motivation of the general manager, these expatriates need to serve under specific conditions. First, they need to serve for a limited and specified period of time. Second, they must work with their locally hired counterparts. In particular, this means that they must transfer their knowledge and authority quickly to the local managers and then leave. Delay in exit only delays the time when the IJV feels it is standing tall and operating under its own direction. To ensure that the general manager has as much start-up responsibility and autonomy as possible (which is necessary), it is also useful for parents to attenuate any desire to establish an extensive book of rules and procedures according to which the IJV must operate.

Conflicts of loyalty

For both parent companies, the work of the planning teams is essentially completed. The financial controller (a U.S. expatriate) is scheduled for a three-year term, after which a local will take over. The staff will then be entirely Davidson-Marley BV, and conflicts

of loyalty to either parent company should be minimal – particularly as the venture grows and achieves success. The general manager and his key staff members are employed by Davidson-Marley BV and as such have career paths anchored within the joint venture rather than the parent companies. Mr. Cilissen, Mr. Theuns, and Mr. Vaasen believe that their future is with Davidson-Marley BV. The business potential is very significant for the firm and thus there is a great potential for growth and expansion of the operations in the Netherlands.

Progress to date

To date, the two parent companies and Davidson-Marley BV appear to be benefiting from a careful, although perhaps too detailed, planning process and a longer-term perspective with regard to profitability. In July 1992, the IJV started its first shipments (100 instrument panels for the Chrysler minivan). These shipments were largely assemblies based upon parts supplied by the Davidson plant in Port Hope, Ontario. By January 4, 1993, shipments to its major customer, Ford, commence. These shipments will represent products manufactured and assembled at the Born plant.

As of January 4, 1993 the Born plant will have approximately 200 people, mostly production associates. Because of its sole supplier status with Ford, it operates under just-in-time manufacturing and delivery procedures. Increasingly, however, the trend is for customers such as Ford to insist upon their suppliers using sequential manufacturing and delivery procedures. The managers at Davidson-Marley BV are confident that their associates will be capable of performing effectively even under this more exacting production schedule. Exactly how these people are selected and managed is described in the next section.

Human resource management (HRM) in the Netherlands: realities and possibilities

Starting a greenfield site always means considerable work has to be done in establishing new policies and practices in every field, including human resource (HR) management. Starting an IJV means that not only do the perspectives of both parents have to be considered, but also the policies and practices must be kept in line with local circumstances (laws, culture and labor market conditions). Both parents of the Born IJV initially formulated the strategy for recruitment, training, and compensation. However, as mentioned earlier, involvement of the HR manager, Mr. Theuns, at an earlier stage of the planning process could have prevented some of the necessary adjustments to local and national circumstances that had to be made. Three months after Mr. Theuns was appointed, a detailed HR strategy was formulated wherein quite a substantial number of changes were incorporated with respect to the initial parents' plan. However, both parents fully acknowledge the necessity of these changes, and Mr. Theuns is now clearly responsible for the HR activities.

Obviously, the first operational challenge for Mr. Theuns, the HR manager, was to fully staff the IJV with the required number of people who possessed the proper qualifications. To do so, however, a number of preparatory activities in the area of *terms of employment* had to be planned and executed. Among others, these involved the establishment of job descriptions, the salary structure, the employment terms, and safety regulations. Once these had been approved by the parents, the actual recruiting started.

Starting from scratch in the Netherlands made it possible to define an HR strategy without having to consult either the unions or a company works council, simply because there were no parties yet with which to discuss issues. Once the IJV was operating, however, unions or work council representatives could become involved in issues related to HR strategy and working conditions.

There were, however, some national laws concerning working conditions and shift work which, together with cultural issues, had to be taken into account when designing a new plant. Also, Mr. Theuns firmly believed that companies had a moral obligation to offer attractive work to people with diverse backgrounds. This was in line with the company policy of establishing workforce flexibility, minimal job classifications, and use of teams with a total quality strategy. This tradition of group work, and the related sociotechnical systems design, has been widely used by various companies throughout the Netherlands since the 1960s. It was clearly reflected in the way the IJV executes its activities regarding human resource management. This is illustrated in more detail in the following presentation.

Some national characteristics affecting firms in the Netherlands

Before we turn to more specific HR issues and practices, more has to be said concerning legal issues, particularly industrial relations, that relate to work and organization in the Netherlands.

Industrial relations

Dutch industrial relations can be characterized by the great emphasis that is placed on mutual consultation and cooperation at all levels. On a national level, employers' federations and trade unions meet in various institutions, with or without government representatives and individual members. At this level, discussions take place about incomes policies, prices, labor markets, and employment and other macroeconomic and noneconomic issues such as social security. Resulting from these discussions are recommendations to the central government as well as to the various employers' federations and unions.

However, one of the main characteristics of Dutch industrial relations is that the influence of the unions, at the company level, is relatively small when compared to that in other countries like the United States or the United Kingdom. It is at the industry/sector level that the unions play their most important role. The percentage of employees unionized in the Netherlands is also relatively low when compared to other industrial countries (about 30 percent).

At the industry/sector levels, employers' federations and unions meet primarily to negotiate collective agreements per sector. The main focus within these agreements is concerned with the terms of employment, but less financially oriented aspects are also part of many collective agreements, such as working times, vacations, safety, and vocational training. The collective agreements contain a general set of agreed-upon regulations which have to be taken into account when establishing individual labor contracts at company level.

On a company level, the number of company agreements, replacing the broader industry-wide collective agreements, is growing. On the company level are the company works councils. These councils are regulated by law, and the employer is obligated to install a works council if there are more than thirty-five employees. Members of the works council are directly elected and the management of the company is not part of it. Management and works council meet at least six times a year. Competency and responsibilities of the works council contain the right for advice pertaining to decisions or plans regarding, for instance, restructuring, major investments, major changes in activities of the company, and changes in the geographical place where the activities are carried out. Also important is the right for approval: management needs the approval of the works council regarding decisions about pension schemes, working time, and vocation regulations, compensation and job classification systems and regulations pertaining to, for instance, recruitment,

training, appraisal, group work discussions, and dealing with complaints. Approval is not necessary, however, when these issues are being dealt with in the collective agreement.

As mentioned earlier, the unions play a rather small role at the company level. Like many individual companies, Davidson-Marley BV prefers to deal with the works council rather than with the unions, because the works council is more likely to be oriented toward the well-being of the company and its employees, whereas the unions are more oriented towards the general relations between employers and employees on a national and industry/sector level. However, in many cases the unions have members taking part in the company works councils, creating a situation in which a works council can be built up of union members of different unions and independent members (nonunion members). Although it is not the case at Davidson-Marley BV, unions can have some indirect influence at the company level, and recently in a number of companies the union started to discuss technological innovations separately with the management. Technology has for a long time been a neglected issue within the unions and they are now paying more attention by, for instance, establishing so-called technology agreements with the management at the company level.

A final aspect of the specific Dutch circumstances we would like to mention here is the Law on Working Conditions. In this law, rules and regulations are formulated pertaining to the safety, health, and well-being of employees. Regulations are directed towards the quality of work, the quality of working conditions, and the perception of the working situation. For instance, work should be adjusted to the person (ergonomics), short-cyclic work or machine-packed work should be avoided, work should add to the technical and personal development of employees, and the use of dangerous materials and equipment should be avoided. The law also stipulates that regular consultation should take place between employers and employees concerning working conditions. In this respect, the works council is required to fulfill certain obligations, although in certain related fields it has limited authority.

In general, it is clear that the industrial relations system concerning working conditions has an influence on the organization, on the quality of work, and on physical working conditions such as lighting, noise, ventilation, the layout of offices and production halls, hygienic circumstances, etc. Not complying with the law is considered to be an economic offence.

Organization

The Davidson-Marley IJV is organized as a flexible, flat, and lean organization with no more than four hierarchical layers, based on the ideas of group work wherein responsibilities are shared by all members of the group. Production work operates in three eight-hour shifts, headed by shift coordinators. It is obligatory in the Netherlands to rotate shifts, and this is being done from day shift to evening shift and night shift (on a three-week basis). Each group within the shifts consists of various associates: (1) trainees; (2) semi-skilled operators who execute relatively simple tasks, including maintenance and quality assurance; and (3) skilled all-round operators who are responsible for the more difficult tasks such as the adjustment of the machines. In addition, twenty-five trainer/operators were appointed who are responsible for training the other associates on how to execute the various tasks. These trainer/operators were sent to a Davidson plant in Canada for a general training in operating the machines and teaching skills to other associates. These trainer/operators are being offered normal production associate positions once the initial training has been done and the production is in full swing.

Recruitment and selection

In a greenfield situation, recruiting and selecting the employees is one of the major HR tasks. In June 1992, the IJV was staffed with a number of professionals including the product engineer, quality engineer, tooling engineer, and facility engineer as well as some ten production associates of around 200 started in May 1992. The staffing process was executed in a well-planned manner.

The input for the recruitment process was formed by governmental agencies, external recruitment services, and activities carried out by Davidson-Marley BV itself through newspaper advertisements and attendance at a regional job fair. Although one of the reasons for locating the IJV in Born was the relatively high unemployment figure, most of the people who reacted as potential employees were already employed by other companies in the region.

Initially a total of 6,000 applicants applied, of whom 2,000 were potential production associates. All of these 6,000 were soon sent a letter, indicating either nonacceptance of their application or informing them about the IJV and the next step in the selection procedure. This was part of the public relations activities carried out during the recruitment period, aimed at reaching as many people as possible. Of these 2,000, some 1,500 remained and were invited to visit the IJV for more information. This was done in groups whose function it was also to allow the assessment of the candidates by the HR manager and a production associate. The remaining 600 candidates were given psychological tests, designed by a consulting firm, assessing their personality, flexibility, and sociability. They were also sent a videotape presenting the Davidson-Marley BV plant. Next, 400 people were invited for an interview with the HR manager and one of the production associates to see whether he or she would fit the job and the organization and had the right motivation to work in teams. The last filter in the selection process was a very general medical examination, assessing general physical fitness. Applicants were not tested for drugs, alcohol, or AIDS. Finally, 200 people were offered a labor contract.

The entire recruitment and selection process was very time-consuming. However, Davidson-Marley IJV thought it was necessary to execute it like this in order to be able to attract the right people for the teamwork being offered. Since it is very difficult in the Netherlands to fire people once they are hired, a number of people were hired on a temporary contract basis by the IJV itself. As sole supplier to Ford, Davidson-Marley BV is operating by just-in-time manufacturing and sequential delivery procedures. This puts special emphasis on production and transport procedures. In order to meet the demands, Davidson-Marley BV is planning to send production associates to the Ford plant for one day to learn about the assembly work there and the issues that may be important for the production work at the Born plant. This is a particularly important aspect of the training effort of the IJV, because of the growing strength of the production and assembly links between Davidson-Marley BV and Ford. At the same time, it clearly shows the emphasis the Born plant puts on the importance and responsibilities of the production associates.

Obviously, being able to set training needs requires detailed descriptions of the work to be executed and the skills needed for the work. Since working in teams is a major aspect of working at Davidson-Marley BV, the IJV decided not to describe every job in detail but to focus on the team level. Assisted by the employers' federation, it has focused on making department descriptions rather than job descriptions. The workers in the teams can then divide the various department tasks among themselves and can organize a system of rotation between tasks.

Appraisal and remuneration

Davidson-Marley BV appraises the performance of every person within the company on a yearly basis. This is in accordance with management by objectives. That is, every year, each employee has a meeting with his or her supervisor and discusses performance and the work itself. Together they will set objectives for the year to come, and these objectives will form the basis for the next appraisal.

Directly linked with this appraisal system is the remuneration system used. Salary determination is partly collective and partly individual. Because the company will not make any profit during the next few years, there is no scheme for profit-sharing. Regarding holidays: the average number of holidays for production workers in the Netherlands is twenty-three plus eleven days. These eleven days are the result of a national plan to shorten individual working weeks (work time shortening, ATV) so as to be able to offer more people a job. The number of these so-called ATV days is typically set during the process of collective bargaining with the unions. Being a new greenfield, Davidson-Marley BV decided to offer employees only six ATV days per year. This again is one of the situations where it is evident that the unions were not involved.

Another aspect of the compensation system is closely related to career development. As previously mentioned, the production associates are divided into four groups, according to the amount of knowledge they possess about the production process. This amount of knowledge also forms the basis for salary. In order to judge how much knowledge they have, Davidson-Marley BV is considering using formal tests to establish this. In addition, these four levels of knowledge possession also form the basis for careers within the production department and also for decisions concerning additional training and education.

Security and safety

Several recent HR issues that receive a great deal of attention in the Netherlands are employees' health, absenteeism, and early retirement for health reasons. It is especially this last issue that has been the center of attention for the past few years. The Netherlands has had a rather generous system for the early retirement of people for health reasons, as part of the entire welfare system. It started out as a good scheme for taking care of people unable to work, but many organizations were able to transfer people to this retirement scheme, using it as a relatively easy way to lay off their surplus of employees. With the growing number of people now in this scheme and its escalating costs, measures have been taken to make it more difficult to transfer people to the scheme. Also, the Law on Working Conditions has had some influence on employers to direct more of their attention to the working conditions as a means of preventing absenteeism and early retirement due to health reasons.

Davidson-Marley BV is also paying much attention to the health of employees and to absenteeism. The average absenteeism percentage in the region is around 10 to 12 percent. Initially, Davidson, being one of the parents, had set out a percentage of 5 percent absenteeism which would be acceptable. General management, however, strives for a figure of 3 percent, which seems to be a minimum that has to be accepted. The initial responsibility for absenteeism lies with the direct supervisor. Therefore the shift coordinator has to take action when production associates are absent, at least by talking to the person to find out what is wrong, but preferably to really look for a solution to the problem, especially if it is directly related to the work situation. To facilitate this, a social team has been installed, consisting of a doctor, a representative of a regional governmental medical agency, and somebody from the HR department.

The IJV regards the health and the general well-being of its employees as being very important. Because it expects not only physical work from their employees, but also thinking, working in teams, and sharing responsibilities, it also, in return, wants to give something back. Feeling at least partly responsible for the well-being of its employees, it also subsidizes individual memberships in sports clubs, in addition to the company health services, individual medical evaluation every two years, and subsidized meals in the company cafeteria.

Planning for the future

Once again, starting a new enterprise involves the establishment of an entirely new package of HR policies and practices. To be able to do this in an effective and efficient manner, planning the activities is very important. Mr. Theuns has acknowledged this from the beginning and indeed has set up an impressive and comprehensive planning scheme. During our interview with him, when asked about several aspects of the HR issues, he more than once stood up and walked to his planning board to indicate when he had planned for some of the activities to be executed. It is beyond the scope of this article to reproduce the entire planning scheme. However, some of the items show the importance of thinking ahead when starting up a new plant.

Under the heading of "Terms of Employment" activities have been planned in immense detail – activities such as drawing up job descriptions, salary structure, employment terms, staff insurances, company regulations, quality procedures, plans for training and education, rewards and recognition schemes, safety regulations, and work instructions. Similarly, the heading "Coaching and Reviewing" covers the planning of activities in the fields of career development, function review, personal coaching, and sickness program. A similar list could be reproduced for the various HR fields: recruitment, selection and assessment, training and education, external mobility (turnover), recruitment planning for key personnel, and miscellaneous (i.e., culture setting, staff guide, company works council, unions, relations, catering, and cleaning).

Planning for the future is very important but is only one aspect of managing a new IJV initiative. Keeping up the vision is one of the major challenges of the near future. In a small company, internal communication is not that difficult, but once it starts to expand, a stronger focus will have to be put on maintaining the vision at every level of the organization. In the event of growth, Davidson-Marley BV has already considered the installation of more decentralized units consisting of working teams with all their own tasks and responsibilities, in line with the idea of empowerment of personnel and teamwork. To retain the vision, it is resisting the practice of wallpapering the entire company with various slogans, productivity reports, etc. It prefers to accomplish this verbally, by regularly stepping out of the daily routine of business and once again discussing with everybody their intentions, what they are doing at the moment and, finally, where they are going as a company, as teams, and as individuals.

Conclusion

We believe the Davidson-Marley BV case is a good example of an IJV where both partners have worked hard to develop the initial relationship and have taken human resource issues into consideration throughout the planning process. Future success will depend upon how well they work with their IJV, Davidson-Marley BV. At this time it appears as if the IJV is a Dutch company fitting in well with the local economy and social community of Born. It also appears that the best relationship the parents can have for the IJV's success is one of initial guidance and structure, supportiveness and independence.

Note

The authors express their appreciation for the support provided by the Human Resource Planning Society, New York, and the Dutch research programme Technology, Work and Organization (TAO), industrial sector, which is carried out by Maastricht Economic Research Institute on Innovation and Technology and for generous time and assistance from Huub Cilissen, general manager, and Jean Theuns, human resource manager, both of Davidson-Marley BV.

As the IJV grows: lessons and progress at Davidson-Marley BV

Ed van Sluijs, GTIP, The Netherlands, and Randall S. Schuler, Rutgers University, U.S.A.

The international joint venture (IJV) of Davidson-Marley BV is located in Born, the Netherlands. It is in its second year of full-time operation with approximately 200 employees. The two parents of this IJV are Davidson-Textron of the United States and Marley Automotive of the United Kingdom.

The two parents came together to form this joint venture for several reasons. The reasons and the characteristics of each parent are detailed in earlier articles. Characteristics of the IJV itself, Davidson-Marley BV, are also described in an earlier article in this journal (December 1992).

At the time of writing of the last article (spring 1992), Davidson-Marley was erecting its plant and installing its equipment. Preparations were being made to run prototypes for its main customer, the Ford Motor plant in Genk, Belgium, that produces the Mondeo. Staffing procedures had been put in place with the majority of hiring yet to be done. Full-time production and just-in-time deliveries to Ford were to begin on January 4, 1993. Although the impression was left that the IJV was "all but done" and the rest of what needed to be done was just perfunctory, this article attempts to describe the reality of it all. In so doing, there are several insights that might be of interest for followers of international joint ventures. There are also several suggestions, particularly regarding human resource management issues, for professionals involved in setting up IJVs.

Introduction

Strategic alliances, particularly of international joint ventures, appear to be a major way firms are globalizing their operations (Main, 1990). As stated in earlier articles, IJVs can make it easier and increase the chances of a firm being successful abroad. They can capitalize on the strengths of each parent and minimize the weaknesses of either. Working together, two firms can spread the risk and gain a greater understanding about doing business in the global environment. Thus, IJVs can be seen as ways to grow, learn, and become profitable, ways that are more attractive than almost any other alternative (Harrigan, 1987a, b; Shenkar and Zeira, 1987a, b, 1990).

But, as with any other business venture, nothing is a sure thing. In IJVs, partners might not get along, markets may disappear (or in some cases, they may never appear), the relationship between the parents and the IJV itself may produce friction and failure, and/or the staffing of the IJV may result in an unsuccessful business under any conditions (Datta, 1989; Gomes-Casseres,

1987). As a way of helping to reduce these downsides, potential partners are implored to get to know each other, to investigate each other's styles and philosophies of doing as much as possible. In many respects, potential partners are urged to treat the process of identifying an IJV partner as equivalent to seeking a marriage partner (Brown, 1990; Tichy, 1988).

As described in the preceding articles, Davidson-Textron and Marley Automotive followed the textbook on IJVs almost line-by-line (Schuler and van Sluijs, 1992; Schuler et al. 1992). If there were a marriage of IJV partners made in heaven, Davidson-Marley BV is it. If the market, financial conditions, complementary skill sets of the partners, and management philosophies were ever to be more appropriate for the establishment and predicted success of an IJV, they would be harder to find than Davidson-Marley BV itself (Schuler and van Sluijs, 1992).

In this article we pick up on the progress of the IJV itself, to see if the prediction of success has come true and to see if there are any lessons to be learned from this joint venture. In doing so, the marriage metaphor is extended. Not surprisingly, however, the focus shifts more to looking at IJV issues from the viewpoint of the IJV itself.

The child grows

Because this child, Davidson-Marley BV, has a customer that consumes almost the entire capacity of the firm, it is like a child with a vitamin-enriched diet; it grows fast! For an IJV, growing fast means encountering problems of joint venture development faster than under normal, less enriched conditions! Full *scale* production is the *first* order of business. Slow market growth and deliberate organizational development are luxuries. The child, the IJV, has to get on its feet and mature as fast as possible. As a consequence, the state of being a total and willing dependent child lasts a much shorter time period. The child begins searching for its own identity and autonomy: the joint venture managers begin to want to make all of their own decisions without being second-guessed by their parents. Their major focus of attention rapidly becomes the customer rather than the parents.

In some respects, this is where Davidson-Marley BV is today. Huub Cilissen, the general manager, and Jean Theuns, the human resource manager, both seek autonomy in running the business. This is not particularly surprising, given that they were both experienced and successful managers at the time they were hired. Yet, understandably, the parents are the ones who have given birth to the joint venture and thus they expect to have some right to direct and manage the operation. In addition, they did establish the market and provide the means of satisfying customers' demands (i.e., they provided the capital, technology, and knowledge to serve the market). Thus the parents and the child have to understand each other's positions and be patient with each other.

Nonetheless, it is not always easy to find the right balance between autonomy (empowerment) and guidance: patience may be tested to the limit, and not just by those running the operations. But this type of situation applies to any IJV; Davidson-Marley BV just gives us the opportunity to become more aware of it. For example, in an IJV the general manager reports to two individuals, one from each parent. Conflicts, differences, and discussions thus occur among the three individuals. But for the others in the IJV the situation is a bit more complex. For example, the human resource manager reports to the general manager of the IJV itself and to the corresponding functional managers for the two parents. Thus, conflicts, differences, and discussions take place among four individuals! Fortunately, both Davidson-Textron and Marley Automotive share philosophies of managing human resources. Both have participative systems and pursue total quality management in their own operations.

But even this cannot guarantee some differences in how to best manage the work force. For example, it is not surprising to find two equally successful parents both thinking that their way may be the better way. The result of this is that the child may no sooner get advice from one parent than it is receiving advice from the other one. And when this is done in the context where the manager of human resources and the general manager of the IJV may also believe that their way is the better way, everyone needs to draw upon as much patience as possible.

The extended family

The metaphor of the marriage and family needs to grow just a bit and encompass a few more family members to illustrate more events occurring in the IJV. When talking about the parents, it becomes simplistic to suggest that each joint venture parent speaks with a single voice in unity. To say that because both parents practice an empowered philosophy of managing human resources, everyone in their respective firms interprets empowerment in the same way or can ignore exigencies of time pressure can be disingenuous. For example, the joint venture parents have representatives in the IJV itself. The controller and the operations managers are from Davidson-Textron. The operations manager, largely because of the pressure to make the required day-to-day deliveries to Ford on a just-in-time basis, had to forgo the use of participative teams and other forms of group problem-solving activities that had been the established *modus operandi* (Schuler and van Sluijs, 1992). While this is likely to moderate with time, it caused some disappointment to those in the IJV itself because they were expecting otherwise. The lesson here, however, is that the best-laid plans can often go astray, particularly those that under other conditions might be seen as normal, but under time constraints might be rather time-consuming. Thus if the maturation process of an IJV is accelerated, participative activities may require time that can be seen as a luxury, time that otherwise would be utilized as a normal part of managing human resources. Accelerated growth can also impact other plans intended for the IJV, particularly those focused around support for a total quality management environment.

Building the strength of the child

Davidson-Marley BV was to be built using participative management processes and using human resource management practices that supported employee development, teamwork, and full skill utilization. Supportive human resource practices included extensive training, enriched jobs, employee empowerment, and cooperative employee–manager relationships (Wickens, 1987). Based upon experience working with these practices in total quality manufacturing environments, Mr. Theuns developed a rather extensive set of recruitment and selection practices to identify those most likely to work effectively under these conditions (see *European Management Journal*, December 1992, p. 434). Used as designed, these would build the strength of the child to achieve the objectives of the IJV. But the best-laid plans . . .

A dual workforce

While the first 100 employees were hired between April 1992 and October 1992, the remaining employees were hired between December 1992 and April/May 1993. Although all employees were hired using the same selection procedures (described in our December 1992 article), there were differences in the desired profiles and characteristics. For selection of the first 100 employees, the desired profiles and characteristics used were (a) willingness to contribute to the building up of the firm in the pioneering phase; (b) ability to identify problems and develop solutions; and (c) having an international orientation (i.e., willingness to travel for training in either the United Kingdom or the United

States). By contrast, for the other employees hired, the selection criteria were different: (a) willingness to join an already ongoing process; and (b) willingness and ability to work in teams. Because the pioneering days are over, some of the initial group of employees have moved on, being replaced by employees using the second set of selection criteria. Regardless, there are two groups of employees: those who were hired under the first set of criteria and those hired under the second set. Of the 200 or so production workers today, about 75 are union members, mostly from the ranks of those hired after November 1992. To this situation was added the use of group activity descriptions, rather than specific *individual* job descriptions, which tend to produce ambiguity for the individual workers.

So today the workforce is composed of those hired between April 1992 and October 1992 and all those hired later. The slight variation in the time of hiring for what in all practical purposes are people doing the same jobs has created many differences besides those already mentioned. Because all employees are initially hired under a one-year temporary contract first, the first group is now under permanent contract while the second group is still under temporary contract. The first group has also been assigned to the more advanced job category. For the plant production workers there are three job categories: beginners, experienced, and all-rounders. The first group are all-rounders and are paid more than the second group, who are still in the beginner and experienced categories.

Systematic initial hiring and job description are essential in an IJV

Resulting from the conditions described was some confusion and voicing of preference for certainty and direction, particularly among those hired without having experience of working in teams and conditions of worker empowerment. With hindsight, Mr. Theuns thinks the lesson here is to begin operations under more classical management procedures and *then* gradually move to conditions of teamwork and empowerment. The only exception to this might be if time can be taken either to hire everyone to fit the conditions and/or to train those hired to fit before the pressure of full production begins. Conditions such as labour market availability, production pressure, and operating costs might, in the final analysis, determine what is really feasible. Hindsight, however, might suggest that a modest increase in initial cost outlays might be more than compensated for over the longer term. To wit, bringing in all the employees at the same time might have avoided creating the two sets of employees described above. This would have enabled the plant to hire all individuals using the same selection criteria. This, in turn, could have precluded the need to now think of melding the groups together and moving from relatively traditional human resources practices to more team-oriented and empowered human resource practices.

Clearly, however, this scenario suggests the necessity of being systematic about the initial hiring and job description and direction preparation. It also indicates just how significant the realities of accelerated growth can be. But the impact of accelerated growth goes further.

Communicate, communicate

Accelerated growth produces the need to attend to more events in a smaller period of time, make more decisions in a shorter space of time, and disseminate more information more quickly. Especially under the hiring and production conditions described above, the need for communications in the Davidson-Marley BV was considerable, even though communications was not anticipated to be an issue because of the small size of the operation (Schuler and van Sluijs, 1992). Mr. Theuns thus found himself needing to perform two major jobs:

one as human resource director and the other as communications director. And because of the demands of starting up the joint venture, Mr. Theuns had to devote considerable time to his primary job of human resource director. Nevertheless, he did have to serve as a communications director as much as possible. Of course, other members of the management team felt similar pressures.

Three potential lessons evolve from this situation. The first is giving consideration to hiring a full-time communications director to work with the human resource director. In addition to helping convey the mission and philosophy of the business to all employees, a communications director might also develop systems of internal communications and train all employees in communication, listening, and feedback skills. This, of course, depends on cost considerations, at least in the short run. The need for this additional person, however, may be attenuated with the initial use of classical management principles and the application of the second lesson.

The second lesson is locating the human resource department on the production floor, or at least adjacent to it. The human resource department is located on the first floor of the facility, thus making it practically impossible for workers and managers to see and utilize. This has made it difficult for the human resource department to communicate, subtly and not so subtly, its messages. One message that is communicated that is particularly important in the early stages of the IJV is that of *partnership*, the third lesson here.

The reality of the importance of partnership has been identified in many case examples of firms pursuing total quality management, such as Ford, Nissan, Komitsu, ICI, Shell, and Unilever (e.g., see Starkey and McKinlay, 1993). The partnership is among workers, human resource professionals, and the line managers (from the operations manager through to the floor supervisors). The partnership is about managing human resources.

In partnership, literally everyone does something related to attracting, motivating, and retaining employees. And because total quality management and operational success depend upon people, partnership is about everyone managing human resources. Mr. Theuns thinks that locating the human resource department next to the production area can facilitate this partnership substantially in two ways. First, it makes the department more user-friendly to the workers. It removes the walls and floors between them and the human resource department professionals. Ease of interaction breeds interaction, and interaction brings familiarity and understanding. Second, it makes the department more accessible to the line manager and vice versa. This accessibility may act with line managers in the same way it does with the workers. Of course, it also has the potential to work the other way, i.e., for the line managers to dump "personnel matters" on the desks of the human resource professionals.

Predicting which direction it will take depends upon the philosophy and direction of the managers of the parents (and how committed they are to this theme of partnership); the philosophy of the line managers; pressure on the line managers for production that in turn focuses their time and attention on purely production-oriented activities; and the relationship between the human resource professionals and the line managers. The more they share the same philosophy and background, the greater the extent to which partnership can become a reality.

But even with the same philosophy and background, it is still imperative that the issue of partnership be discussed by the management team. For example, at Davidson-Marley BV it would be important for the eight-person management team (Mr. Cilissen and Mr. Theuns are two members along with the managers of engineering, quality, sales, purchasing, operations and finance) to discuss and resolve their views on managing human resources. At the end of the day, it is important to decide and agree upon who is responsible for absenteeism, safety, grievances, shift change requests, workplace complaints, job conditions, and training for group members. Variations in actual behavior from what is agreed upon can cause substantial uncertainty and confusion, resulting in less than optimal operating conditions and employee morale. However, to the extent that agreement is reached and all behave accordingly, the greater the possibility of achieving optimal operating conditions early and of smoothly moving the joint venture from adolescence to adulthood.

From adolescence to adulthood

All within one year? Yes, a majority of the workers have been with the joint venture for only a year. But in the minds of some, Davidson-Marley BV began in 1989, so the joint venture can be viewed as celebrating its fifth birthday this year. In the minds of Mr. Cilissen and Mr. Theuns it is three years old. Remember, we are talking about an enriched joint venture, one growing at an accelerated rate. It is certainly mapping onto this path quite well in some respects. Despite the economic environment and demands for cost reductions that large customers are increasingly asking from their suppliers, the IJV is on track with its profitability goals.

Yes, it does have some facial symptoms of youth remaining. It must improve working conditions, working hours, and safety and health conditions. By the autumn of 1993, these conditions became an issue of concern to the workers. There were two showers, only a few toilets, a few washbasins; some workers were working 9.5 hours rather than the required limit of 8; emergency exits were difficult to reach; and storage of toxic materials did not conform to requirements. An independent labor body in the Netherlands (the Arbeidsinspectie) issued a formal report enumerating these conditions, to which the joint venture has responded. The joint venture responded by drawing up concrete plans for the improvement in working conditions. It also responded by creating two safety teams: one addresses general working conditions and safety and meets weekly with Mr. Theuns; and the other is the ARBO team (Dutch law requires such a team that addresses *arbeidsomstandigheden* or "working conditions"). Actually the plant had conformed to the law regarding toilets, washbasins and emergency exits, but this conformance was at the minimum level. While having more of all these was desirable, the plant layout had already been established when this was noticed by the management team.

Problems of rapid growth

Again, these conditions largely resulted from the rapid growth of the joint venture, and the issue of building in some slack enters. Perhaps these conditions and the report of the Arbeidsinspectie would have been unnecessary had the plant been built to standards above the minimum. Again, earlier involvement of the local managers could have raised the possibility of these conditions becoming an issue with the local workers and in so doing prevented them from becoming issues later. Precise forecasting of worker productivity is nearly impossible. This, combined with the desire not to overhire, resulted in working employees more hours than intended. The rapid start-up also made it more difficult to get everyone attending to the importance of safety and health, even though this was one of the topics in the core training programs. While the problems were largely the result of rapid growth and the lack of time necessary to balance workload with workers, the task forces have been addressing these issues and progress has been made.

Another aspect that is related to the rapid growth of the IJV, and also to the internal operations of the IJV, is the relationship between the technological layout of the plant and the working in teams. We have already mentioned that owing to the time pressure on deliveries, the use of participative teams has not been operationalized to the extent planned. Apart from this time pressure, however, the layout of the production plant is also of importance here. The intrinsically flexible technology used within the IJV had been installed in such a way that teamwork and cooperation were made difficult to implement. In fact, many workers were operating with their backs to each other or were otherwise (i.e., because of the way the machinery had been organized) prevented from having contact with each other. During the summer of 1993, the layout of the production facilities was reorganized in such a way that it became easier for the production associates to interact with each other. And what we wrote earlier about the interaction between the personnel department and the workers applies here as well: ease of interaction breeds interaction, and in the case of the production associates, this interaction should enlarge the possibilities for establishing advanced forms of teamwork and participative problem solving.

In relation to communications and internal operations, the joint venture is also seeking further development. The venture is still staffed with highly qualified individuals from the United Kingdom and the United States as well as the Netherlands. While this is necessary in the early stages, for reasons already identified, this management composition of three nationalities can slow down internal communications and operations (Gomes-Casseres, 1987; Harrigan, 1987a). This is particularly true in a participatory work environment where decisions require a great deal of discussion and information processing, and when the majority of participants need to operate in a second language, discussions tend to become inefficient. As the expatriates from the two parents are repatriated during the year, this may ease the process of internal communications and facilitate internal operating efficiency. This will in turn speed the movement from adolescence to adulthood. Of course, this withdrawal of parental involvement in this joint venture is probably far earlier than would be the case for many IJVs, but it is possible because of the rapid growth path this joint venture is on and the quality of the local nationals selected by the parents in the first place. As scheduled, the U.S. controller is to be repatriated in September 1994 and the Canadian operations manager around July 1994. It is anticipated that they will be replaced with Dutch nationals.

Summary and conclusions

As implied in the above discussion, there are many aspects of an IJV's success that involve managing human resources and the HR department (Shenkar and Zeira, 1990). One of the big aspects is how many, when, and what types of employees to hire. As suggested in the previous article, Mr. Cilissen and Mr. Theuns agree that bringing in local national managers as early as possible in the process of setting up the IJV can bring enormous savings and efficiencies over a very short period of time. In addition to bringing them in early, it is important to identify who to bring in. As suggested earlier, it is important to consider bringing in a local communications manager, particularly when pursuing a competitive strategy that depends upon a great deal of employee empowerment and participation. It also appears to be useful to bring in a logistics manager, a manager to assist in managing and organizing the material flow, especially within the firm, and to a lesser extent the input and output of "raw" materials and parts through to finished products. This did not seem to be a sufficiently vital position to warrant the early hiring of such a person, but it became evident rather soon that this was not the case. This was due largely to the demands of just-in-time delivery of the suppliers to the customer. For others thinking about such a joint venture, the importance of this position should not be underestimated. And interestingly enough, its importance appears to be most vital at the early stages, when the systems and procedures need to be set up. This position, however, remains vital,

especially when the demand schedules of the major customer remain unpredictable. Because of the likelihood of such circumstances, it appears warranted to hire a logistics person early.

Bringing in the nonmanagement staff at least six months prior to full-scale production can also prove to be advantageous to the IJV. This relatively early time frame, however, is consistent with other greenfield sites set up with a total quality management commitment (Wickens, 1987). Workers need to be trained both in the production process and in working with each other: teams take time to develop; there are no shortcuts. Systematic selection can help reduce the time needed, but it is also important to be consistent in the selection criteria used. In the situation of the Davidson-Marley BV, two sets of selection criteria were used, along with a single set of more traditional personnel practices. The initial intention was to use one set of general selection criteria accompanied by a set of specific criteria for the first 100 or so team-oriented and empowered human resource practices. The Limburg region of the Netherlands had been selected in part for its high levels of unemployment (it was and still is more than 10 percent). Again, however, cost considerations can revise the best-intended plans. The result was bringing in one set of workers early and another set later. But these cost advantages may be lost in the longer run as the real impact of this type of deviation from plan becomes evident. This is particularly true of the impact on human resources. Both the parents and the JV are now addressing this situation and appear to be responding very successfully. Traditional personnel practices are being revised. In fact, one of the concerns of the JV is that when the European economic slowdown reverses, other employers may seek to lure away some of the Davidson-Marley BV workers because they have become so well trained and familiar with empowerment practices and total quality management procedures and processes. The joint venture is responding by revising career management and salary and benefit plans to help prevent this from happening. A one-day trip by all the IJV employees to Ford, for example, gave workers greater knowledge and insight into product-quality and just-in-time inventory issues.

Overall, it appears that many of the classic human resource management issues associated with IJV formation and development have surfaced in the Davidson-Marley BV, e.g., issues of career development for the local managers; issues of conflict and control between the two parents *vis-à-vis* the IJV; and desire for the IJV to become an independent and self-sustaining business as soon as possible (Harrigan, 1987a, b; Schuler *et al.*, 1991). And just as these issues have appeared, so they have been addressed and managed fairly successfully. This has been in large measure due to the quality of the parents' relationship with each other, the quality of the local managers selected, and the fact that the major customer was already identified. But just as these factors have been critical in the success of the IJV thus far, they have also produced challenges. And these challenges have arisen primarily because the development of the IJV has been accelerated by having the large customer already arranged. However, they are typical of IJVs and thus are ones that would have had to be faced at some point. Having seen these challenges early has therefore made it possible for this IJV to get on with its evolution from child to adulthood status earlier than other IJVs. Fortunately, the management team recognized these challenges and responded accordingly. Fortunately, too, the management team has been supported by the board (consisting of five members: two presidents and vice presidents from each parent and Mr. Cilissen). Certainly, many of the changes and adjustments that have been made involved all the members of the management team, but particularly Mr. Cilissen and Mr. Theuns. From experiences thus far, Mr. Theuns recommends others thinking of joint ventures not only to systematically prepare for every aspect of the JV's operation (from the earliest point

onward), but also to systematically record events and processes as they unfold. He, in essence, recommends that the HR manager might be the one in charge of keeping a diary or journal for the JV. In turn, this journal can become a road map against which the management team can measure and evaluate and learn from its progress. This can be especially helpful in an IJV that is evolving from childhood to adulthood status earlier than most IJVs. Of course, the parents might do something similar, and then occasionally all could share their progress reports. IJVs could also expand their own learning by meeting with and exchanging ideas and experiences with other suppliers to Ford. In fact, several suppliers have been meeting to cooperate in such activities as joint recruitment and training (after realizing that many of them were using similar HR practices to deliver total quality products to their common customer).

For organizations interested in IJVs, this profile of the Davidson-Marley BV has highlighted several significant HR issues in IJV development and operation. Although there are many other issues in addition to HR ones, read in conjunction with the previous three articles [the earlier parts of their Appendix], this profile might still enhance the potential for a successful launch of an IJV between two hopeful joint venture parents (Cascio and Serapio, 1991; Slocum and Lei, 1993). At minimum, it should help to flag some areas of HRM that IJV parents need to discuss and resolve as early as possible, particularly if major customers are ready for delivery.

Note

The authors express their appreciation for the support provided by the Human Resource Planning Society, New York, and the Dutch Research Programme, Technology, Work and Organization, industrial sector, which is carried out by MERIT, and for the generous time and assistance from Huub Cilissen, general manager, and Jean Theuns, human resource manager, both of Davidson-Marley BV.

Precision Measurement of Japan

A small foreign company in the Japanese labor market*

Precision Measurement of Japan (PM-J) is a joint venture company between Takezawa† Electric Company (TEC), a Japanese electrical equipment manufacturing company, and Precision Measurement, Inc. (PMI), a Minnesota-based manufacturer of measurement devices. Major markets for these devices are chemical processes, pipelines, aircraft and aerospace, and power generation. As a multinational corporation, PMI is faced with the problem of penetrating the Japanese market before one of its Japanese competitors perfects the various gauges and shuts the U.S. company out of the Japanese market. In order to penetrate the Japanese market, PMI has entered into a business relationship with TEC, thus forming an international joint venture, PM-J. This step was intended to increase PMI's credibility with the Japanese, and to forestall a Japanese competitor from using its protected domestic market to work out bugs, employ economies of scale, undercut PMI's pricing scheme, and generally take over the world instrument

market. This would seriously, perhaps fatally, affect PMI's viability.

The problem

The problem faced by his company, according to Joe Smith, president of PM-J, is that the Japanese instrument companies are becoming more visible and are developing broader product lines that may directly affect PM-J's market share. Corporate PMI headquarters is genuinely concerned that the Japanese long-term plan is to capture and dominate the world instrument markets just as they have taken over camera, automobile, video recorder, and other high-tech markets. The instrument market could be the next Japanese strategic industry.

Currently, the Japanese tend to dominate only their domestic instrument markets, says Smith. This could change if they work their familiar strategy: closing the Japanese markets to foreign competition, acquiring

* This case was prepared by James C. Scoville (with the assistance of Christine Hoffman and Eliyahue Stein), Carlson School of Management, Case Development Center, University of Minnesota. Reprinted with permission.

† I am also indebted to referees who commented on the case. One of their suggestions was a brief guide to pronunciation of the Japanese names in this case. In general, each vowel merits a syllable: thus, "Tah.keh.zah.wah." The only exception is when "i" serves as a "y," as in the name of Keio ("Kayo") University. All "sh" combinations in this case are pronounced as in "shoe." This case appears in updated form in R.F. Buller and R. S. Schuler, *Cases on Managing People and Organizations* 7th edn (Southwestern: 2003).

volume and experience in domestic markets, and basing foreign marketing on that experience.

The usual Japanese strategy is either to (a) obtain licenses for advanced technology from other companies (usually from the United States) and then improve the technology and market it alone; or (b) use some company's proven distribution arrangements to establish a market base and then go it alone. Both of these approaches save the Japanese company considerable time and expense, thus freeing resources and capital for quick and effective marketing of the new and/or improved technology. Smith reports that two competitors gained real substance in this manner.

After penetrating the foreign markets with this strategy, excellent service and responsiveness from the Japanese companies are generally reported. The Japanese will, no doubt, continue their patient, persistent way of presenting high-technology, high-performance products that are backed by quality service. Even though they gain market position slowly, says Smith, once the Japanese establish accounts, their outstanding customer relations and excellent service record often mean they keep the accounts; the non-Japanese are then in a position of lost accounts and a declining market share.

Overriding questions

PMI wishes to establish a permanent position in the Japanese domestic market. Additionally, it would be preferable that any Japanese competition be retarded by PMI's establishment of a strong sales and manufacturing posture in Japan. To acquire and maintain a market share in the instrument industry, PMI must establish credibility as a viable company; this it sought to do by combining with TEC. By establishing PM-J, PMI is demonstrating a long-term commitment and significant investment in Japan.

In its efforts to form this joint venture, PMI was faced with several overriding questions including:

1 Does PMI really know TEC? Can TEC be trusted? Has the IJV been well planned?
2 Who will really run PM-J? Who will make the HR-related decisions, such as about selection, promotion, performance appraisal, etc.? What will be the HR practices used?
3 Is PMI prepared to learn from this joint venture? Is PMI prepared to learn about and from TEC and PM-J?

The answers to these questions need to be considered by PMI management. In the absence of systematic thinking about and planning for them, the chances for failure increase.

In its efforts to capture the Japanese market, PM-J is faced with two overriding questions:

1 Is it possible to hire a sufficient number of qualified sales engineers (preferably recent graduates) to increase sales, establish quality accounts, and achieve a reasonable profit growth?
2 In what manner might PM-J increase its market position and distribution in the Japanese market?

The answers to these questions for PM-J are complicated by a variety of socioeconomic factors unique to Japan.

The country

Japan has a small amount of habitable land located on a number of mountainous islands, with few natural resources but abundant human resources. Pressured by the need to import almost all raw materials, including 100 percent of all oil, the Japanese economy grew at phenomenal rates during the 1960s and 1970s. During this period, Japanese industrial products moved from having a reputation as cheap and flimsy to a position known for quality and reliability. This achievement was attained in part through

Table B.1 Projected staffing patterns for Precision Measurement of Japan, 2001–2003

	April '01	*Dec '01*	*Dec '02*	*Dec '03*
Administration	5	5	5	5
Secretarial/clerical	5	5	5	5
Engineering	8	11	13	15
Sales & marketing	(3)			
Engineering services group	(3)			
Production	(2)			
Production technicians	2	3	3	3
	20	24	26	28

protective import practices and a coordinated industrial strategy featuring cooperation between major manufacturing groups and the government, especially through activities of the Ministry of International Trade and Industry (MITI).

The company

Precision Measurement, Inc. was founded in the mid-1960s to produce a wide range of measurement and instrumentation equipment. Over the years, the company has remained at the forefront of this industry and continues to this day to pursue cutting-edge research. In recent years, the company's financial strength has been sustained by a classic "cash cow" – a gauge for measurement of flow and pressure. The success of this gauge relies on two factors: (a) very fine and precise machining of high-quality material to strict quality standards; and (b) an ingenious application of elementary principles of physics. Neither of these constitutes a substantial barrier to Japanese competition: machining materials to high standard is straightforward; and even the casewriter's late-1950s high school physics allows him to understand the way the gauge works!

Staffing implications

To penetrate the Japanese domestic market, an optimal staffing pattern must be generated which would yield the desired sales capability. (Manufacturing takes place in the United States, with the gauge being modified to the customer's needs in Japan by production engineers and technicians.) PM-J's president supplied a table (Table B.1) of desired staffing patterns from the beginning of 2001 through 2003, which focuses on their probable staffing needs. Although PM-J found it very difficult to hire the eight engineers who presently represent the company, it is now faced with the need to engage seven more in just two and one-half years.

Engineering labor markets in Japan

The nature of Japanese labor markets, particularly for professionals and managers, directly affects attainability of the staffing patterns outlined by the company. Although the practice is less popular today, large Japanese organizations generally hire people as they finish school for "lifetime employment." The employee then receives a traditional training that consists of considerable job rotation and general training intended to develop broad skills; the employee, therefore, expects a pay system based primarily on length of service with the company rather than job-specific performance. Thus PM-J's competitors would typically hire engineers on completion of university training and employ them until their early to mid-fifties. Then, as is the practice with many managers, the senior employees are transferred to subsidiaries, client organizations, smaller plants, or less demanding jobs.

A small company like PM-J cannot easily compete in the labor market because it cannot guarantee its own survival for the career lifetime of the employees. Small organizations are more likely to go out of business, and, even if they survive, are less likely to obtain a major share of the product market. This fact does little to instill confidence in the new graduate who expects lifetime employment as a condition of employment. The same weakness generally applies to foreign companies in Japan. They often do not share a commitment to lifetime employment, traditional pay systems, or a long business presence in Japan. This image, formed by some foreign companies that came to Japan and then laid off many people or totally withdrew, is widespread among Japanese professionals.

PM-J has generally been unable to recruit immediate postgraduates because it is both small and foreign. This has necessitated acquiring its engineering force in various ad hoc ways, predominantly relying on recommendations from its joint venture partner, TEC. While not optimal, this has at least allowed the company to develop a skeleton staff.

The first two columns of Table B.2 show the name and recruiting source of engineers currently employed by PM-J. The third and fourth columns show the salaries of these people (millions of yen per year) as compared with the average pay of employees of the same age and education in large companies in Japan. The final column shows each employee's job performance evaluation as reported by company president Smith. Table B.2 clearly demonstrates that PM-J's hiring pattern has strongly deviated from the stereotypical postuniversity hire/lifetime employment pattern of Japanese industry in general.

Alternatives to the current situation

Given the staffing and recruiting patterns of Japanese industries and the staffing dilemmas faced by PM-J, what alternative plans of action are available to a small, foreign company that will promote its stated objectives of expanded sales and increased market share? If PM-J is to predominate in the Japanese market, what alternatives to its current pattern of hiring mid-career engineers could move the company toward hiring newly graduated qualified engineers? Are there changes occurring in the Japanese labor culture that might benefit PM-J if the company recognizes the changes and adapts them to fit its needs?

Attracting younger engineers

How might PM-J increase its hiring ratio of younger engineers directly out of school? Will it be as difficult to hire new graduates in the future as previous experience suggests? The latter situation seems to be loosening a bit as professors' influence in directing students has declined. Indeed, some students are more willing to consider employers other than just the very largest and more traditional Japanese companies. Furthermore, the typical lifetime employment pattern seems to be eroding as some younger professionals with relatively recent dates of hire move to new companies after only three or four years of employment. Organizations like the Recruit Center (a major recruiting and placement organization providing extensive published information on companies as prospective employers) and "headhunters" are supporting these changes in employment patterns by publicizing employment opportunities and company characteristics. Young professionals in engineering and other technical fields are beginning to rely on such data in making career decisions.

Table B.2 Precision Measurement of Japan's sales and support force, spring 2001

Name and experience	Annual salary (million yen) including bonuses	Average pay at large companies* (million yen)	Performance evaluation
Sato, small company experience, recommended by the general manager of PM-J	9.5	9.7	55% effort rating; lower segment on performance
Suzuki, formerly a representative for PM-J	7.3	5.8	80%
Takahashi, TEC (age: late 40s)	7.3	7.2	75–85%
Watanabe Nihon Medical (age: early 50s), recommended by a classmate who is now a professor	9.5	9.5	Very high
Tanaka, junior high school education plus 20 years in the instrumentation sales business; answered an ad in a trade journal			N/A
Ito, TEC (age: 32)	5.8	5.8	90%
Kobayashi, new university graduate	2.9	3.0	N/A
Saito, TEC (age: about 40)	6.3	6.3	Very high
Yamamoto, TEC (age: mid 40s)	8.4	7.8	Very high

Source: Japan Institute of Labor Statistical Reports; and Japanese Ministry of Labor (www.mol.go.jp/info/toukei.english/b-01.htm

* Equal to eighteen months' salary in the average large company, no housing or other allowances figured in. The extra six months' pay reflects the average level of bonuses in Japan. At present, large Japanese companies pay roughly two months' salary as a bonus three times a year (late spring, late summer, and at the Christmas–New Year season).

The advantages of this alternative, i.e., to employ personnel agencies, are straightforward. First, PM-J can more readily advertise the benefits and opportunities it is able to provide to career-minded professionals via the agencies, and headhunters, as third parties, can confer as they present the company as a stable organization that demonstrates Japanese characteristics. Third, recruitment agents are financially motivated to match employers and employees; PM-J can capitalize on this by requesting younger, well-educated, technically qualified engineers who have a potentially longer career life with the company.

The principal disadvantages of personnel agencies are their high cost to the small organization, in terms of money and CEO time. Further caveats must be noted: graduates of the best Japanese universities and engineering programs (the University of Tokyo and Keio University) would probably not be interested in employment agencies, because they would most likely be recruited by the large domestic companies via contacts with university professors. Likewise, headhunters would be less able to lure young new hires from large companies to work for a smaller foreign-based firm. Additionally, if PM-J accepted a large proportion of graduates from second- and third-tier universities, it would be unable to generate a level of credibility that a workforce of "better"-educated employees from top-rated universities would confer.

Attracting female engineers

One intriguing labor market strategy might be to get women into PM-J's labor force as sales engineers. A growing number of women are enrolled in engineering programs of Japanese universities. Their employability, at least in principle, should be enhanced by equal opportunity legislation recently passed by the Diet (Japan's parliament). More distant observers, including some at the corporate offices of PMI, have occasionally brainstormed about job redesign and the use of women engineers; U.S.-based students may almost think this a natural option.

Practical reaction at PM-J, however, stresses that the acceptability of women in many Japanese work roles is not immediately forthcoming. Moreover, it will be even longer in coming within the industrial setting, where men are employed almost exclusively and where evening entertainment of customers is an expected job component.

Engineers versus salespeople

A variant on the idea of increasing the number of engineers at PM-J is to reduce the company's reliance on engineers by employing nontechnically trained salespeople; the sales component of the engineers' positions would be eliminated or substantially decreased. After all, engineers don't do all the selling in the United States; rather, they provide technical backup and design work after the salesperson has made the pitch.

Perhaps it is feasible to explore hiring graduates of technical high schools and vocational schools for sales, following the example set when Tanaka was hired (Table B.2). This could be accomplished by multiple testing (which is less restricted in Japan than in the United States), and increased training to identify and qualify strong sales candidates. In fact, PMI in the United States and other organizations in Japan succeeded in using a combination of both occupations in marketing products.

By using nonengineering salespeople, PM-J could easily expand its labor force with younger employees. Unfortunately, the company is small and foreign; in reducing the perceived qualifications of its salesforce it will suffer a further loss of the credibility that is conferred on employees holding an engineering degree from a respected university.

Maintaining the status quo

Staying with the status quo is another strategy. PM-J could continue using mid-career people. Most of these employees have been recruited from the joint venture partner, TEC. This method is relatively inexpensive, because the initial recruitment, selection, and training costs are absorbed by TEC since the engineers began employment there. An advantage of this method is that the engineers with twenty-five to thirty years' experience have far more business contacts than do fresh graduates. The principal disadvantage is that one cannot be certain that the TEC engineers are quality employees. After all, why should TEC give up its best people to PM-J and retain the marginal employees for its own use? It is quite conceivable that the joint venture could be receiving some of the less productive TEC personnel. This also perpetuates the current dilemma of a salesforce in its early to mid-fifties, which does not assist the company's image, credibility, or ability to capture the difficult Japanese market.

A further complication in PM-J's reliance on TEC's transferred employees is that many mid-career professionals may be loyal to their previous employer; this will not result in a highly motivated salesforce that will be prepared to endeavor diligently to promote a new employer in the market.

Supplementing the status quo

Another strategic option is to supplement the status quo (hiring mid-career professional engineers) with headhunters and/or employment agencies such as the Recruit Center. Headhunters have become more prevalent in the Japanese labor market recently, and many Japanese companies report some successes in employing their services. Even though such agencies and headhunters are quite expensive and time-consuming, they do represent one means of filling gaps created by internal rotations of employees or vacancies resulting from terminated employees. Perhaps the most likely recruit from headhunting would be in the 28- to 30-year-old range who is making a career move. Although not fresh from school, these engineers would still be relatively recent university graduates with longer career lives ahead of them. This would tend to stabilize PM-J's engineering and salesforce turnover while simultaneously conferring the credibility to be gained from the honored university degree.

Toward an appraisal of these options

The likely success of these various strategies clearly depends on the prospective state of the Japanese engineer labor market. PM-J's

hiring success will be directly enhanced by any developments that reduce the number of engineers absorbed by the rest of Japanese industry and by its ability to gain credibility as a stable "Japanese" company. Indirect effects are also possible.

For example, it is likely that any developments that loosen the supply of male engineers will make it even more difficult for female engineers to be accepted, especially in sales. Thus, a reliable forecast of engineering labor market conditions in Japan is central to any strategy recommendation to PM-J.

Future labor market developments

Effects of an aging workforce

The Japanese labor force and population has aged in recent years, putting pressure on the social insurance and retirement systems, similar to the U.S. situation. This has led the government to explore postponing pension age from about 60 to 65. The Japanese employment system for engineers (among other professions) initially moves employees in the 50 to 55 age range to secondary employment (within the firm) or to other employers.* Since the government has made early pensions less likely, it seems that in coming years more men will seek longer second careers. As noted, this would dampen women's employability. It would also increase the availability of engineering resources to a company like PM-J.

Decline in the number of new workers

The declining number of young people entering the labor market and the declining pool of new engineering graduates implies that small companies like PM-J are more

---

* The age-related pay system (*nenko*), plus the common decline of productivity after a certain age, means that older workers tend rapidly to become more and more expensive.

likely to be squeezed out of the market. On present hiring patterns, 80 percent of the graduates of the top ten Japanese engineering schools would be recruited and absorbed by a select group of employers consisting of the largest domestic and foreign organizations. This tightening of the youth market decreases the viability of a strategy aimed at hiring fresh graduates into small, foreign companies.

Foreign product competition and the Japanese labor market

One must consider the labor market effects of opening Japanese product markets to foreign competition. If Japan concedes to growing pressure from its allies to reduce import tariffs and trade barriers, who will be hit hardest? Which Japanese industries will be hurt by a policy of greater import penetration into Japan? First of all, it is not probable that agriculture will be hit heavily. Even though Japanese food prices are three to six times the world level, it is unlikely that the government would chance eroding its support base among small farmers. This is due to the fact that import restriction policies have supported the relatively large agricultural population, who have in turn faithfully supported the incumbent government party, the Liberal Democrats, since the late 1940s.

Are import penetration liberalizations for nonagricultural products apt to affect big companies like Matsushita, Hitachi, or Asahi? These firms run the Japanese "economic miracle" and are closely tied to government policy through the coordinating activities of MITI. Such an alliance between government and big business is likely to forestall serious import impacts on the key companies. Thus, will not any opening of Japanese markets to U.S. imports probably be designed to have the most impact on items produced by smaller businesses? As these smaller businesses cut back on employment, won't they have the effect of loosening the labor market exactly where PM-J is located (in terms of company size)?

Political considerations aside, it is also true that small-scale industry in Japan has much higher labor costs (relative to larger enterprises) than in the United States or Germany (another major trading country). Increased foreign product-market competition and a resulting loosening of the smaller-company labor market would increase a surviving small foreign company's ability to recruit and retain qualified employees.

To the extent that Japanese trade policy is liberalized, PM-J should be more successful on all fronts in trying to hire engineers in competition with Japanese firms. On the other hand, the staffing demands of other foreign firms which either expand or enter Japan as a result of this trade policy liberalization will have to be taken into account.

Product market issues

Having considered some major human resource dynamics affecting PM-J's penetration into the Japanese market, it is necessary to review what product market considerations are relevant to the success of PM-J in the Japanese market.

Standards are most frequently mentioned as problems or barriers by would-be U.S. importers of technical equipment. Japanese standards are simply not the same as the United States' and are very difficult to understand or change. With respect to the "cash cow gauge," PM-J spent six or seven years on the standards acceptance process.

The biggest issue regarding the product market is the prospect for increased penetration of imports into the Japanese market. Japanese government policy on this is evolving. Whether this will help sell PM-J's product, only time will tell. But if it becomes easier for foreign firms to bid on government jobs (pursuant to GATT and WTO agreements), PM-J might see a direct sales payoff in major government projects.

Further issues from this case

There are at least four further issues
to address in this case. First, is TEC
doing its job? Is it providing qualified
people to the joint venture, PM-J, or is
it "dumping" marginal employees who
are past their peak performance and on
the downslide?

A second issue that needs to be addressed
is whether PM-J's pay scale is appropriate.
Data in Table B.2 provide comparisons with
big companies' pay levels.

The longer-run labor market strategy options

One can identify the risks, benefits, and
costs of various alternatives (including
staffing options) against the backdrop of
various "states of the world." Those states
of the world will be dominated by the degree
to which government policy changes so that
PM-J (or, more radically, a lot of foreign
competition) is able to penetrate domestic
markets in Japan. Some engineering labor
market strategies will be higher risk and
lower risk, with higher and lower costs

and payoffs, depending what one thinks
will happen to the engineering labor market
and PM-J's ability to penetrate the product
market. Although Japanese government
policies on foreign access to markets may
dominate the scene, other things that will
impinge upon the labor market should be
considered:

- the aging population;
- shortages of youth entering the labor
  force;
- increased numbers of people (early to
  mid-fifties) seeking longer second
  careers;
- an increased number of women seeking
  positions;
- changing Japanese culture and labor
  markets;
- changing values; and
- economic and banking conditions.

A third issue is how should PM-J attempt to
recruit enough people to permit an effective
penetration of the Japanese product market
on which the survival not only of PM-J but
of its parents PMI and TEC may depend?
What can be done to help ensure that the
parents and the IJV itself learn from their
experiences as they develop the IJV and
move on to other joint ventures?

Bibliography

Abelson, R. (1996) "Welcome mat is out for gay investors," *New York Times*, September 1: section 3: 1, 7.

Abrahamson, E. (1991) "Managerial fads and fashions: The diffusion and rejection of innovations," *Academy of Management Review* 16: 586–612.

Adams, M. (2002) "Mergers and acquisitions: Making a merge," *HR Magazine*, March: 53–57.

Adler, N.J (2001) *International Dimensions of Organizational Behavior*, 4th edn., Cincinnati: Southwestern College Publishing.

Adler, N.J. and Bartholomew, S. (1992) "Academic and professional communities of discourse: Generating knowledge on transnational human resource management," *Journal of International Business Studies* 23: 551–569.

Adler, N.J. and Jelinek, M. (1986) "Is 'organization culture' culture bound?" *Human Resource Management* 25: 73–90.

Aguinis, H. and Henle, C.A. (2002) "The search for universals in cross-cultural organizational behavior," in J. Greenberg (ed.) *Organizational Behavior: The State of the Science*, 2nd edn., Mahwah, NJ: Lawrence Erlbaum Associates.

Ahmadjian, C. and Robinson, P. (2001) "Safety in numbers: Downsizing and the deinstitutionalization of permanent employment in Japan," *Administrative Science Quarterly* 46: 622–654.

Aldrich, H.E. (1979) *Organizations and Environments*, Englewood Cliffs, NJ: Prentice Hall.

Alexander, L. (2000) *Corporate Governance and Cross-Border Mergers*, The Conference Board, New York.

Allport, G.W. (1954) *The Nature of Prejudice*, Reading, MA: Addison-Wesley.

Anderson, C. (2000) "Survey: The young: Tomorrow's child," *The Economist*, December 23, 2000–January 5, 2001.

Andrews, E. and Bradsher, K. (2000) "This 1998 model is looking more like a lemon," *New York Times*, November 26, section 3: 1–11.

Andrews, E.L. (2002) "Becoming less German: New Swiss chief attacks Deutsche Bank's costly habits," *New York Times*, May 21: C1.

Anfuso, D. (1994) "Novell idea: a map for mergers," *Personnel Journal*, March: 48–55.

Apfelthaler, G., Muller, H.J., and Rehder, R.R. (2002) "Corporate global culture as competitive advantage: Learning from Germany and Japan in Alabama and Austria?" *Journal of World Business* 37: 108–118.

Armour, S. (2000) "Merging companies act to keep valuable employees," *USA Today*, November 24, Section B.

Armstrong, D. and Cole, P. (1996) "Managing distances and differences in geographically distributed work groups," in S.E. Jackson and M.N. Ruderman (eds.) *Diversity in Work Teams: Research Paradigms for a Changing Workplace*, Washington, DC: American Psychological Association, pp. 187–215.

Arndt, M. (2000) "Let's talk turkeys," *Business Week*, December 11: 44–48.

Arndt, M. (2001) "A merger's bitter harvest," *Business Week*, February 5: 112–114.

Arndt, M. (2002) "How companies can marry well," *Business Week*, March 4: 28.

Ashkanasy, N.M. and Jackson, C.R.A. (2001) "Organizational culture and climate," in N. Anderson, D.S. Ones, H.K., Sinangil, and C. Viswesvaran (eds.) *Handbook of Industrial, Work and Organizational Psychology*, vol. 2, London: Sage, pp. 399–415.

Ashkanasy, N.M., Wilderom, C.P.M., and Peterson, M.F. (eds.) (2000a) *Handbook of Organizational Culture and Climate*, Thousand Oaks, CA: Sage.

Ashkanasy, N.M., Broadfoot, L., and Falkus, S. (2000b) "Questionnaire measures of organizational culture," in N.M. Ashkanasy, C.P.M. Wilderom, and M.F. Peterson (eds.) *Handbook of Organizational Culture and Climate*, Thousand Oaks, CA: Sage, pp. 131–146.

Ashkenas, R.N. and Francis, S.C. (2000) "Integration managers: Special leaders for special times," *Harvard Business Review*, November–December: 108–114; Delta Consulting Group Study.

Ashkenas, R.N., DeMonaco, L.J., and Francis, S.C. (2000) "Making the deal real: How GE Capital integrates acquisitions," *Harvard Business Review*, January–February: 165–178.

Atlas, R.D. (2002) "How banks chased a mirage: Costly acquisitions of investment houses proved a bad fit," *New York Times*, Section 3.

Badaracco, J.L. (1991) *The Knowledge Link*, Boston: Harvard Business School Press.

Barkema, H.G., Shenkar, O., Vermeulen, F., and Bell, J. (1997) "Working abroad, working with others: How firms learn to operate international joint ventures," *Academy of Management Journal* 42 (2): 426–442.

Barney, J. (1991) "Firm resources and sustained competitive advantage," *Journal of Management* 17: 99–120.

Bartlett, C.A. and Ghoshal, S. (1989) *Managing across Borders: The Transnational Solution*, London: Hutchinson.

Bartlett, C.A. and Ghoshal, S. (1992) *Transnational Management*, Homewood, IL: Irwin.

Beamish, P.W. (1985) "The characteristics of joint ventures in developed and developing countries," *Columbia Journal of World Business*, 20 (3): 13–19.

Beamish, P.W. and Inkpen, A.C. (1995) "Keeping international joint ventures stable and profitable," *Long Range Planning* 28 (3): 26–36.

Becker, B.E. and Huselid, M.A. (1998) "High performance work systems and firm performance: A synthesis of research and managerial implications," in *Research in Personnel and Human Resources Management*, ed. G. Ferris, Greenwich, CT: JAI Press.

Becker, B.E., Huselid, M.A., Pinkus, P.S., and Spratt, M.F. (1997) "HR as a source of shareholder value: Research and recommendations," *Human Resource Management* 36 (1) (Spring): 39–48.

Becker, B.E., Huselid, M.A., and Ulrich, D. (2001) *The HR Scorecard*, Boston, MA: Harvard Business School Press.

Becker, G.S. (1964) *Human Capital*, New York: National Bureau of Economic Research.

Bere, J.F. (1987) "Global partnering: Making a good match," *Directors and Boards* 11 (2): 16.

Berger, J., Cohen, B.P., and Zelditch, M. Jr. (1966) "Status characteristics and expectation states," in J. Berger, M. Zelditch Jr., and B. Anderson (eds.) *Sociological Theories in Progress*, Boston, MA: Houghton Mifflin, pp. 47–73.

Berlew, F.K. (1984) "The joint venture: A way into foreign markets," *Harvard Business Review*, July–August: 48–54.

Berry, J.W. (1994) "Acculturation and psychological adaptation," in A.M. Bouvy, F.J.R. van de Vijver, P. Boski, and P. Schmitz (eds.), *Journeys into Cross-cultural Psychology*, Lisse, the Netherlands: Swets & Zeitlinger, pp. 129–141.

Best, D.L. and Williams, J.E. (2001) "Gender and culture," in D. Matsumoto (ed.) *The Handbook of Culture and Psychology*, Oxford: Oxford University Press, pp. 195–219.

Beyer, J.M. (1981) "Ideologies, values, and decision making in organizations," in P.C. Nystrom and W.H. Starbuck (eds.) *Handbook of Organizational Design*, vol. 2, New York: Oxford University Press, pp. 166–202.

Bhagat, R.S., Kedia, B.L., Harveston, P.D., and Triandis, H.C. (2002) "Cultural variations in the cross-border transfer of organizational knowledge: An integrative framework," *Academy of Management Review* 27 (2): 204–221.

Bianco, A. (2000) "When a merger turns messy," *Business Week*, July 17: 90–93.

Black, J.S., Gregersen, H.B., Mendenhall, M.E., and Stroh, L.K. (1999) *Globalizing People through International Assignments*, Reading, MA: Addison-Wesley.

Blodgett, L.L. (1991) "Partner contributions as predictors of equity shares in international joint ventures," *Journal of International Business Studies* 22: 63–78.

Bloom, H. (2002) "Can the United States export diversity?" *Across the Board*, March/April: 47–51.

Bobier, S. (2000) Personal communication in company seminar for J&J, November 7.

Bond, R.A. and Smith, P. (1996) "Culture and conformity: A meta-analysis of studies using the Asch line judgment task," *Psychological Bulletin* 119: 11–137.

Bottger, P.C. and Yetton, P.W. (1988) "An integration of process and decision-scheme explanations of group problem-solving performance," *Organizational Behavior and Human Decision Processes* 42: 234–249.

Bourdreau, J.W. and Berger, C.J. (1985) "Decision-theoretic utility analysis applied to employee separations and acquisitions," *Journal of Applied Psychology* 70: 581–612.

Boudreau, J.W. and Rynes, S.L. (1985) "Role of recruitment in staffing utility analysis," *Journal of Applied Psychology* 70 (2): 354–366.

Bower, J.L. (2001) "Not all M&As are alike – and that," *Harvard Business Review*, March: 93–101.

Bradley, P., Hendry, C., and Perkins, S. (1988) "Global or multi-local? The significance of international values in reward strategy," in C. Brewster and H. Harris (eds) *International HRM: Contemporary Issues in Europe*, London: Routledge.

Brass, D.J. (1984) "Being in the right place: A structural analysis of individual influence in organization," *Administrative Science Quarterly* 29: 518–539.

Brewer, M.B. (1979) "In-group bias in the minimal intergroup situation: A cognitive–motivational analysis," *Psychological Bulletin* 86: 307–324.

Brewster, C. (1995). "Towards a European model of human resource management," *Journal of International Business Studies* 26: 1–21.

Brewster, C. and Harris, H. (1999) *International HR*, London: Routledge.

Brodbeck, F.C. *et al.* (2000) "Cultural variation of leadership prototypes across 22 European countries," *Journal of Occupational and Organizational Psychology* 73: 1–29.

Bromiley, P. and Cummings, L.L. (1993) "Organizations with trust: Theory and measurement," Paper presented at the meeting of the Academy of Management Meetings, Atlanta, GA.

Brown, R.C. (1995) "Employment and labor law: Considerations in international human resource management," in O. Shenkar (ed.) *Global Perspectives of Human Resource Management*, Englewood Cliffs, NJ: Prentice Hall, pp. 37–59.

Brown, R.J. (1990) "Mixed marriages," *International Management*, December: 84.

Brown, R.J. (1991) "Testing times," *Personnel Today*, February 5: 5.

Buckley, P.J. and Casson, M. (1998) "A theory of cooperation in international business," in F. Contractor and P. Lorange (eds.) *Cooperative Strategies in International Business*, Lexington, MA: Lexington Books, pp. 31–53.

"Business: The amazing portable sarariman" (1999) *The Economist*, 20 November.

Caligiuri, P.M. and Lazarova, M. (2000) "Strategic repatriation policies to enhance global leadership development," in M. Mendenhall, T. Kuehlmann, and G. Stahl (eds.) *Developing Global Business Leaders: Policies, Processes, and Innovations*, New York: Quorum Books.

Carli, L.L. (1989) "Gender differences in interaction style and influence," *Journal of Personality and Social Psychology* 56: 565–576.

Cascio, W.F. (1991) *Costing Human Resource: The Financial Impact of Behavior in Organization*, Boston: PWS-Kent.

Cascio, W.F. and Bailey, E. (1995) "International human resource management: The state of research and practice," in O. Shenkar (ed.) *Global Perspectives of Human Resource Management*, Englewood Cliffs, NJ: Prentice Hall, pp. 15–36.

Cascio, W.F. and Serapio, M.G. Jr. (1991), "Human resource systems in an international alliance: The undoing of a done deal?" *Organizational Dynamics*, Winter: 63–74.

Charman, A. (1999) "Global mergers and acquisitions: The human resource challenge," *International Focus* (Alexandria, VA: Society for Human Resource Management).

Charman, A. and Carey, D. (2000) "A CEO roundtable on making mergers succeed," *Harvard Business Review*, May–June: 145–154.

Chattopadhyay, P. (1999) "Beyond direct and symmetrical effects: The influence of demographic dissimilarity on organizational citizenship behavior," *Academy of Management Journal* 42: 273–287.

Chi, T. and McGuire, D.J. (1996) "Collaborative ventures and value of learning: Integrating the transaction cost and strategic option perspectives on the choice of market entry modes," *Journal of International Business* 2: 285–307.

Child, J. (1977) *Organization*, New York: Harper & Row.

Child, J. and Faulkner, D. (1998) *Strategies of Cooperation*, Oxford: Oxford University Press.

Child, J. and Markoczy, L. (1993) "Host-country managerial behavior and learning in Chinese and Hungarian joint ventures," *Journal of Management Studies* 30: 611–631.

Child, J., Faulkner, D., and Pitkethly, R. (2001) *The Management of International Acquisitions*, Oxford: Oxford University Press.

Chiu, W.C.K., Chan, A.W., Snape, E., and Redman, T. (2001) "Age stereotypes and discriminatory attitudes towards older workers: An East–West comparison," *Human Relations* 54: 629–661.

Chronicle of Higher Education (1992) "The *Chronicle of Higher Education* Almanac," *Chronicle of Higher Education* 39: 15.

Cohen, W.M. and Levinthal, D.A. (1990) "Absorptive capacity: A new perspective on learning and innovations," *Administrative Science Quarterly* 35: 128–152.

Colvin, G. (1998) "M&A and you: Career power," *Fortune*, June 22: 173–175.

Colvin, G. (2001) "The changing art of becoming unbeatable," *Fortune*, November 12: 299.

Conference Board (2000) *Employee Communication during Mergers*, New York.

Conlin, M. (2001) "Where layoffs are a last resort," *Business Week*, October 8: 42.

Conner, K.R. (1991) "A historical comparison of resource-based theory and five schools of thought within industrial organization economics: Do we have a new theory of the firm?" *Journal of Management* 17 (1): 121–154.

Conner, K.R. and Prahalad, C.K. (1996) "A resource base theory of the firm: Knowledge vs opportunism," *Organization Science* 7: 77–501.

Contractor, F.J. and Lorange, P. (eds.) (1988) *Cooperative Studies in International Business*, Lexington, MA: Lexington Books.

Contractor, F.J. and Ra, W. (2002) "How knowledge attributes influence alliance governance choices: A theory development note," *Journal of International Management* 8: 11–27.

Coy, P. (1999) "The alliance manager: I'M O.K., YOU'RE O.K.," *Business Week*, October 5: 134.

Creswell, J. (2001a) "When a merger fails: Lessons from Sprint," *Fortune*, April 30: 185–187.

Creswell, J. (2001b) "First cold front," *Fortune*, February 5: 26.

Cyr, D.J. (1995) *The Human Resource Challenge of International Joint Ventures*, Westport, CT: Quorum Books.

Daft, R.L. and Weick, K.E. (1984) "Toward a model of organizations as interpretation systems," *Academy of Management Review* 9: 284–295.

Datta, D.K. (1988) "International joint ventures: A framework for analysis," *Journal of General Management* 14 (2): 78–91.

Datta, D.K. and Guthrie, J.P. (1994) "Executive succession: Organizational antecedents of CEO characteristics," *Strategic Management Journal* 15: 432–452.

Davenport, T. (2000) "Workers are not assets," *Across the Board*, June: 30–34.

Delaney, J.T. (1996) "Workplace cooperation: Current problems, new approaches," *Journal of Labor Research* 17 (1) (Winter): 45–61.

Denison, D.R. (1996) "What is the difference between organizational culture and organizational climate? A native's point of view on a decade of paradigm wars," *Academy of Management Review* 21: 619–654.

Deogun, N. and Scannell, K. (2001) "Market swoon stifles M & A's red-hot start, but old economy supplies a surprise bounty," *Wall Street Journal*, January 2: R4.

"Deutsche Bank is shedding all its shares of Munich Re" (2002) *New York Times*, June 19: W1.

"Deutsche learns well from UK, US models" (2001) *Financial Times*, October 15.

Dickson, M.W., Aditya, R.M., and Chhokar, J.S. (2000) "Definition and interpretation in cross-cultural organizational culture research: Some pointers from the GLOBE research program," in N.M. Ashkanasy, C.P.M. Wilderom, and M.F. Peterson (eds.) *Handbook of Organizational Culture and Climate*, Thousand Oaks, CA: Sage, pp. 447–464.

DiMaggio, P.J. and Powell, W.W. (1983) "The iron cage revisited: Institutional isomorphism and collective rationality in organizational fields," *American Sociology Review* 35: 147–160.

Donaldson, T. and Preston, L.E. (1995) "The stakeholder theory of the corporation: Concepts, evidence, and implications," *Academy of Management Review* 20: 65–91.

Dowling, P.J., Welch, D.E., and Schuler, R.S. (1999) *International Human Resource Management: Managing People in a Multinational Context*, Cincinnati, OH: Southwestern Publishing.

Doz, Y. (1996) "The evolution of cooperation in strategic alliances: Initial conditions or learning processes?" *Strategic Management Journal* 17: 55–83.

Doz, Y.L. and Hamel, G. (1998) *Alliance Advantage: The Art of Creating Value through Partnering*, Boston: Harvard Business School Press.

Doz, Y. and Prahalad, K. (1981) "Headquarters influence and strategic control in MNCs," *Sloan Management Review* 23 (1): 15–29.

Doz, Y., Hamel, G., and Prahalad, C.D. (1986) "Strategic partnerships: Success or surrender?" Paper presented at the Conference on Cooperative Strategies in International Business, The Wharton School and Rutgers University.

Dreyfuss, J. (2001) "AXA: Here comes the hard part," *Bloomberg News*, pp. 57–62.

Drucker, P. (2001) "The next society," *The Economist*, November 3: 5.

Drucker, P.F. (1989) *The New Realities*, New York: Harper & Row.

Dyer, J.H. (1997) "Effective interfirm collaboration: How firms minimize transaction costs and maximize transaction value," *Strategic Management Journal* 18: 535–556.

Dyer, L. (1990) *Human Resource Planning*, Washington, DC: Bureau of National Affairs.

Eagly, A.H. and Carli, L.L. (1981) "Sex of researchers and sex-typed communications as determinants of sex differences in influenceability: A meta-analysis of social influence studies," *Psychological Bulletin* 90: 1–20.

Eagly, A.H. and Johnson, B.T. (1990) "Gender and leadership style: A meta-analysis," *Psychological Bulletin* 108: 223–256.

Earley, P.C. and Mosakowski, E.M. (2000) "Creating hybrid team cultures: An empirical test of international team functioning," *Academy of Management Journal* 43: 26–49.

Economist, The (2000) "The DaimlerChrysler emulsion," July 29–August 4.

Economist, The (2001) "The great mergers wave breaks," January 27: 59–60.

Economist Intelligence Unit Report (1999) *Managing Alliances and Acquisitions in Latin America*, New York: The Economist Intelligence Unit.

Edwards, P., Ferner, A., and Sisson, K. (1996) "The conditions for international human resource management," *International Journal of Human Resource Management* 7 (1): 20–40.

Egelhoff, W.G. (1991) "Information-processing theory and the multinational enterprise," *Journal of International Business Studies* 22 (third quarter): 341–367.

Eisenhardt, K.M. (1988) "Agency and institutional explanations of compensation in retail sales," *Academy of Management Journal* 31: 488–511.

Elder, G.H. Jr. (1974) *Children of the Great Depression*, Chicago: University of Illinois Press.

Elsass, P.M. and Graves, L.M. (1997) "Demographic diversity in decision-making groups: The experiences of women and people of color," *Academy of Management Review* 22: 946–974.

Emerson, V. (2001) "An interview with Carlos Ghosn, President of Nissan Motors, Ltd. and Industry Leader of the Year (*Automotive News*, 2000)," *Journal of World Business* 36 (1): 3–10.

"Employee communication during mergers" (2000) New York: The Conference Board.

Evans, P., Pucik, V., and Barsoux, J.-L. (2002) *The Global Challenge: Frameworks for International Human Resource Management*, Boston, MA: McGraw-Hill.

"Face value: Kozlowski's colours" (2002) *The Economist*, January 26: 60.

Fairlamb, D. (2000) "The Continent regains its allure," *Business Week*, June 26: 226–227.

Fairlamb, D. (2002) "Can this man crank up Deutsche?" *Business Week*, 56–57.

Fealy, E., Kompare, D., and Howes, P. (2001) "Compensation and benefits in global mergers and acquisitions," in C. Reynolds (ed.) *Guide to Global Compensation and Benefits*, 2nd edn., San Diego, CA: Harcourt, pp. 25–54.

Festinger, L., Schachter, S., and Black. K. (1950) *Social Pressures in Informal Groups: A Study of Human Factors in Housing*, New York: HarperCollins.

Finkelstein, S. and Haleblian, J. (2002) "Understanding acquisition performance: The role of transfer effects," *Organization Science* 13 (1): 36–47.

Fischmann, M. and Levinthal, D.A. (1991) "Honeymoons and the liability of adolescence: A new perspective on duration dependence in social and organizational relationships," *Academy of Management Review* 6: 442–468.

Flamholtz, E.G. and Lacey, J.M. (1981) *Personnel Management: Human Capital Theory, and Human Resource Accounting*, Los Angeles: Institute of Industrial Relations, University of California.

Florkowski, G.W. and Nath, R. (1993) "MNC responses to the legal environment of international human resource management," *International Journal of Human Resource Management* 4: 305–324.

Florkowski, G.W. and Schuler, R.S. (1994) "Auditing human resource management in the global environment," *International Journal of Human Resource Management* 5: 4.

Foss, N.J. and Pedersen, T. (2002) "Transferring knowledge in MNCs: The role of sources of subsidiary knowledge and organizational context," *Journal of International Management* 8: 49–67.

Frayne, C.A. and Geringer, J.M. (1990) "The strategic use of human resource management practices as control mechanisms in international joint ventures," *Research in Personnel and Human Resources Management*, suppl. 2: 53–69.

Frayne, C.A. and Geringer, J.M. (2000) "Challenges facing general managers of international joint ventures," unpublished paper.

Frederiksen, N. (1986) "Toward a broader conception of human intelligence," *American Psychology* 41: 445–452.

Freeman, E. and Liedtka, J. (1997) "Stakeholder capitalism and the value chain," *European Management Journal* 15 (3) (June): 286–296.

Freidheim, C.F. Jr. (1998) *The Trillion-Dollar Enterprise: How the Alliance Revolution Will Transform Global Business*, Reading, MA: Perseus Books.

Friedman, M.A. (1970) "Friedman Doctrine: The social responsibility of business is to increase its profits," *New York Times Magazine*, September 13: 32ff.

Galpin, T.J. and Herndon, M. (1999) *The Complete Guide to Mergers and Acquisitions*, San Francisco: Jossey-Bass.

Garvin, D.A. (1993) "Building a learning organization," *Harvard Business Review* 71 (July–August): 78–92.

Gates, S. (2001) *Performance Measurement during Merger and Acquisition Integration*, New York: The Conference Board.

Georgas, J. (1998) "Intergroup contact and acculturation of immigrants," Paper presented at the Fourteenth International Congress of the International Association for Cross-cultural Psychology, Bellingham, WA, August.

Geringer, J.M. and Hebert, L. (1989) "Control and performance of international joint ventures," *Journal of International Business Studies* 20 (Summer): 235–254.

Geringer, J.M. and Hebert, L. (1991) "Measuring performance of international joint ventures," *Journal of International Business Studies* 22: 253–267.

Ghemawat, P. (2001) "Distance still matters," *Harvard Business Review*, September: 137–147.

Ghemawat, P. and Ghadar, F. (2000) "The dubious logic of global megamergers," *Harvard Business Review*, July–August: 65–72.

Gibney, F. Jr. (1999) "Daimler-Benz and Chrysler merge to DaimlerChrysler," *Time*, May 24, www.geocites.com/MotorCity/Downs/9323/dc.htm, p.5

Gibson, C.B. (1999) "Do they do what they believe they can? Group-efficacy beliefs and group performance across tasks and cultures," *Academy of Management Journal* 42: 138–152.

Giles, P. (2000) "The importance of HR in making your merger work," Workspan, August: 16–20.

Ginsberg, A. (1990) "Connecting diversification to performance: A sociocognitive approach," *Academy of Management Review* 15: 514–535.

Glass, L.G. (1992) *He Says, She Says: Closing the Communication Gap between the Sexes*, New York: Putnam.

Glunk, U., Heijltjes, M.C., and Olie, R. (2001) "Design characteristics and functioning of top management teams in Europe," *European Management Journal* 19: 291–300.

Gomes-Casseres, B. (1987) "Joint venture instability: Is it a problem?" *Columbia Journal of World Business* 22 (2): 97–102.

Gomes-Casseres, B. (1989) "Joint ventures in the face of global competition," *Sloan Management Review* 30 (Spring): 17–26.

Graham, J.L., Mintu, A.T., and Rodgers, W. (1994) "Exploration of negotiation behaviors in 10 foreign cultures using a model developed in the United States," *Management Science* 40: 72–95.

Grant, R.M. and Spender, J.C. (1996) "Knowledge and the firm: An overview," *Strategic Management Journal* 12: 83–103.

Green, S.C. and Walsh, A. (1988) "Cybernetics and dependence: Reframing the control concept," *Academy of Management Review* 13 (2): 287–301.

Greengard, S. (2000) "Due diligence: The devils in the details," *Workforce*, October: 69

Greenhalgh, L. (2000) "Ford Motor Company's CEO Jac Nasser on transformational change, e-business, and environmental responsibility," *Academy of Management Executive* 14 (3): 46–51.

Grunroos, C. (1990) *Service Management and Marketing*, Lexington, MA: Lexington Books.

Gunther, M. (2001) Understanding AOL's grand unified theory of the media cosmos," *Fortune*, January 8: 72–82.

Gupta, A.K. and Govindarajan, V. (2002) "Cultivating a global mindset," *Academy of Management Executive* 16 (1): 116–126.

Habeck, M.M., Kröger, F., and Träm, M.R. (2000) *After the Merger: Seven Rules for Successful Post-merger Integration*, New York/London: Financial Times/Prentice Hall.

Hakim, D. (2002) "G.M. rises and Nissan falls in J.D. power quality survey," *New York Times*, May 31: C4.

Hakim, D. with Maynard, M. (2002) "Hot dogs, apple pie and Toyota," *New York Times*, February 17: C3.

Hall, R. (1992) "The strategic analysis of intangible resources," *Strategic Management Journal* 13: 135–144.

Hambrick, D.C., Li, J., Xin, K., and Tsui, A.S. (2001) "Composition gaps and downward spirals in international joint venture management groups," *Strategic Management Journal* 22: 1033–1053.

Hamel, G. (1991) "Competition for competence and inter-partner learning within international strategic alliances," *Strategic Management Journal* 12 (special issue): 83–104.

Hamel, G. (2001) "Avoiding the guillotine," *Fortune*, April 2: 139–144.

Hamel, G. and Prahalad, C.K. (1994) *Competing for the Future: Breakthrough Strategies for Seizing Control of Your Industry and Creating the Markets of Tomorrow*, Boston: Harvard Business School Press.

Hammonds, K.H., Zellner, W., and Melcher, R. (1997) "Writing a new social contract," *Business Week*, March 11: 60–61.

Hanoka, M. (1997) "Effective rightsizing strategies in Japan and America: Is there a convergence of employment practices?" *Academy of Management Executive* 11 (2): 57–67.

Handy, C. (1998) "A better capitalism," *Across the Board*, April: 16–22.

Harbison, J.R. (1996) *Strategic Alliances: Gaining a Competitive Advantage*, New York: The Conference Board.

Harrigan, K.R. (1986) *Managing for Joint Venture Success*, Boston, MA: Lexington.

Harrigan, K.R. (1987a) "Managing joint ventures," *Management Review* 76 (2): 24–42.

Harrigan, K.R. (1987b) "Strategic alliances: Their new role in global competition," *Columbia Journal of World Business* 22 (2): 67–69.

Harrison, J. and St. John, C. (1996) "Managing and partnering with external stakeholders," *Academy of Management Executive* 10 (2): 46–60.

Harvey, M., Speier, C., and Novicevic, M.M. (1999) "The impact of emerging markets on staffing the global organization: A knowledge-based view," *Journal of International Management* 5 (3): 167–186.

Hedberg, G.L.T. (1981) "How organizations learn and unlearn," in P.C. Nystrom and W.H. Starbuck (eds.) *Handbook of Organizational Design*, vol. 1, New York: Oxford University Press.

Hedlund, G. and Nonaka, I. (1993) "Models of knowledge management in the West and Japan," in P. Lorange, B. Chakravarthy, J. Roos, and Van de Ven, A.H. (eds.) *Implementing Strategic Processes: Change, Learning, and Cooperation*, Oxford: Blackwell, pp. 117–144.

Hellriegel, D., Jackson, S.E., and Slocum, J.W. Jr. (1999) *Management*, 9th edn., Cincinnati: Southwestern Publishing.

Hennart, J.F. (1988) "A transaction cost theory of equity joint ventures," *Strategic Management Journal* 9: 36–74.

Hennart, J.F. and Reddy, S. (1997) "The choice between mergers/acquisitions and joint ventures: The case of Japanese investors in the United States," *Strategic Management Journal* 18: 1–12.

Hergert, M. and Morris, D. (1988) "Trends in international collaborative agreements," in F. Contractor and P. Lorange (eds.) *Cooperative Strategies in International Business*, Toronto: Lexington Books, pp. 1–28.

Hill, C.W.L. (1990) "Cooperation, opportunism, and the invisible hand: Implications for transaction cost theory," *Academy of Management Journal* 15: 500–513.

Hitt, M.A., Harrison, J.S., and Ireland, R.D. (2001) *Mergers and Acquisitions: A Guide to Creating Value for Stakeholders*, Oxford: Oxford University Press.

Hodgkinson, G.P. (2001) "Cognitive processes in strategic management: Some emerging trends and future directions," in N. Anderson, D.S. Ones, H.K. Sinangil, and C. Viswesvaran (eds.) *Handbook of Industrial, Work and Organizational Psychology*, vol. 2, London: Sage, pp. 416–440.

Hoffman, E. (1985) "The effect of race-ratio composition on the frequency of organizational communication," *Social Psychology Quarterly* 48: 17–26.

Hofstede, G. (1970) *Culture's Consequences: International Differences in Work-Related Values*, Beverly Hills, CA: Sage.

Hofstede, G. (1991) *Cultures and Organizations: Software of the Mind*, London: HarperCollins.

Hofstede, G. (1993) "Cultural constraints in management theories," *Academy of Management Executive* 71 (1): 81–93.

Hofstede, G. (1997) *Culture and Organizations: Software of the Mind*, rev. edn., New York: McGraw-Hill.

Hofstede, G. (1998) "Organization culture," in M. Poole and M. Warner (eds.) *The ICBM Handbook of Human Resource Management*, ITP: London, pp. 237–255.

Hofstede, G., Neuijen, B., Ohayav, D.D., and Sanders, G. (1990) "Measuring organizational culture: A qualitative and quantitative study across twenty cases," *Administrative Science Quarterly* 25: 286–316.

Holson, L.M. (2000) "Whiz kid: Young deal maker is a force behind a company's growth," *New York Times on the Web*, June 28.

Hooijberg, R. and Petrock, F. (1993) "On cultural change: Using the competing values framework to help leaders execute a transformational strategy," *Human Resource Management* 32: 29–50.

Hopkins, H.D. (1999) "Cross-border mergers and acquisitions: Global and regional perspectives," *European Management Journal* 5 (3): 207–219.

House, R.J., Hanges, P.J., Ruiz-Quintanilla, S.A., Dorfman, P.W., Javidan, M., Dickson, M., Gupta, V., and 170 country investigators (1999) "Cultural influences on leadership and organizations: Project GLOBE," in W. Mobley, J. Gessner, and V. Arnold (eds.) *Advances in Global Leadership*, vol. 1, Stamford, CT: JAI Press, pp. 171–234.

Huber, G.P. (1991) "Organizational learning: The contributing processes and literatures," *Organization Science* 2 (1): 88–115.

Huff, A.S. (ed.) (1990) *Mapping Strategic Thought*, Chichester, U.K.: Wiley.

Huff, A.S. and Jenkins, M. (eds.) (in press) *Mapping Strategic Knowledge*, London: Sage.

Huff, A.S. and Schwenk, C.R. (1990) "Bias and sensemaking in good times and bad," in A.S. Huff (ed.) *Mapping Strategic Thought*, Chichester, U.K.: Wiley, pp. 89–108.

Hui, C.H. and Luk, C.L. (1997) "Industrial/organizational psychology," in J.W. Berry, M.H. Segall, and C. Kagitçibaşi (eds.) *Handbook of Cross-cultural Psychology*, vol. 3, Boston, MA: Allyn & Bacon, pp. 371–411.

Hunt, M.S. (1972) "Competition in the major home appliance industry," unpublished doctoral dissertation, Harvard University.

Huselid, M.A, Jackson, S.E., and Schuler, R.S. (1997) "Technical and strategic human resource management effectiveness as determinants of firm performance," *Academy of Management Journal* 40: 171–188.

Hyatt, J. (1988) "The partnership route," *INC.*, December: 145–148.

Ilgen, D., LePine, J., and Hollenbeck, J. (1999) "Effective decision making in multinational teams," in C. Earley and M. Erez (eds.) *New Approaches to Intercultural and International Industrial/Organizational Psychology*, San Francisco: New Lexington Press, pp. 377–409.

Inkpen, A. (1995) *The Management of International Joint Ventures: An Organizational Learning Perspective*, London: Routledge.

Inkpen, A.C. and Beamish, P.W. (1997) "Knowledge, bargaining power and international joint venture stability," *Academy of Management Review* 22: 177–202.

Inkpen, A.C. and Crossan, M.M. (1995) "Believing is seeing: Joint ventures and organization learning," *Journal of Management Studies* 32 (5): 595–618.

Inkpen, A.C. and Currall, S. (1997) "International joint venture trust: An empirical examination," in P.W. Beamish and J.P. Killing (eds.) *Cooperative Strategies: North American Perspectives*, San Francisco: New Lexington Press, pp. 308–334.

Inkpen, A.C. and Dinur, A. (1997) "Knowledge management processes and international joint ventures," *Organizational Science* 8: 267–289.

Isen, A.M. and Baron, R.A. (1991) "Positive affect as a factor in organizational behavior," in L. Cummings and B.M. Staw (eds.) *Research in Organizational Behavior*, vol. 13, Greenwich, CN: JAI Press, pp. 1–53.

Jackson, S.E. (1992a) "Team composition on organizational settings: Issues in managing an increasingly diverse work force," in S. Worchel, W. Wood, and J.A. Simpson (eds.) *Group Process and Productivity*, Newbury Park, CA: Sage, pp. 204–261.

Jackson, S.E. (1992b) *Diversity in the Workplace: Human Resources Initiatives*, New York: Guilford.

Jackson, S.E. (1996) "The consequences of diversity in multidisciplinary teams," in M.A. West (ed.) *Handbook of Workgroup Psychology*, New York: Wiley, pp. 53–76.

Jackson, S.E. and Schuler, R.S. (1995) "Understanding human resource management in the context of organizations and their environments," in M. Rosenzweig and L. Porter (eds.) *Annual Review of Psychology*, Palo Alto, CA: Annual Reviews, Inc., pp. 237–264.

Jackson, S.E. and Schuler, R.S. (2000) *Managing Human Resources: A Partnership Perspective*, 7th edn., Cincinnati, OH: Southwestern Publishing.

Jackson, S.E. and Schuler, R.S. (2003) *Managing Human Resources: A Partnership Perspective*, 8th edn., Cincinnati, OH: Southwestern Publishing.

Jackson, S.E., Brett, J.F., Sessa, V.I., Cooper, D.M., Julin, J.A., and Peyronnin, K. (1991) "Some differences make a difference: Individual dissimilarity and group heterogeneity as correlates of recruitment, promotions, and turnover," *Journal of Applied Psychology* 76: 675–689.

Jackson, S.E., May, K.E., and Whitney, K. (1995) "Under the dynamics of diversity in decision-making teams," in R.A. Guzzo and E. Salas (eds.) *Team Effectiveness and Decision Making in Organizations*, San Francisco: Jossey-Bass, pp. 204–61.

Jaeger, A.M. (1986) "Organization development and national culture: Where's the fit?" *Academy of Management Review* 11: 178–190.

Jaffe, M.P. (1987) "Workforce 2000: Forecast of occupational change," in the technical appendix to W.B. Johnston and A.E. Packer, *Workforce 2000: Work and Workers for the 21st Century*, Washington, DC: U.S. Department of Labor, p. 23.

Javidan, M. (2002), "Siemens CEO Heinrich von Pierer on cross-border acquisitions," *Academy of Management Executive* 16 (1): 13–15.

Jensen, M and Meckling, W. (1976) "Theory of the firm: Managerial behavior, agency costs, and ownership structure," *Journal of Financial Economics* 3: 305–360.

Johnson, J.L., Cullen, J.B., Sakano, T., and Takenouchi, H. (1996) "Setting the stage for trust and strategic integration in Japanese–U.S. cooperative alliances," *Journal of International Business Studies* 27: 981–1004.

Johnson, J.W. (1996) "Linking employee perceptions of service climate to customer satisfaction," *Personnel Psychology* 49: 831–846.

Johnston, W.B. and Packer, A.E. (1987) *Workforce 2000: Work and Workers for the 21st Century*, Washington, DC: U.S. Department of Labor.

Jones, T.M. (1995) "Instrumental stakeholder theory: A synthesis of ethics and economics," *Academy of Management Review* 20: 404–437.

Kamoche, K. (1997) "Knowledge creation and learning in the international firm," *International Journal of Human Resource Management* 8 (3): 213–225.

Kaplan, R.S. and Norton, D.P. (1996) *The Balanced Scorecard: Translating Strategy into Action*, Boston: Harvard Business School Press.

Kapner, S. (2002a) "Banking mergers gain momentum in Europe," *New York Times*, April 24.

Kapner, S. (2002b) "Deal for Miller Brewing may be first in a series," *New York Times*, May 31: C2.

Kashima, Y. (2001) "Culture and social cognition: Toward a social psychology of cultural dynamics," in D. Matsumoto (ed.), *The Handbook of Culture and Psychology*, Oxford: Oxford University Press, pp. 325–360.

Katz, D. and Kahn, R.L. (1978) *The Social Psychology of Organization*, New York: Wiley.

Katz, P.A. and Taylor, D.A. (1988) *Eliminating Racism: Profiles in Controversy*, New York: Plenum Press.

Kay, I.T. and Shelton, M. (2000) "The people problems in mergers," *McKinsey Quarterly* 4: 29–37.

Khanna, T., Gulati, R., and Nohria, N. (1998) "The dynamics of learning alliances: Competition, cooperation, and relative scope," *Strategic Management Journal* 19: 193–210.

Killing, J.P. (1983) *Strategies for Joint Venture Success*, New York: Praeger Publishers.

Kogut, B. (1988) "Joint ventures: theoretical and empirical perspectives," *Strategic Management Journal* 9: 319–332.

Kogut, B. and Zander, U. (1996) "What firms do? Coordination, identity and learning," *Organizational Science* 7: 502–518.

KPMG (2000) *KPMG Mergers and Acquisitions: A Global Research Report*, New York: KPMG.

Kraly, E.P. and Hirschman, C. (1990) "Racial and ethnic inequality among children in the United States – 1940 and 1950," *Social Forces* 69: 33–51.

Kramer, R.M. and Brewer, M.B. (1984) "Effects on group identity of resource use in a simulated common dilemma," *Journal of Personality and Social Psychology* 46: 1044–57.

Krass, P. (2001) "Why do we do it?" *Across the Board*, May–June: 22–29.

Kroger, F. and Tram, M.R. (2000) *After the Merger: Seven Rules for Post-merger Integration*, New York/London: Prentice Hall/Financial Times.

Lane, P.J., Salk, J.E., and Lyles, M.A. (2001) "Absorptive capacity, learning, and performance in international joint ventures," *Strategic Management Journal* 22: 1139–1161.

Lasserre, P. (1983) "Strategic assessment of international partnership in Asian countries," *Asia Pacific Journal of Management*, September: 72–78.

Lau, D.C. and Murnighan, J.K. (1998) "Demographic diversity and faultlines: The compositional dynamics of organizational groups," *Academy of Management Review* 23: 325–340.

Laurent, A. (1986) "The cross-cultural puzzle of international human resource management," *Human Resource Management* 25: 91–102.

Lei, D., Slocum, J.W. Jr., and Pitts, R.A. (1997) "Building cooperative advantage: Managing strategic alliances to promote organizational learning," *Journal of World Business* 32 (3): 202–223.

Leung, K. (1997) "Negotiation and reward allocation across cultures," in P.C. Earley and M. Erez (eds.) *New Perspectives on International Industrial/Organizational Psychology*, San Francisco: New Lexington, pp. 640–675.

Leung, K., Au, Y.F., Fernandez-Dols, J.M., and Iwawaki, S. (1992) "Preference for methods of conflict processing in two collectivist cultures," *International Journal of Psychology* 27: 195–209.

Levine, J.B. and Byrne, J.A. (1986) "Corporate odd couples," *Business Week*, July 21: 100–105.

Levine, J.M. and Moreland, R.L. (1990) "Progress in small group research," *Annual Review of Psychology* 41: 585–634.

Liberatore, M.D. (2000) "HR's relative importance in mergers and acquisitions," *Human Resource Executive*, March 2: 48.

Liebeskind, J.P., Oliver, A.L., Zucker, L., and Brewer, M. (1996) "Social networks, learning, and flexibility: Sourcing scientific knowledge in new biotechnology firms," *Organization Science* 7: 428–443.

Light, D.A. (2001) "Who goes, who stays?" *Harvard Business Review* 39: 35–46.

Lin, X. and Germain, R. (1998) "Sustaining satisfactory joint venture relationships: The role of conflict resolution strategy," *Journal of International Business Studies* 29 (1): 179–196.

Lincoln, E. (1999) "Job security in Japan," *Brookings Review*, Fall.

Lincoln, J.R. and Miller, J. (1979) "Work and friendship ties in organizations: A comparative analysis of relational networks," *Administrative Science Quarterly* 24: 181–199.

Lorange, P. (1986) "Human resource management in multinational cooperative ventures," *Human Resource Management* 25: 133–148.

Lowry, T. (2000) "AOL Time Warner: The thrill is gone," *Business Week*, October 16: 158–160.

Lucenko, K. (2000) "Strategies for growth," *Across the Board*, September: 63.

Luo, Y. (1998) "Joint venture success in China: How should we select a good partner," *Journal of World Business* 33 (2): 145–166.

Luo, Y. (1999) "Toward a conceptual framework of international joint venture negotiations," *Journal of International Management* 5: 141–165.

Luo, Y. (2001) "Antecedents and consequences of personal attachment in cross-cultural cooperative ventures," *Administrative Science Quarterly* 46: 177–201.

Luo, Y. (2002) "Capability exploitation and building in a foreign market: Implications for multinational enterprise," *Organization Science* 13 (1): 48–63.

Luo, Y. and Tan, J.J. (1998) "A comparison of multinational and domestic firms in an emerging market: A strategic choice perspective," *Journal of International Management* 4 (1): 21–40.

Lyles, M.A. (1987) "Common mistakes of joint venture experienced firms," *Columbia Journal of World Business* 22 (2): 79–85.

McGill, M.E., Slocum, J.W. Jr., and Lei, D. (1992) "Management practices in learning organizations," *Organizational Dynamics*, Summer: 5–17.

Main, J. (1990) "Making global alliance work," *Fortune*, December 17: 121–126.

Makhija, M.V. and Ganesh, U. (1997) "The relationship between control and partner learning in learning related joint ventures," *Organizational Science* 8 (2): 508–524.

Mann, L. (1980) "Cross-cultural studies of small groups," in H.C. Triandis and R.W. Brislin (eds.) *Handbook of Cross-cultural Psychology*, vol. 5, Boston, MA: Allyn & Bacon, pp. 155–209.

Marks, M.L. and Mirvis, P.H. (2000) "Creating an effective team structure," *Organizational Dynamics*, Winter: 35–47.

Marschan, R., Welch, D., and Welch, L. (1997) "Control in less hierarchical multinationals: The role of personal networks and informal communication," *International Business Review* 5 (2): 137–150.

Martinez, Z.L. and Ricks, D.A. (1989) "Multinational parent companies influence over human resource decisions of affiliates: U.S. firms in Mexico," *Journal of International Business Studies* 20 (3): 465–468.

Mayer, M.C.J. and Whittington, R. (1999) "Strategy, structure, and 'systemness': National institutions and corporate change in France, Germany, and the UK, 1950–1993," *Organization Studies* 20: 933–959.

Mendenhall, M. and Oddou, G. (1985) "The dimensions of expatriate acculturation," *Academy of Management Review* 10: 39–47.

Metha, S.N. (2000) "Lucent's new spin," *Fortune*, August 14: 30–31.

Meyer, J.W. and Rowan, B. (1977) "Institutionalized organizations: Formal structure as myth and ceremony," *American Journal of Sociology* 83: 340–363.

Miller, J.G. (1984) "Culture and the development of everyday social explanation," *Journal of Personality and Social Psychology* 46: 961–978.

Miller, J.G. (1987) "Cultural influences on the development of conceptual differentiation in person description," *British Journal of Developmental Psychology* 5: 309–319.

Millikin, F.J. and Martins, L.L. (1996) "Searching for common threads: Understanding the multiple effects of diversity in organizational groups," *Academy of Management Review* 21: 402–433.

Mirvis, P.H. and Marks, M.L. (1992) *Managing the Merger: Making It Work*, Englewood Cliffs, NJ: Prentice Hall.

"Mr. Ackermann expects" (2002) *The Economist*, May 2: 70.

Moran, R.T. and Abbott, J. (1994) *NAFTA: Managing the Cultural Differences*, Houston, TX: Gulf Publishing.

Morgan, P.V. (1986) "International human resource management: Fact or fiction?" *Personnel Administrator* 31 (9): 44.

Morosini, P. (1998) *Managing Cultural Differences: Effective Strategy and Execution across Cultures in Global Corporate Alliances*, Oxford: Elsevier.

Morris, D.A. and Hergert, M. (1987) "Trends in international collaborative agreements," *Columbia Journal of World Business* 22 (2): 15–21.

Morrison, E.W. (1997) "When employees feel betrayed: A model of how psychological contract violation develops," *Academy of Management Review* 22: 226–256.

Mudambi, R. (2002) "Knowledge management in multinational firms," *Journal of International Management* 8: 1–9.

Muller, J., Green, J., and Tierney, C. (2001) "Chrysler's rescue team," *Business Week*, January 15: 48–50.

Muson, H. (2002) "Friend? Foe? Both? The confusing world of corporate alliances," *Across the Board*, March–April: 19–25.

Nee, E. (2001) "Cisco: How it aims to keep right on growing," *Fortune*, February 5: 91–96.

Newburry, W. and Zeira, Y. (1997) "Implications for parent companies," *Journal of World Business* 32 (2): 87–102.

Nonaka, I. and Johansson, J.K. (1985) "Organizational learning in Japanese companies," in R.B. Lamb (ed.) *Advancement in Strategic Management*, Greenwich, CT: JAI Press.

Nonaka, I. and Takeuchi, H. (1995) *The Knowledge-Creating Company: How Japanese Companies Create the Dynamics of Innovation*, New York: Oxford University Press.

Nooteboom, J., Berger, H., and Noorderhaven, N.G. (1997) "Effects of trust and governance on relational risk," *Academy of Management Journal* 40: 308–338.

Numerof, R.F. and Abrams, M. (1998) "Integrating corporate culture from international M & A's," *HR Focus* 75 (6): 11–12.

Ohmae, K. (1989a) "The global logic of strategic alliance," *Harvard Business Review*, March–April: 143–154.

Ohmae. K. (1989b) "Managing in a borderless world," *Harvard Business Review*, May–June: 152–161.

Ohmae, K. (1989c) "Planting for a global harvest," *Harvard Business Review*, July–August: 136–145.

Ohmae, K. (1995) *Triad Power: The Coming Shape of Global Competition*, New York: Free Press.

Olmeda, E.L. (1979) "Acculturation: A psychometric perspective," *American Psychologist* 34: 1061–1070.

O'Reilly, A.J.F. (1988) "Establishing successful joint ventures in developing nations: A CEO's perspective," *Columbia Journal of World Business* 23 (1): 65–71.

O'Reilly, C. and Pfeffer, J. (2000) *Hidden Value: How Great Companies Achieve Extraordinary Results with Ordinary People*, Boston, MA: Harvard Business School Press.

Osterman, P.O. (1984) *Internal Labor Markets*, Cambridge, MA: Ballinger.

Parkhe, A. (1991) "Interfirm diversity, organizational learning, and longevity in global strategic alliances," *Journal of International Business Studies* 22: 579–602.

Parkhe, A. (1993) "Strategic alliance structuring: A game theoretic and transaction cost examination of interfirm cooperation," *Academy of Management Journal* 36: 794–829.

Pelled, L.H. and Xin, K.R. (1997) "Birds of a feather: Leader–member demographic similarity and organizational attachment in Mexico," *Leadership Quarterly* 8: 433–450.

"Performance measurement during mergers and acquisitions integration" (2000) New York: The Conference Board.

Perlmutter, H.V. and Heenan, D.A. (1986) "Cooperate to compete globally," *Harvard Business Review* 64 (2): 136–152.

Peterson, M.F. and Hofstede, G. (2000). "Culture: National values and organizational practices," in N.M. Ashkanasy, C.P.M. Wilderon, and M.F. Peterson (eds.) *Handbook of Organizational Culture and Climate*, Thousand Oaks, CA: Sage, pp. 401–416.

Pettigrew, T.F. (1997) "Generalized intergroup contact effects on prejudice," *Personality and Social Psychology Bulletin* 23: 173–185.

Pettigrew, T.F. (1998) "Intergroup contact theory," *Annual Review of Psychology* 49: 65–85.

Pfeffer, J. (1994) *Competitive Advantage through People*, Boston, MA: Harvard Business School Press.

Pfeffer, J. (1996) "When it comes to 'best practices' – why do smart organizations occasionally do dumb things?" *Organizational Dynamics*, Summer: 12–25.

Pfeffer, J. and Cohen, Y. (1984) "Determinants of internal labor markets in organization," *Administrative Science Quarterly* 29: 550–572.

Porter, M.E. (1980) *Competitive Strategy: Techniques for Analyzing Industries and Competitors*, New York: Free Press.

Porter, M.E. (1985) *Competitive Advantage: Creating and Sustaining Superior Performance*, New York: Free Press.

Porter, M.E. and Fuller, M. (1986) "Coalitions and global strategy," in M.E. Porter (ed.) *Competition in Global Industries*, Boston, MA: Harvard Business School Press, pp. 315–344.

Prahalad, C.K. and Doz, Y.L. (1987) *The Multinational Mission: Balancing Local Demands and Global Vision*, New York: Free Press.

Prahalad, C.K. and Hamel, G.C. (1990) "The core competence of the corporation," *Harvard Business Review* 68 (May–June): 79–91.

Prahalad, C.K. and Hamel, G.C. (1994) "Strategy as a field of study: Why search for a new paradigm?" *Strategic Management Journal* 15: 5–16.

Pucik, V. (1988) "Strategic alliances, organizational learning and competitive advantage: The HRM agenda," *Human Resource Management* 27 (1): 77–93.

Quinn, R.E. and Rohrbaugh, J. (1983) "A spatial model of effectiveness criteria: Toward a competing values approach to organizational analysis," *Management Science* 29: 363–377.

Rafeli, A. and Worline, M. (2000) "Symbols in organizational culture," in N.M. Ashkanasy, C.P.M. Wilderom, and M.F. Peterson (eds.) *Handbook of Organizational Culture and Climate*, Thousand Oaks, CA: Sage, pp. 71–84.

Ralston, D.A., Yu, K.-C., Wang, X., Terpstra, R.H., and He, W. (1996) "The cosmopolitan Chinese manager: Findings of a study on managerial values across the six regions of China," *Journal of International Management* 2: 79–109.

Ranft, A.L. and Lord, M.D. (2002) "Acquiring new technologies and capabilities: A grounded model of acquisition implementation," *Organizational Science* 13 (4): 420–441.

Reid, D., Bussier, D., and Greenway, K. (2001) "Alliance formation issues for knowledge-based enterprises," *International Journal of Management Reviews* 3 (1): 79–100.

Reuer, J.J. and Miller, K.D. (1997) "Agency costs and the performance implications of international joint venture internalization," *Strategic Management Journal* 18 (6): 425–438.

Reve, T. (1990) "The firm as a nexus of internal and external contracts," in M. Aoki, B. Gustafson, and O. Williamson (eds.) *The Firm as a Nexus of Treaties*, Newbury Park: Sage, pp. 133–161.

Rhodes, S.R. (1983) "Age-related differences in work attitudes and behavior: A review and conceptual analysis," *Psychological Bulletin* 93: 328–367.

Ridgeway, C.L. (1982) "Status in groups: The importance of motivation," *American Sociological Review* 47: 76–88.

Ridgeway, C. and Johnson, C. (1990) "What is the relationship between socioemotional behavior and status in task groups," *American Journal of Sociology* 95: 1189–1212.

Ring, P.S. and Van de Ven, A.H. (1992) "Structuring cooperative relationships between organizations," *Strategic Management Journal* 13: 483–498.

Ring, P.S. and Van de Ven, A.H. (1994) "Developmental processes of cooperative interorganizational relationship," *Academy of Management Review* 19: 90–118.

Robertson, C. and Jett, T. (1999) "Pro-environmental support: The environmental and industrial benefits of project XL at Merck & Co., Inc.," *Organizational Dynamics*, Summer: 81–88.

Robson, D. (2001) "The green utility that's in the black," *Business Week*, March 26: 108.

Roehl, T.W. and Truitt, J.F. (1987) "Stormy open marriages are better evidence from U.S., Japanese and French cooperative ventures in commercial aircraft," *Columbia Journal of World Business* 22 (2): 87–95.

Root, F. (1988) "Some taxonomies of international cooperative agreements," in F. Contractor and P. Lorange (eds.) *Cooperative Strategies in International Business*, Lexington, MA: Lexington Books.

Rosenkopf, L., Metiu, A., and George, V.P. (2001) "From the bottom up? Technical committee activity and alliance formation," *Administrative Science Quarterly* 46: 748–772.

Ruf, B.M., Muralidhar, K., and Paul, K. (1998) "The development of a systematic, aggregate measure of corporate social performance," *Journal of Management* 24: 119–133.

Russell, C.J., Colella, A., and Bobko, P. (1993) "Expanding the context of utility: The strategic importance of personnel selection," *Personnel Psychology* 41: 781–801.

Rynes, S. and Rosen, B. (1995) "A field survey of factors affecting the adoption and perceived success of diversity training," *Personnel Psychology* 48: 247–270.

Sager, I. (1996) "The new biology of big business," *Business Week*, April 15: 19.

Salk, J.E. and Shenkar, O. (2001) "Social identities in an international joint venture: An exploratory case study," *Organization Science* 12 (2): 161–178.

Schaan, J.L. (1983) "Parent control and joint venture success: The case of Mexico," unpublished doctoral dissertation, University of Western Ontario.

Schaan, J.L. (1988) "How to control a joint venture even as a minority partner," *Journal of General Management* 14 (1): 4–16.

Schiesel, S. (2002) "AOL suggests move by Malone and other risks," *New York Times*, October 14: C1.

Schneider, S.C. and Barsoux, J. (1997) *Managing across Cultures*, London: Prentice Hall.

Schonfeld, E. (1997) "Merck vs. the biotech industry: Which one is more potent?" *Fortune*, March 29: 161–162.

Schuler, R.S. (2001) "HR issues in international joint ventures," *International Journal of Human Resource Management*, February: 1–50.

Schuler, R.S. and Jackson, S.E. (1987) "Linking competitive strategy and human resource management practices," *Academic Management Executive* 3: 207–219.

Schuler, R.S. and Jackson, S.E. (1999) *Strategic Human Resource Management: A Reader*, Oxford: Blackwell.

Schuler, R.S. and Jackson, S.E. (2001) "HR issues in mergers and acquisitions," *European Management Journal*, June: 253–287.

Schuler, R.S. and MacMillan, I.C. (1984) "Gaining competitive advantage through HR management practices," *Human Resource Management* 23: 241–255.

Schuler, R.S. and van Sluijs, E. (1992) "Davidson-Marley BV: Establishing and operating an international joint venture," *European Management Journal* 10 (4): 428–437.

Schuler, R.S., Jackson, S.E., Dowling, P.J., and Welch, D.E. (1991) "The formation of an international joint venture: Davidson Instrument Panel," *Human Resource Planning* 15 (1): 50–60.

Schuler, R.S., Dowling, P.J., and De Cieri, H. (1992) "The formation of an international joint venture: Marley Automotive Components Ltd.," *European Management Journal*, September: 304–309.

Schweiger, D.M. and Power, F.R. (1987) "Strategies for managing human resources during mergers and acquisitions," *Human Resource Management* 10 (1): 19–35.

Schweiger, D.M., Ridley, J.R. Jr., and Marini, D.M. (1992) "Creating one from two: The merger between Harris Semiconductor and General Electric Solid State," in S.E. Jackson (ed.) *Diversity in the Workplace: Human Resources Initiatives*, New York: Guilford Press, pp. 167–201.

Scott, W.R. (1987) "The adolescence of institutional theory," *Administrative Scientific Quarterly* 32: 493–511.

Selmer, J. (2001) "Human resource management in Japan: Adjustment or transformation?" *International Journal of Manpower* 22: 235–243.

Serapio, M.G. Jr. and Cascio, W.F. (1996) "End-games in international alliances," *Academy of Management Executive* 10 (1): 63–73.

Seriver, A. (2001) "Swiss–American Bank mergers – while one works?" *Fortune*, February 5: 201–202.

Seth, A., Song, K.P., and Pettit, R.R. (2002) "Value creation and destruction in cross-border alliances: An empirical analysis of foreign acquisitions of U.S. firms," *Strategic Management Journal* 2: 921–940.

Shenkar, O. (ed.) (1995) *Global Perspectives of Human Resource Management*, Englewood Cliffs, NJ: Prentice Hall.

Shenkar, O. (2002) "International joint ventures," Paper presented at the Academy of Management Annual Meetings, August 10.

Shenkar, O. and Li, J. (1999) "Knowledge search in international cooperative ventures," *Organizational Science* 10 (2): 34–44.

Shenkar, O. and Yan, A. (2002) "International joint venture issues," Paper presented at the Academy of Management Annual Meetings, August 10.

Shenkar, O. and Zeira, Y. (1987a) "Human resource management in international joint ventures: Direction for research," *Academy of Management Review* 12 (3): 546–557.

Shenkar, O. and Zeira, Y. (1987b) "International joint ventures: Implications for organization development," *Personnel Review* 16 (1): 30–37.

Shenkar, O. and Zeira, Y. (1990) "International joint ventures: A tough test for HR," *Personnel*, January: 26–31.

Shirley Bobier, V.P. (2000) *HR*, November 7. This study is referred to here as the "J&J Study." Also see "Merger Success," A.T. Kearney Study, 1998.

Silver, S.D., Cohen, B.P., and Crutchfield, J.H. (1994) "Status differentiation and information exchange in face-to-face and computer-mediated idea generation," *Social Psychology Quarterly* 57: 108–123.

Sirower, M.L. (1997) *The Synergy Trap*, New York: Free Press.

Slocum, J.W. and Lei, D. (1993) "Designing global strategic alliances: Integrating cultural and economic factors," in G.P. Huber and W.H. Glick (eds.) *Organizational Change and Redesign: Ideas and Insights for Improving Performance*, New York: Oxford University Press, pp. 295–322.

Smith, P.B. (2001) "Cross-cultural studies of social influence," in D. Matsumoto (ed.) *The Handbook of Culture and Psychology*, Oxford: Oxford University Press, pp. 361–374.

Snell, S.A. (1992) "Control theory in strategic human resource management: The mediating effect of administrative information," *Academic Management Review* 35: 292–327.

South, S.J., Bonjean, C.M., Markham, W.T., and Corder, J. (1982) "Social structure and intergroup interaction: Men and women of the federal bureaucracy," *American Sociological Review*, 47: 587–599.

Sparks, D. (1999) "Partners," *Business Week*, October 5: 106.

Starkey, K. and McKinlay, A. (1993) *Strategy and the Human Resource: Ford and the Search for Competitive Advantage*, Oxford: Blackwell.

Stasser, G. and Titus, W. (1985) "Pooling of unshared information in group decision making: Biased information sampling during discussion," *Journal of Personality and Social Psychology* 48: 1467–1478.

Steensma, H.K. and Lyles, M.A. (2000) "Explaining IJV survival in a transitional economy through social exchange and knowledge-bases perspective," *Strategic Management Journal* 21: 831–851.

Steiner, I.D. (1972) *Group Process and Productivity*, San Diego, CA: Academic Press.

Stephan, W.G., Ybarra, P., Martinez, C.M., Schwartzwald, J., and Tur-Kaspa, M. (1998) "Prejudice toward immigrants to Spain and Israel: An integrated threat theory analysis," *Journal of Cross-cultural Psychology* 29: 559–576.

Stewart, T. (1999) "See Jack. See Jack run," *Fortune*, September 17: 124.

Stewart, T.A. (1990) "How to manage in the new era," *Fortune*, January 15: 58–72.

Storey, J. (ed.) (2001) *Human Resource Management: A Critical Text*, London: Thomson Learning.

Sun, H. and Bond, M.H. (1999) "The structure of upward and downward tactics of influence in Chinese organizations," in J.C. Lasry, J.G. Adair, and K.L. Dion (eds.) *Latest Contribution to Cross-cultural Psychology*, Lisse, the Netherlands: Swets & Zeitlinger, pp. 286–299.

Tajfel, H. (1978) *Differentiation between Social Groups: Studies in the Social Psychology of Intergroup Relations*, San Diego, CA: Academic Press.

Tannen, D. (1990) *You Just Don't Understand: Men and Women in Conversation*, New York: Ballatine.

Tannen, D. (1995) *Talking from 9 to 5*, New York: Avon Books.

Taylor, A. (2000) "Bumpy roads for global auto makers," *Fortune*, December 18: 284.

Taylor, A. (2001) "Can the Germans rescue Chrysler?" *Fortune*, April 30: 106–112.

Taylor A. III (2002) "Can J & J keep the magic going?" *Fortune*, May 27: 117–122.

Teece, D.J. (1987) "Profiting from technological innovation: Implications for Integration, collaboration, licensing and public policy," in D.J. Teece (ed.) *The Competitve Challenge: Strategies for Industrial Innovation and Renewal*, Cambridge, MA: Ballinger.

Themstrom, S. (1973) *The Other Bostonians: Poverty and Progress in the American Metropolis, 1880–1970*, Cambridge, MA: Harvard University Press.

Thomas, T. (1987) "Keeping the friction out of joint ventures," *Business Review Weekly*, January 23: 57–59.

Thompson, A.A. and Strickland, A.J. (1998) "Crafting and implementing strategy," New York: McGraw-Hill.

Tichy, N.M. (1988) "Setting the global human resource management agenda for the 1990s," *Human Resource Management* 27 (1): 1–18.

Tierney, C. (2000) "Defiant Daimler," *Business Week*, August 7: 89–93.

"To cut or not to cut" (2001) *The Economist*, February 10: 61–62.

Tierney, C, and Green, J. (2000) "Daimler's board: Not exactly crisis managers," *Business Week*, December 11: 47–48.

Triandis, H.C., Dunnette, M.D., and Hough, L.M. (eds.) (1994) *Handbook of Industrial and Organizational Psychology*, 2nd edn., vol. 4, Palo Alto, CA: Consulting Psychologists Press.

Trice, H.M. and Beyer, J.M. (1993) *The Culture of Work Organizations*, Englewood Cliffs, NJ: Prentice Hall.

Tung, R.L. (1981) "Selection and training of personnel for overseas assignments," *Columbia Journal of World Business* 16 (1): 57–71.

Tung, R.L. (1994) "Human resource issues and technology transfer," *International Journal of Human Resource Management* 5: 807–826.

Tyson, L.D. (2001) "The new laws of nations," *New York Times*, July 14: A15.

Ulrich, D. (1998) *Delivering Results: A New Mandate for Human Resource Professionals*, Boston, MA: Harvard Business School Press.

Useem, M. (1996) "Shareholders as a strategic asset," *California Management Review*, Fall: 8–27.

van Sluijs, E. and Schuler, R.S. (1994) "As the IJV grows: Lessons and progress at Davidson-Marley BV," *European Management Journal* 12 (3): 315–321.

Very, P. and Schweiger, D. (2001) "The acquisition process as a learning process: Evidence from a study of critical problems and solutions in domestic and cross-border deals," *Journal of World Business* 36 (1): 11–31.

Viscio, A.J., Harbison, J.R., Asin, A., and Vitaro, R.D. (1999) "Post-merger integration: What makes mergers work?" http://www.strategy-business.com/bestpractice/99404/page1.html (accessed December 7, 1999).

Vlasic, B. and Stertz, B.A. (2000) "Taken for a ride," *Business Week*, June 5: 84–92.

von Bertalanffy, L. (1950) "The theory of open systems in physics and biology," *Science* 111: 23–29.

Walker, J.W. (1995) "The ultimate human resource function with the business," *Handbook of Human Resource Management*, New York: Human Resource Planning Society.

Ward, C. (2001) "The A, B, C's of acculturation," in D. Matsumoto (ed.) *The handbook of culture and psychology*, Oxford: Oxford University Press, pp. 411–445.

Watkins, K.E. and Marsick, V.J. (1993) *Sculpting the Learning Organization*, San Francisco: Jossey-Bass.

Watson Wyatt Survey (2000) http://www.watsonwyatt.com /homepage/eu/res/Surveys/ MergersandAquisitions/0600/page (accessed December 19, 2000).

Weber, Y. (2000) "Measuring cultural fit in mergers and acquisitions," in N.M. Ashkanasy, C.P.M. Wilderom, and M.F. Peterson (eds.) *Handbook of Organizational Culture and Climate*, Thousand Oaks, CA: Sage, pp. 309–320.

Webster, D.R. (1989) "International joint ventures with Pacific Rim partners," *Business Horizon* 32 (2): 65–71.

Welbourne, T.M. and Andrews, A.O. (1996) "Predicting the performance of initial public offerings: Should human resource management be in the equation?" *Academy of Management Journal* 39: 891–919.

Westney, D.E. (1998) "Domestic and foreign learning curves in managing international cooperative strategies," in F. Contractor and P. Lorange (eds.) *Cooperative Strategies In International Business*, Lexington, MA: Lexington Books.

Wibulswadi, P. (1989) "The perception of group self-image and other ethnic group images among the Thai, Chinese, and Americans in the Province of Chiang Mai," in D. Keats, D. Munro, and L. Mann (eds.) *Heterogeneity in Cross-cultural Psychology*, Lisse, the Netherlands: Swets & Zeitlinger, pp. 204–209.

Wickens, P. (1987) *The Road to Nissan: Flexibility, Quality, Teamwork*, London: Macmillan.

Wiersema, M. and Bird, A. (1993) "Organizational demography in Japan: Group heterogeneity, individual dissimilarity and top management team turnover," *Academy of Management* 36: 996–1025.

Wilkinson, A., Godfrey, G., and Marchington, M. (1997) "Bouquets, brickbats and blinkers: Total quality management and employee involvement in practice," *Organization Studies* 18 (5): 799–819.

Williams, J.E., and Best, D.L. (1990) *Measuring Sex Stereotypes: A Multination Study*, Newbury Park, CA: Sage.

Williams, K. and O'Reilly, C.A. (1998) "Demography and diversity in organizations: A review of 40 years of research," in B. Staw and L. Cummings (eds.) *Research in Organzational Behavior*, vol. 20, Greenwich, CT: JAI Press, pp. 77–140.

Williamson, O.E. (1979) "Transaction-cost economics: The governance of contractual relations," *Journal of Law and Economics* 22 (2): 233–261.

Williamson, O.E. (1981) "The modern corporation: Origins, evolution, attributes," *Journal of Economic Literature* 19: 1537–1568.

Wong, N. (2000) "Let spirit guide leadership," *Workforce*, February: 33–36.

Wood, S. (1999) "Human resource management and performance," *International Journal of Management Reviews* 1 (4): 367–413.

"Work attitudes: Study reveals generation gap" (1986) *Bulletin to Management*, October 2: 326.

Wright, P.M. and McMahan, G.C. (1992) "Theoretical perspectives for strategic human resource management," *Journal of Management* 18: 295–320.

Wright, P.M. and Snell, S.A. (1991) "Toward an integrative view of strategic human resource management," *Human Resource Management Review* 1: 203–225.

Xenikou, A. and Furnham, A. (1996) "A correlational and factor analytic study of four questionnaire measures of organizational culture," *Human Relations* 49: 349–371.

Yan, A. (1998) "Structural stability and reconfiguration of international joint ventures," *Journal of International Business Studies* 29 (4): 733–796.

Yan, A. and Gray, B. (1994) "Bargaining power, management control, and performance in United States–China joint ventures: A comparative case study," *Academy of Management Journal* 37: 1478–1517.

Yan, A. and Luo, Y. (2001) *International Joint Ventures: Theory and Practice*, Armonk, NY: Sharpe.

Yang, C. (2001) "Show true for AOL Time Warner," *Business Week* (January 15): 57–64.

Ybarra, O. and Stephan, W.G. (1994) "Perceived threats as a predictor of stereotypes and prejudice: Americans' reactions to Mexican immigrants," *Boletín de Psicología* 42: 39–54.

Zenger, T.R. and Lawrence, B.S. (1989) "Organizational demography: The differential effects of age and tenure distribution on technical communications," *Academy of Management Journal* 32 (2): 353–376.

Zucker, L.G. (1977) "The role of institutionalization in cultural persistence," *American Sociology Review* 42: 726–743.

Zucker, L.G. (1987) "Institutional theories of organization," *Annual Review of Sociology* 1987: 443–464.

Internet resources

Further information about topics in these chapters are available (subject to deletion) on these Internet Web sites:

http://jackson.swcollege.com

http://www.ilo.org

http://www.haygroup.com

http://www.expatriates.com

http://webofculture.com

http://www.culturebank.com

http://www.shrm.org

http://www.watsonwyatt.com

http://www.towers.com

http://www.mercer.com

http://www.acrossfrontiers.com

http://home3.americanexpress.com

http://www.odci.gov/cia/publications/factbook/

http://www.eurobru.com

http://www.jil.go.jp

www.anderson.ucla.edu/research/japan Global Window – The Guide to Business Success – Japan.

www.japaneseculture.about.com/culture/japaneseculture

www.executiveplanet.com – "The Japanese corporation of the future and understanding the Japanese business mind." Also visit the Web site www.recruit.com.

www.jinjapan.org/insight/html/focus02/challenges_in_the.html

http://www-15.nist.gov/atp/conf /jvsummar.htm

www.valueintegration.com/csint.htm

Index